THE BOOK
OF
Blessings

New Jewish Prayers for Daily Life,

the Sabbath, and the New Moon Festival

סֵפֶר הַבְּרָכוֹת
סִדּוּר בְּגִרְסָה חֲדָשָׁה
לִימוֹת הַחֹל, לְשַׁבָּת וּלְרֹאשׁ חֹדֶשׁ

MARCIA FALK

Beacon Press, Boston

Beacon Press
25 Beacon Street
Boston, Massachusetts 02108-2892
www.beacon.org

Beacon Press books
are published under the auspices of
the Unitarian Universalist Association of Congregations.

The first Beacon Press edition of this book was published in 1999.

Grateful acknowledgment is made to the following copyright holders for permission to include in this volume the original language versions and Marcia Falk's translations of the following material: Hakibbutz Hameuchad Publishers for Zelda's poems "Golden Butterfly," "Strange Plant," "Moon Is Teaching Bible," "When I Said the Blessing over the Candles," "Each of Us Has a Name," "Pause," "First Rain," and "Leisure"; Sifriat Poalim Publishers for Leah Goldberg's poems "The Blade of Grass Sings to the River," "The River Sings to the Stone," "From My Mother's House," and "In Everything"; Dalia Ravikovich for her poem "Moon in the Rain"; Davar Publishing House for Rachel's poem "To My Land"; Joseph Tussman for Malka Heifetz Tussman's poems "Humble Hour," "Water Without Sound," "Last Apple," "Nasturtiums," "With Teeth in the Earth," "Eating an Apple," "I Am Woman," "Leaves," "Today Is Forever," and "Holy Quiet."

The translations of Malka Heifetz Tussman's poems originally appeared in *With Teeth in the Earth: Selected Poems of Malka Heifetz Tussman*, translated, edited, and introduced by Marcia Falk (Wayne State University Press, 1992). Some of the original poems by Marcia Falk included here are from the collection *This Year in Jerusalem* (State Street Press, 1986). Other original poems and translations by Marcia Falk appeared first in the following magazines and journals: *American Poetry Review, Ariel, Choice, Dark Horse, European Judaism, Jerusalem Quarterly, Lilith, Ma'ariv, Midstream, Modern Poetry in Translation, Moment, Open Places, Poet & Critic, Poetry/LA, Primavera, Reconstructionist, Reform Judaism, Response, Tikkun,* and *Triquarterly.*

05 04 03 02 01   8 7 6 5 4 3

This book is printed on acid-free paper that meets the uncoated paper ANSI/NISO specifications for permanence as revised in 1992.

Library of Congress Cataloging-in-Publication Data can be found on page 534.

The Book of Blessings

לחיים שיע

בְּרֹב שַׂרְעַפַּי בְּקִרְבִּי
תַּנְחוּמֶיךָ יְשַׁעַשְׁעוּ נַפְשִׁי.

FOR STEVE
When cares abound within me
your comforts refresh my soul.

———————

לאברהם גילעד

שִׂישׂ וְגִיל עֲדֵי־עַד!

FOR ABRAHAM GILEAD
Joy forever!

———————

ולכלל ישראל

יִהְיוּ לְרָצוֹן אִמְרֵי פִי
וְהֶגְיוֹן לִבִּי לְפָנֶיכֶם.

AND FOR THE COMMUNITY OF ISRAEL
May the words of my mouth
and the meditations of my heart
find favor.

Contents

PART ONE

The Daily Cycle: The Weekdays

PART TWO

The Weekly Cycle: The Sabbath

*English only

תֹּכֶן הָעִנְיָנִים

חלק א׳

מַחֲזוֹר הַיּוֹם: יְמוֹת הַחֹל

חלק ב׳

מַחֲזוֹר הַשָּׁבוּעַ: שַׁבָּת

*בְּאַנְגְּלִית

PART THREE

The Monthly Cycle:
The New Moon Festival and Surrounding Rituals

Commentary*

*English only

חלק ג׳

מַחֲזוֹר הַחֹדֶשׁ:
רֹאשׁ חֹדֶשׁ וּטְקָסִים הַקְּשׁוּרִים בּוֹ

פֵּרוּשִׁים וְהֶאָרוֹת*

*בְּאַנְגְּלִית

Acknowledgments

A friend recently asked how I had the chutzpah to write this book—weren't all prayer books produced by committees? So I confessed that I had my own committee—poets, artists, scholars, friends—without whom I could not have seen this book through the thirteen years from its inception to its completion.

How could I have done this work without Snira Klein, who sat with me in the sunroom overlooking her garden and on the telephone halfway across the state of California, discussing the history and associations of virtually every word in my Hebrew blessings? For her love and respect for the Hebrew language and its literature, for her marvelous sensitivity to nuance, and for her abounding patience with this project, I cannot thank her enough.

And what would it have been like to do this work without Alison Jordan, who sat with me over tea at my dining room table, discussing everything from theology in the Commentary to instructions in the footnotes? For the lucidity and logic with which she approached texts and issues, for the pointed insights that so often broke through stalemates in my thinking, as well as for her thoughtfulness and care, I thank her deeply.

And I thank Deborah Enelow, whose ideas often spurred me, whose clarity always grounded me, and whose friendship encouraged and sustained me, especially during the book's crucial final stages.

Rachel Adler and Hillel Furstenberg, brilliant and learned talmudists, graciously shared their knowledge and understanding with me. Liturgy scholar Lawrence Hoffman generously gave me the benefit of his remarkable expertise. My ongoing conversations with theologian Judith Plaskow greatly stimulated my writing and helped me clarify my thinking. I am indeed blessed to have such wonderful colleagues, some of whom hold beliefs quite different from my own but all of whom were willing to respond to my work and to share their truths with me. They are a challenge and an inspiration.

And still there are more. Linguist and Hebraist Ezri Uval reviewed all the Hebrew with an exacting eye and the heart of someone who truly loves the language; on top of that, he answered my endless queries with promptness and good humor. Philosopher Dorit Bar-On brought a sharp linguistic discrimination to bear on many portions of my Hebrew texts; our conversations during the early stages of the book helped move this project off the ground. At a later stage, Yair Zakovitch contributed his perspective as a scholar of Hebrew Bible. Over the course of several years, poet Lucille Day read and critiqued my English poetry and poetic prose. Linguist and Yiddishist Eli Katz reviewed the Yiddish texts for accuracy and my translations of them for fidelity. I thank each of these friends, whose unique gifts are reflected throughout, especially in the details.

I am grateful to the members of B'not Esh, the Jewish feminist collective to which I belong, who have responded supportively over the past decade to my developing liturgy. I am also grateful to the women of the Grail in Cornwall, New York, and to the members of the academic communities with which I have been affiliated at Stanford and at the University of California at Berkeley. I thank the following individuals, who responded to queries or shared resources with me: Judith K. Eisenstein, Ira Eisenstein, Lillian Steinfeld, Ron Kuzar, Penina Beck, David Ellenson, Ruth Linden, Lisa Handwerker, Minoo Moallem, Elizabeth Castelli, Marilyn Yalom, Sonya Herman, Daniel Matt, Martha Ackelsberg, Arthur Waskow, Nancy Flam, Ramie Arian, Judith Brin Ingber, Howard Eilberg-Schwartz, Linda Kaplan, Daniel Schroeter, Susan Berrin, Chaim Seidler-Feller, Denni Liebowitz, David Brin, and Arlene Agus. Thanks also to those who offered help in a variety of ways to move this work into the world: Judith Saffer, Naamah Kelman, Ari Tzuk, Nancy Felton, Joel Dansky, Ellen Umansky, Nancy Andell, Helene Aylon, David Enelow, Gwyneth Sinizer, Ari Davidow, Rose Katz, Herb Bivins, Efrat Lev, Leora Zeitlin, Stephen Yenser, Rivka Greenberg, David Cooper, and Heather McHugh. Special thanks to Ron Yohai-Rifkin for generously sharing his graphic skills. And deep, heartfelt gratitude to Steve Marsh—for his wisdom.

My appreciation goes to my editors at Harper San Francisco and to other members of the staff. In particular, I want to thank Marie Cantlon, who faithfully and lovingly saw the project through every stage of its development. Marie's wise counsel improved the book in many ways, and her steady support of its author went way beyond the call of duty. I am indebted to Kandace Hawkinson for giving the book the benefit of her finely honed editorial skills. I thank Ann Moru for her thorough and excellent copyediting. David Bullen provided a brilliant design; Terri Leonard and Martha Blegen expertly guided the book through production. The book also benefited from the specialized knowledge and skills of David Golomb, Joel Hoffman, and Jonathan Schwartz, and from the meticulous typesetting of Wilsted & Taylor.

I am indebted to the staff and supporters of the MacDowell Colony in Peterborough, New Hampshire, which provided fellowship residencies of undisturbed time in 1983, 1984–85, and 1994–95, without which I could not have begun this project or completed it. I thank the MacArthur Foundation for a travel grant enabling me to get to MacDowell.

I am appreciative of the creativity of several talented composers who have set many of my blessings to music: Fran Avni, Linda Hirschhorn, Faith Rogow, Aviva Rosenbloom, Arkadi Serper, Craig Taubman, and Alan Weiner. Linda and Fran, working in collaboration, have produced an exciting CD and cassette entitled "Selections from Marcia Falk's Blessings in Song" (Half Note Productions). I hope that the music of these composers will be heard—and that others, too, will try their hand—because each melody, like each reader, brings a new voice to the whole, adding to it richness and depth.

As this book was going to press, the world lost a foremost scholar and composer of Jewish music—and I lost a dear friend. Judith K. Eisenstein contributed in a significant way to this book, and I am sad that I cannot share the final work with her. Remembering her is a blessing.

Special gratitude goes to my mother, Frieda Goldberg Falk, my first teacher of Judaism, who followed the development of this project and believed in it all along—who, indeed, believed in Jewish feminism long before it became the influential movement that it is today. Special appreciation also goes to my father, Abraham Abbey Falk, whose memory is a blessing. And, of course, as always, to my brother, Sam.

My thanks go unbounded to the world's most wonderful childcare provider, Ann Bilbao, who shepherded Abby, along with a flock of his peers, through his preschool and kindergarten years, giving me the peace of mind without which I could not have even considered doing this project.

And to Abraham Gilead (Abby) himself, without whom I would have had so much less to bless!

And *most of all*, my vast, inexpressible appreciation to Steve Rood—poet, critic, partner, spouse, and friend—*without whom not*.

NOTE TO THE 1999 PAPERBACK EDITION

Almost three years have sped by since this book first appeared between covers—three years of joys and sorrows, unanticipated rewards, and inevitable disappointments. Of the gifts I've received, none has touched me more deeply than the personal expressions of the women and men and—most delightful surprise!—children who have told me what the book has meant to them. Their words arrived by letter and phone, via fax and e-mail, and, best of all, in person—after a talk or a reading, at a conference dinner or in a hotel elevator, in a bookstore or classroom or chance meeting on the street. Each story has been unique, and I want to thank each storyteller—you know who you are—for what you have given me.

As for the inevitable losses—most painful was the death of my friend of thirty years, Hebraist and educator Ezri Uval, who contributed so much lively intelligence to this book.

May his memory be a blessing to those who knew him, as his life was to all *am yisra'eyl*, the people of Israel, whose language and civilization he cherished and enriched.

And there is now. I am filled with delight to see *The Book of Blessings* appear in this paperback edition, a format that will be accessible, I hope, to all those who have wanted the book and waited to have it for their own. I thank Amy Caldwell, my editor at Beacon Press, for shepherding the book to its new publication. I am very happy indeed to be working with the staff of this literature-loving independent publishing house.

I dedicate this new edition of *The Book of Blessings* to the memory of my friend Ezri and to the future of my joy-loving son, Abby—and of *all* our children, for they are all *our* children. In a world of unfettered, globally ranging capitalism, with its cynical values and shortsighted vision, our children faithfully remind us, day by day and moment by moment, of the need to cultivate and preserve humane literary, social, and spiritual traditions. May our words and deeds prove worthy of their faith.

Author's Preface

Hannah rose after eating and drinking at Shiloh while Eli the priest was sitting at the entrance to God's sanctuary. Her spirit was greatly pained and she prayed to God, weeping profusely. . . . As she continued praying to God, Eli watched her mouth. Now Hannah, she spoke in her heart; her lips moved, but she uttered no sound; and Eli took her for a drunkard. Eli said to her, "How long will you go on behaving like a drunkard! Put away your wine!" Then Hannah replied, saying, "No, my lord, I am a woman in anguish, and I have had neither wine nor liquor, but have been pouring my heart out before God. Do not regard your servant as a worthless woman, for I have been speaking all this time out of the greatness of my concern and out of my vexation."

I SAMUEL 1:9–10, 12–16

How many great laws can be learned from these verses relating to Hannah! *Now Hannah, she spoke in her heart.* From this we learn that one who prays must direct his heart.

TALMUD, B. BERAKHOT 31A

Hannah replied, saying, "No, my lord." Some say that she said to him: "You are no person of authority, nor is the Shekhinah or the Spirit-of-Holiness with you, since you have presumed me guilty rather than innocent. Are you not aware that I am a woman in anguish?"

TALMUD, B. BERAKHOT 31B

There is, for me, a plumbline that drops from the center of my being down to the beginning of my history. At one end, *álef*, at the other, *taf*. If human language is, in large measure, what gives us our humanity—allowing me to communicate with you, distinguishing us from other parts of creation—then Hebrew is sign and symbol of my particular human identity, giving me my home as a Jew. Although my first language is English, I cannot imagine myself without the millennia-old language of my people. When I was fifteen, visiting Israel for the first time, an Israeli asked me what was my "mother tongue," my *s'fat eym*. English, I replied, is my *s'fat eym*, but Hebrew is my *s'fat dam*—the language of my blood.

If you are looking for the heart and soul and bones of Hebrew prayer, you will find them all in the blessing. A blessing—in Hebrew, *b'rakhah*—is a special kind of utterance that can turn a moment into an event. Blessings intensify life by increasing our awareness of the present even while awakening our connections to the past. In a richly faceted world, full of surprise and infinite variation, the source of blessings is everywhere to be found. No wonder the rabbis of the Talmud (b. Berakhot 35a) proclaimed it forbidden to enjoy anything of this world without first saying a blessing.

As a poet, I have long been drawn to the power—the lyric intensity—of the Hebrew *b'rakhah*. I first began to write blessings of my own, however, because I was extremely uncomfortable with the heavily patriarchal image of God in the traditional blessings. I have now been writing new Hebrew blessings for over a dozen years, and during the course of that time my understanding of the greater context, the greater whole—my theology, if you will—has evolved, revealing itself to me in unexpected ways, each of which became part of the creative process, influencing my liturgical forms. Because I never completely abandoned any station on the journey—I did not reject my earlier blessings, I just moved on to write new ones—what I find today as I look over this first volume of *The Book of Blessings* is a variegated collection. To no one's surprise more than my own, *The Book of Blessings* has emerged as a *siddur*—a prayer book—for use in both the home and the community on weekdays, Sabbaths, and Rosh Hodesh, the festival of the New Moon. More volumes are in progress: for the major and minor festivals, the High Holidays, and the ordinary and extraordinary events of the life cycle.

Looking back to the genesis of the journey, I see that my first blessings were based closely on the traditional blessing form: they exhorted the community to bless or praise, celebrate or seek out the presence of the divine in relation to specific occasions, such as beginning a meal or ushering in a holiday. Yet they departed sharply from the traditional blessings by offering new images for divinity—images that called into question the rabbinic depictions of God as the Lord and king. Because I crafted my theological metaphors to connect specifically to the occasions they marked, and because my language was rooted in biblical and rabbinic sources as well as other texts from later Hebrew literature, my first blessings could be read as a kind of midrash, or commentary, on the historical tradition. ("Tradition" is a word I use broadly to mean everything in Jewish civilization that has come down to us from the past—and also what we contribute to it today.) For example, I composed my **Blessing Before the Meal** as an adaptation of the traditional *hamótzi* prayer, which praises God for "bringing forth bread from the earth." Yet by imaging divinity as *eyn haḥayim*, "wellspring (or fountain, or source) of life," rather than as *adonay elohéynu, mélekh ha'olam*, "Lord our God, king of the world," I was suggesting another way to apprehend the divine and to awaken gratitude for the body's nurturance.

I first presented my blessings publicly in 1983 at an educational institute held at Rutgers University, and then a second time in 1984 at a Jewish women's conference in Los Angeles.[1] As a result of those presentations and the publication of a magazine article early in 1985,[2] these new blessings began to circulate informally across the United States and also in Israel, where they were adopted by communities and individuals from a range of orientations—Reconstructionist, Reform, Conservative, *havurah*-style, feminist, progressive, and unaffiliated Jews. It wasn't long before people were extrapolating from them to write new blessings of their own.

This response was gratifying in several ways. First of all, I was moved that my work was finding a place in the Jewish community, the home for which I had intended it. And I was especially glad to see it inspire a burst of new writing in Hebrew, since most liturgical innovation of recent times has been in English.[3] But the results were not quite what I had anticipated. My early blessings were, for me, starting points in the creative process; I had never intended them to be used as blueprints or formulas. So I was taken aback when I heard people inserting the phrase *eyn hahayim* into the traditional Hebrew prayers in the place of *adonay elohéynu, mélekh ha'olam*. To me, *adonay elohéynu, mélekh ha'olam* is an example of dead metaphor, that is, I see it as a greatly overused image that no longer functions to awaken awareness of the greater whole. Moreover, because this image has had absolute and exclusive authority in Jewish prayer, it has reinforced forms of patriarchal power and male privilege in the world. But I have never believed that the alternative to this icon is a substitute image for the divine, since any single name or image would necessarily be partial and would, potentially, be the basis for further exclusivity and distortion. Rather, from the very beginning I maintained that we should set in motion *a process of ongoing naming* that would point toward the diversity of our experiences and reach toward a greater inclusivity within the encompassing, monotheistic whole.[4] As an example of what I was calling for, I offered *several* new images of my own—among them, *eyn hahayim*.

I was even less prepared to see the opening of my **Blessing Before the Meal**, *N'vareykh et eyn hahayim*, "Let us bless the source of life," removed from the context in which it originally emerged and treated as a new formula—that is, inserted into a traditional blessing, often without any other substantive changes made to the rest of the content.[5] Although I had myself repeated this phrase in a few other contexts where I thought it had resonance, I had never intended it to substitute *universally* or *automatically* for the traditional rabbinic opening of the *b'rakhah*. Indeed, the creation of formulas was far from my earliest designs. Rather, as a poet, I sought to create an organic whole with each new blessing; and, as a liturgist, I firmly believed that no convention of prayer ought to become completely routine, lest it lose its ability to inspire authentic feeling. I had strived to embody these convictions in my work right from the start.

For example, in my *Havdalah: Parting Ritual for the Sabbath*, written in 1982, I had offered two new theological images besides *eyn haḥayim: nishmat kol ḥay*, literally, "the soul (or breath) of all that lives," and *nitzotzot hanéfesh*, literally, "the sparks of the spirit." As *eyn haḥayim* was an image of water, water drawn from the earth, so *nishmat kol ḥay* and *nitzotzot hanéfesh* were images of air and of fire. I had hoped that this cluster of images, taken as a whole, might begin to suggest the presence of the divine in the whole of creation—suggest it in a way not possible using any single image alone. My *Havdalah* also introduced two variations for the verb *n'vareykh*, "let us bless": *n'haleyl*, "let us praise (or celebrate)" and *n'vakeysh*, "let us seek." It seemed to me that just as divinity could be imaged in a myriad of ways, so prayerful action could take a great variety of forms—and the search for these, too, was part of the poetic process.

Indeed, each variation led to further ones. Over the years, as I continued composing blessings, I experimented with lyric forms, probing their potential to evoke spiritual awareness. I found myself varying not just words and images but syntax and, ultimately, literary genres. The creative process replicated the spiritual journey—or perhaps I should say that it *was* a spiritual journey, rich with the gifts of discovery and surprise. And I hoped that the products of my labor would evoke these also in the reader, the pray-er.[6] As I moved further and further away from the exhortative syntax ("Let us bless . . .") of my original blessings, I found myself attempting to suggest the presence of the sacred in less obvious, less predictable ways—until, at a certain stage, I was no longer using images to point directly toward divinity at all.

That is how it came to be that different kinds of blessings and different liturgical genres appear side by side in this new prayer book. All of it is intended to be a form of prayer—those offerings that are easily recognizable as blessings and those that take less familiar forms; the introductory prose meditations, which I call *kavanot haleyv*, "intentions of the heart"; and the poems of Jewish women poets writing in Hebrew, Yiddish, and English, offered here in the original languages alongside my new English translations. But the heart of the book is the Hebrew blessing, itself presented in a variety of forms and always accompanied by an English transliteration (for those who cannot read the Hebrew alphabet) and by an English version (which is not a literal translation but a counterpart, an English poem designed to re-create the effect of the original Hebrew). And yes, the heart of the heart of the book is what appears in Hebrew letters, those ancient forms that spell the civilization of the Jewish people, for no combination of English letters can ever fully render the history, the meanings, the connections borne by the twenty-two characters of the Hebrew *álef-beyt*.

Among the different blessings in the book are many that may seem to contain no specific reference to the divine. For example, the **Morning Blessing** and the **Blessing Before Going to**

Sleep—which frame THE DAILY CYCLE, beginning and ending the day—focus on personal gratitude while leaving open its object, its focus. **Handwashing upon Awakening** and **Handwashing Before the Meal** call to mind the *k'dushah*, "holiness," of the unified body-spirit-self. The **Blessing of the Children**—which is part of the Sabbath home ritual found in THE WEEKLY CYCLE—echoes words spoken by the biblical God to suggest divinity within the individual child. **Blessing the Beloved** adapts lines from the biblical Song of Songs to convey reciprocal human love. The new blessings of commandment, such as **Sabbath Candle-lighting, Torah Blessings,** and **Putting on the Prayer Shawl**, focus on our intentions—the alignment of heart and mind—during the performance of ritual acts. The blessings for cycles of time—the **Blessing for the New Week** and the **Prayer for the New Month**—express wishes for the fulfillment of self and community. *Aléynu L'shabéyaḥ:* **It Is Ours to Praise**, a closing prayer of the *Shaḥarit:* **Morning Service for the Sabbath**, makes a commitment to work to redeem the world through acts of *tikun*, "repair." **Renewal of the Moon**, which concludes THE MONTHLY CYCLE, takes the form of an extended reverie contemplating the redemptive state.

Where is the divine in all of these? Nowhere in particular—yet potentially everywhere that attention is brought to bear. If everything is capable of being made holy, as rabbinic Judaism teaches with its scrupulous attention to the details of ordinary life, then surely we need not—we *ought* not—localize divinity in a single apt word or phrase. We may find it wherever our hearts and minds, our blood and souls are stirred.

Having a sense of how this book is organized will help you decide how you wish to use it. The body of the book is the liturgy, presented in three parts: THE DAILY CYCLE, THE WEEKLY CYCLE, and THE MONTHLY CYCLE. Each cycle contains an introduction providing a general orientation and an overview of the cycle's contents, as well as general suggestions for use. THE DAILY CYCLE offers individual blessings and poems to be read during the course of the day—any day. For the most part, I assume, these offerings will be used by individuals, although some may also be recited with other people as, for example, when one is sharing a meal. THE WEEKLY CYCLE and THE MONTHLY CYCLE are intended for use in both the home and the community, and they each have several sections, for different times and settings. THE WEEKLY CYCLE contains home rituals and complete prayer services for Sabbath eve and Sabbath morning, as well as a ritual for the Sabbath's closing. THE MONTHLY CYCLE provides a new Rosh Hodesh ceremony for use in either the community or the home, as well as rituals for announcing the date of the Rosh Hodesh festival and for blessing the moon in its waxing phase. It also includes inserts with which to render the Sabbath morning service suitable for Rosh Hodesh day observance. For each ceremony, ritual, and service in THE WEEKLY CYCLE and THE MONTHLY CYCLE, I have offered specific suggestions for implementation; these are found following the section's title page. Each cycle is for the most part self-contained, but for occasions when the Sabbath and Rosh Hodesh coincide, I have provided instructions for combining the celebrations. The *List of Liturgical Offerings*, on pp. xxvi–xxxvii, outlines the complete contents of the liturgy in their order of presentation.

In the outside lower corner of each page of liturgy, a cross-reference to the Commentary appears (indicated by the abbreviation "Comm."). The Commentary, which is for general readers and scholars alike, provides linguistic information about the new offering, with particular emphasis on the Hebrew version. It also discusses the offering's counterpart in the traditional liturgy,[7] sometimes providing historical background and theological analysis. When Hebrew texts are discussed, they are always presented in transliterated form along with a literal translation into English. (A guide to the system of transliteration follows this Preface.) For those who do not read Hebrew but wish to gain a more precise sense of the meaning of the Hebrew offerings, the Commentary is a good place to begin. For purposes of cross-reference back to the liturgy, the Commentary headings provide the page numbers where the corresponding liturgy offerings may be found.

Thus the Commentary may be consulted in segments; however, I recommend that it be read through once as a whole, because terms are defined and conventions are explained only the first time that they appear, and later discussions often build upon earlier ones. Themes that are only touched upon in this Preface—such as the implications of the traditional language for divinity and the relationship between spontaneity and fixed words of prayer—are treated in greater depth in the Commentary (and, to some extent, in the cycle introductions). The Commentary also discusses other general issues relevant to the understanding and use of this liturgy, such as what it means to pray without having I-Thou dialogue with an Other. In the introduction to the Commentary, I offer a brief statement of my theology, setting it in the context of other contemporary Jewish thinkers.

Because this book is, more than anything else, a prayer book, the best way to put it to use will be determined, in the end, by you. My intention in creating *The Book of Blessings* was to provide a resource for the forging of fully inclusive and embracing communities. While I do not expect all its offerings to appeal equally to any one reader, I hope you will find at least something in it that speaks for you.

The Book of Blessings is intended for those who are in the habit of praying—and for those who are not. It is for those dissatisfied or frustrated with the traditional prayers and for those who appreciate the traditional texts and wish to build upon them. The aim of *The Book of Blessings* is to be part of an ongoing conversation that will help keep Judaism alive and responsive to our spiritual needs and moral concerns.

The Book of Blessings is a branch of a tree whose seeds were planted three millennia ago by a woman who prayed from her heart. It is a branch of Hannah's tree—Hannah, who found her own voice by uttering her own words of prayer and who spoke up to defend that voice, those words, when she was challenged by a man of authority. It is a branch of Hannah's tree—Hannah, who centuries later became the rabbis' very model of authenticity. It is a branch of the tree that the rabbis cultivated, tended, and pruned, so that it grew and changed shape throughout their era, hundreds of years before Jewish prayers were codified. It is a branch of a tree that flowered in the hands of the *paytanim*, the liturgical poets of rabbinic times and of later centuries. It is a branch of a tree that did not ossify even after the printing press was invented and prayer books became standardized, a tree that remained an organic thing, ever adapting and evolving. The Book of Blessings sprouts from a living tree that seeks to go on bearing fruit into the future.

The Book of Blessings is for those immersed in Judaism, and for those standing at its gates, looking for a way in. It is, especially, for those of us who have, at some time in our lives, stood like Hannah outside the sanctuary's walls, suffused with longing, or anger, or pain. May these words be, for you, for us—all of us—a new beginning, a new healing. Above all, may this book invite you to add your own voices to the whole—the diversified whole of *k'lal yisra'eyl*, the community of Israel, and the greater wholes of all humanity, all creation.

Marcia Falk
Berkeley, California
Iyar 5756

Guides for the Reader

GUIDE TO THE TRANSLITERATION

Beside each Hebrew blessing, in small English letters, is a nonlanguage sometimes referred to as "transliteration" or "transcription." The system used here is neither perfectly scientific (because that would be too clumsy to read) nor perfectly phonetic (because that would obliterate certain phonemic distinctions and, in any case, is nearly impossible to produce). Rather, what is provided should help English readers who know little or no Hebrew to approximate the sounds of the original and to recognize basic sentence structure through punctuation and capitalization. Note that because Hebrew has no capital letters, capitals appear in the transliteration only where they would appear in English for purposes of form and syntax (i.e., at the beginnings of sentences and in titles) and not to indicate proper names. Punctuation follows modern conventions for Hebrew, which are considerably more flexible than, and not always in line with, those of standard English.

All words are stressed on the final syllable except those marked with accents for penultimate stress. Most letters are pronounced as they would be in English. Note that "g" is hard, as in "good"; "kh" is a guttural (the letter *khaf*), pronounced as in the final consonant of "Bach"; "ḥ" represents another guttural letter (*ḥeyt*), which, in the speech of most Israelis, is indistinguishable from the letter represented by "kh." The vowel sounds are as follows: "a" as in the first syllable of "pasta," "e" as in "egg," "i" as in "pit," "o" as in "core," "u" as in the "oo" of "food," "ay" as in the "ye" of "rye," "ey" as in "whey," "uy" as in the Spanish *muy* or the "ewy" of "chewy." The letters *álef* and *áyin*, pronounced as glottal stops in modern Hebrew, are indicated by apostrophes when they appear in the middle of a word. Apostrophes also stand for the mobile *sh'va*, which is a very short vowel usually pronounced like the "u" in "suppose." (Those readers familiar with the nuances of Hebrew pronunciation and grammar should note that the vowel *tzeyrey* is represented here by "ey" to distinguish it from the vowel *segol*, which is represented by "e," even though many Israeli speakers pronounce the two identically. *Sh'va m'raḥeyf* is treated as a *sh'va naḥ*, according to the rule of *sh'va*, and hence it is not indicated with an apostrophe, as in the words *lidvaréynu* and *unkadeysh*.)

Like any system of rules, this one has its predictable exceptions. Words that may be familiar to English readers, either because they have entered the English language (e.g., "Kaddish," which becomes *kaddish* in transliteration) or because they often go untranslated in Jewish contexts (e.g., *shabbat* and *kiddush*), retain the use of doubled letters, which are otherwise absent in the transliteration.

Note that the proper nouns "Rosh Hodesh" and "Shekhinah," which are becoming increasingly familiar in Jewish-English parlance, are treated as English words in the English sections of the book and are spelled according to one of the conventions in common use. However, when they appear in the liturgy or Commentary as transliterations of Hebrew text, they conform to the transliteration system of the book (*rosh ḥódesh* and *sh'khinah*). So too, titles of Talmud tractates and other rabbinic texts are spelled according to one of the scholarly conventions and do not necessarily conform to this book's system of transliteration.

Note on the Hebrew and Yiddish Orthography

In general, the Hebrew in this book, including punctuation, follows the grammatical and orthographical conventions of modern usage. Thus *makaf* (hyphen) is not introduced, and *dageysh kal* is retained at the beginnings of words and not dropped following words ending in an open syllable. However, exceptions to these conventions will be found in quotations and close adaptations of biblical and rabbinic passages, as well as certain well-known phrases borrowed from the traditional liturgy, which are presented in their received forms. So too, **L'khu, Rey'ot V'rey'im: Greeting the Sabbath Bride** retains the idiosyncratic vocalization of the kabbalistic hymn *l'khah, dodi*, from which it is adapted (as found in traditional prayer books).

Words that get penultimate stress are marked with a *méteg* (the small vertical line under the consonant to the left of the vowel), as in סֵפֶר (*séyfer*). *Kamatz katan* (which is pronounced like "o" rather than "a") is indicated with an elongated *kamatz*, as in כָּל (*kol*); this is in contrast to the standard *kamatz*, as found in נְשָׁמָה (*n'shamah*).

Spelling in the original Yiddish poems presented in this book has been modernized to conform to the standards of the YIVO Institute for Jewish Research. The punctuation of the original poems has not, for the most part, been changed.

Note on Attributions, Translations, and Abbreviations

All poems not written by the author of this book are attributed, with the poet's name appearing at the end of the poem. All translations of such poems into English, as well as all unattributed English poems, are by the book's author, as are the translations of biblical and rabbinic texts found throughout the book. Whenever a substantial biblical passage (as opposed to just a word or phrase) appears in a liturgical offering, either intact or in adapted form, the biblical source is cited with that offering. The Commentary explains all such adaptations; it also points out further allusions to biblical and rabbinic texts. (Exceptions to this practice of citation are found in the *Sh'ma:* **Personal Declaration of Faith** and the *Sh'ma:* **Communal Declaration of Faith**; the several biblical sources of these offerings are not cited with the offerings themselves but are discussed at length in the Commentary.)

Standard abbreviations for the names of biblical books are used whenever these titles appear in parentheses (in the Commentary and other explanatory sections of the book). References to the Babylonian Talmud (which is traditionally called "the Bavli") have a "b." before the tractate name; references to the Jerusalem Talmud (traditionally called "the Yerushalmi") are marked with a "y."

List of Liturgical Offerings

רְשִׁימַת הַבְּרָכוֹת וְהַתְּפִלּוֹת

PART TWO

The Weekly Cycle: The Sabbath

SABBATH EVE

חלק ב׳

מַחֲזוֹר הַשָּׁבוּעַ: שַׁבָּת

לֵיל שַׁבָּת

DEPARTURE OF THE SABBATH, ENTRANCE OF THE WEEK

מוֹצָאֵי שַׁבָּת וּכְנִיסַת הַשָּׁבוּעַ

PART THREE

The Monthly Cycle: The New Moon Festival and Surrounding Rituals

AWAITING THE NEW MOON

EVE OF THE NEW MOON FESTIVAL

חלק ג׳

מַחֲזוֹר הֶחָדָשׁ:
רֹאשׁ חֹדֶשׁ וּטְקָסִים הַקְּשׁוּרִים בּוֹ

לִקְרַאת רֹאשׁ חֹדֶשׁ

לֵיל רֹאשׁ חֹדֶשׁ

DAY OF THE NEW MOON FESTIVAL

IN THE PRESENCE OF THE MOON

ראש חֹדֶשׁ

לְאוֹר הַלְּבָנָה

בְּכָל־יוֹם אֲבָרְכֶךָּ
וַאֲהַלְלָה לְעוֹלָם וָעֶד.

Each day, I will bless
and evermore sing praise.

PART ONE

The Daily Cycle

The Weekdays

מַחֲזוֹר הַיּוֹם

יְמוֹת הַחֹל

Introduction

The Feast

The laden arms of the oak, the elm,
and the agitated hunger of the small jays,

the fat globes of white sugarmum
where bees suck love,

and you, in the morning shade,
sipping hot coffee,

the taste of the new day sharp
and alive on your tongue,

are a chorus that says,
Indulge: the world is abundant—

this loving, dying world
to which we are given,

out of which we have come—
O body of the world,

eat with joy
the body of the world.

We are embodied selves, and Judaism acknowledges our embodiment. *This* life, *this* world, *this* moment in time: we acknowledge, we embrace, we claim. In Jewish religious practice, the ordinary—the quotidian—does not go unmarked or unattended: one blesses not just on the holiday but *every* day.

And indeed, the ordinary, the commonplace, the *everyday* is an ongoing source of blessing in our lives. In a life lived attentively, we experience daily the world's great fullness, for which we are filled with gratefulness.

So, in the Talmud (b. Menaḥot 43b), Rabbi Meir tells us to utter daily one hundred blessings. In rabbinic times, this mandate was largely fulfilled by attendance at daily prayer services in the morning, afternoon, and evening. Such attendance was made obligatory by the rabbis at the end of the first century—obligatory, that is, for men. Women were exempted from "time-bound" commandments and therefore were not required to pray at specific times. This exemption has been widely explained as the rabbis' way of "freeing" women to perform their duties as childbearers, childrearers, and homemakers. Some scholars, however, believe this explanation to be a rationalization, masking the painful truth that the rabbis saw women as children, unreliable and unable to adhere to strictures of time. Whatever the reason, the rabbinic exemption of women ultimately turned daily communal worship into an explicitly male domain.

In addition to communal services, the rabbis provided blessings to be recited by individuals on a daily basis—upon waking in the morning, upon retiring at night, and upon eating and drinking. Blessings were also said at other times, such as upon seeing wondrous sights in nature, upon hearing good or bad news, and upon smelling fragrant plants or fruits, but since such events do not necessarily occur every day, the blessings for them were not mandated daily. According to the Talmud (b. Berakhot 20b), women, too, were expected to say certain blessings, such as the grace after meal. Unfortunately, the Talmud speaks of blessings mainly as the practice of men, leaving us with scant record of women's liturgical lives.

It is the intention of this book to make both communal and individual prayer available, accessible, and potentially meaningful to all members of the community. To do this, however, one must be realistic about how prayer is currently used in Jewish life. And the reality is that while communal prayer services are still attended daily by many Orthodox Jewish men, the great majority of non-Orthodox Jews who attend synagogue services do so mostly on the Sabbath and holidays; this is also true of most Orthodox Jewish women.

Still, even for those who are unaccustomed to any form of daily prayer, there may be moments in the day that evoke the desire to say a blessing. We may come upon these moments when we are not expecting them, perhaps when we are least expecting them; at such times they are pure gifts. But we may also deliberately call these moments into being at other times, set times of day, when we are most likely to be receptive to them. THE DAILY CYCLE of this book is for this purpose.[8] Thus it provides blessings for mealtimes, when we may awaken our gratitude for sustenance, and blessings for the beginning and end of the day when, withdrawn from activity, we may pause to reflect on our relationship to the propelling forces and sustaining currents in our lives. THE DAILY CYCLE also offers psalms for those times of the day when we may wish to pause and reflect on the passage of time itself, and on life's greater connections. When we are able to apprehend and grasp such moments, they become opportunities to appreciate life more deeply and more purely and to gather inner strength—or, as a friend of mine put it, to find our place in the lap of the world.

"The lap of the world"—this phrase draws me back to Judaism's awareness of our embodiment. For what is daily life but a sequence of embodied acts: we rise, we wash, we eat, we work, we play, we sleep. The traditional morning prayers, collectively known as *birkhot hasháḥar*, "blessings of the dawn," mirror the embodied movements of rising in the morning as they praise God for such things as "opening the eyes of the blind," "clothing the naked," "straightening up those who are bent over," "giving strength to the weary," and "removing sleep from my eyes and slumber from my eyelids."[9] Two prayers from this sequence—the blessing for handwashing, known as *n'tilat yadáyim*, "lifting of the hands," and the blessing immediately following it, known as *asher yatzar*, "who has created [human beings]"—were originally intended to accompany bodily activities performed upon awakening. The latter prayer, especially, provides testimony to the rabbis' recognition of human flesh as a glorious achievement of creation; surprisingly earthy, this blessing notes the wondrous functioning of the body's "orifices and cavities," without which human life would not be sustained. Taken together with another prayer from this compilation—*elohay, n'shamah*, which focuses on the purity of the breath, or spirit—these blessings contain the seeds of an integrated awareness of the self as a locus of life.

And yet, these seeds are *only* seeds: they are not a fully flowered recognition of the interdependence—indeed, the oneness—of body and spirit, a recognition that might ultimately acknowledge the holiness of the body itself. Rather, the rabbinic blessings reflect the dominant perspective of traditional Jewish liturgy, which, as I read it, glorifies the spirit, or soul, *over and above* the body. The following passage from the Talmud (b. Berakhot 10a) illustrates the point: "Just as The-Holy-One-Blessed-Be-He fills the world, so the soul fills the body; just as The-Holy-One-Blessed-Be-He sees but is not seen, so the soul sees but is not seen; just as The-Holy-One-Blessed-Be-He feeds the whole world, so the soul feeds the whole body; just as The-Holy-One-Blessed-Be-He is pure, so the soul is pure; just as The-Holy-One-Blessed-Be-He resides in the innermost rooms, so the soul resides in the innermost rooms. Let whoever has these five attributes come and praise the One who has these five attributes." Thus, in the rabbinic view, it is through the soul that we are expected to know and communicate with divinity; immutable and eternal, the human soul belongs to God and returns to God, ultimately giving humanity its likeness to God. In contrast, the body is seen as *the work of God* but as *fundamentally unlike God* in its imperfection and in its mutability—as it grows ill, ages, dies, and decays.

From a feminist point of view, this hierarchy of body and spirit has problematic ramifications. It does not seem coincidental that in Judaism, as in other religions and cultures, females are often associated with the domain of the body while males are given dominion over the mind and the soul. Moreover, the elevation of the soul over the body would seem to ignore the truth that through our bodies we come to know the world: through our senses we reach out, communicate, learn, appreciate, love—and thus, we may also say, we experience the divine. A spirituality that does not *fully* embrace sensuality, fully honor our embodiedness as sacred, is not, ultimately, whole.

Still, when re-creating Jewish prayer from a feminist perspective, one must struggle with some painful tensions: one must acknowledge that sometimes it is difficult to love the body—and not just because of patriarchal disparagements. When one is in relentless pain, for example, or suffering from incurable illness, or in the throes of dying, one may wish to dissociate from one's body. I have heard people say things like "I am not my body," "I am alive though my body is fading," and "Though my body is broken, my spirit is whole." Honoring the body, one must not deny its—our—pain.

Even ordinary aches and pains and the normal process of aging often give us the sense that something is happening *to* us—as if *we* were not our bodies, as if *we* were not what was "happening." Our highly conditioned vocabulary and syntax make it hard to avoid making distinctions between one's "self" and one's body. Yet are these distinctions finally true?

By affirming the unity of body and spirit, I do not mean to invalidate those distinctions we sometimes need, distinctions that may help us assert our humanity. I am, rather, seeking an honest language that enables us to articulate our truths. I am aware that these truths differ among individuals and may even shift for a given individual as her or his circumstances change. In the end, though, I cannot help but feel that the dualistic language of Western cultures, which imputes "scientifically" separate domains to the body and the spirit, has perpetrated invisible lies that make it harder for us to discern our needs and speak coherently about our convictions. I am intuitively drawn to the scientific discoveries of our own era that challenge dualistic perceptions, and I am impressed by articulations such as this one by neuroscientist Candace Pert: "The mind is some kind of enlivening energy . . . *throughout the brain and body* that enables the cells to talk to each other, and the outside world to talk to the whole organism" (emphasis mine).[10] I find myself inspired by those individuals who succeed in maintaining such unitary visions in their daily lives, despite the pervasive distortions of the cultural lens. I am especially moved by the words of feminist theologian Nelle Morton, who, in the last stages of her terminal illness, told me, "I have stopped making my own blood." Others would have said—I, in her position, might well have said—"My body has stopped making its own blood." Nelle's ability to claim and embrace the totality of her being, her refusal to split her body off from her self, despite extreme pain and deterioration, were extensions of the way in which she lived her life and a reflection of her deeply feminist vision of wholeness. Such a vision may not always be possible; at times, it may not seem to speak to one's situation. But there must be room for it to exist in our language and a place for it to flower in our liturgical expression.

I have grappled with these issues in all my compositions, but nowhere more pointedly than in my blessings for THE DAILY CYCLE. To create a new morning sequence, **Blessings upon Awakening,** I first composed my **Morning Blessing** out of the seeds of themes in the traditional *asher yatzar* and *elohay, n'shamah* prayers. To this I added another new blessing, **Handwashing upon Awakening,** based on the traditional *n'tilat yadáyim.* Taken together, these two new prayers represent a step toward claiming the body as sacred and toward envisioning the unified wholeness of human life. Awareness of the body is also central to my new evening prayer, **Blessing Before Going to Sleep,** which is based on the traditional blessing said upon retiring. I have coupled this with *Sh'ma:* **Personal Declaration of Faith,** an adaptation of the biblical passage known as *sh'ma,* "Hear, O Israel," which is traditionally said at bedtime. Together these form the evening sequence, **Blessings for the End of the Day.**

THE DAILY CYCLE also introduces a mealtime ritual, **Blessings for Meals,** consisting of three elements: **Handwashing Before the Meal,** which echoes **Handwashing upon Awakening** but is in a plural rather than a singular voice; **Blessing Before the Meal,** which introduces the term *eyn haḥayim,* "wellspring (or source) of life," as an embodied image of the divine to be associated with blessings of sustenance; and **Blessing After the Meal,** which reprises the term *eyn haḥayim,* as it re-creates, in condensed form, the themes of the traditional grace after meals. Together, the blessings in this mealtime ritual focus awareness on the physical-social-spiritual act of nurturing the body with food.

THE DAILY CYCLE concludes with **Daily Psalms,** a sequence of six contemplative poems in English. This section of the cycle is based on the traditional allocation of a distinct biblical psalm for each day of the week. At the beginning of the section is the **Introductory Recitation for the Daily Psalm,** which is intended to give focus to the reading of the poems.

Thus the offerings in THE DAILY CYCLE, which are primarily for personal rather than communal use, have as part of their aim the attainment of wholeness within the self. Yet even when one is praying in solitude, the sharing of a liturgical tradition can situate one communally and historically, thus connecting the self to larger wholes. Above all, these blessings are intended to evoke a sense of belonging to the whole of being.

Blessings upon Awakening

בְּרָכוֹת לִיקִיצָה

Morning Blessing

*The breath of my life
will bless,*

*the cells of my being
sing*

*in gratitude,
reawakening.*

Birkat Hasháḥar   בִּרְכַּת הַשַּׁחַר

Nishmat ḥayay t'vareykh

v'kérev libi yashir:

Kol od n'shamah b'kirbi

modah/modeh ani.
(female)   *(male)*

נִשְׁמַת חַיַּי תְּבָרֵךְ

וְקֶרֶב לִבִּי יָשִׁיר:

כָּל עוֹד נְשָׁמָה בְּקִרְבִּי

מוֹדָה/מוֹדֶה אֲנִי.

Handwashing upon Awakening

*W*ashing the hands, I call to mind
the holiness of body.

נְטִילַת יָדַיִם בְּעֵת הַיְקִיצָה

N'tilat Yadáyim B'eyt Haykitzah

תִּזְכֹּר נַפְשִׁי אֶת קְדֻשַּׁת הַגּוּף
בִּנְטִילַת יָדַיִם.

Tizkor nafshi et k'dushat haguf
bintilat yadáyim.

Blessings for Meals

בְּרָכוֹת לַאֲרוּחוֹת

Handwashing Before the Meal

Washing the hands, we call to mind the holiness of body.

נְטִילַת יָדַיִם לִפְנֵי הָאֲרוּחָה

N'tilat Yadáyim Lifney Ha'aruḥah

תִּזְכֹּר נַפְשֵׁנוּ אֶת קְדֻשַׁת הַגּוּף בִּנְטִילַת יָדַיִם.

Tizkor nafshéynu et k'dushat haguf bintilat yadáyim.

Comm.
p. 426

Blessing Before the Meal

Let us bless the source of life
that brings forth bread from the earth.

Hamotzi'ah   הַמּוֹצִיאָה

N'vareykh et eyn haḥayim

hamotzi'ah léḥem min ha'áretz.

נְבָרֵךְ אֶת עֵין הַחַיִּים
הַמּוֹצִיאָה לֶחֶם מִן הָאָרֶץ.

Blessing After the Meal

Let us acknowledge the source of life,
source of all nourishment.

May we protect the bountiful earth
that it may continue to sustain us,

and let us seek sustenance
for all who dwell in the world.

בִּרְכַּת הַמָּזוֹן

Birkat Hamazon

Nodeh l'eyn haḥayim
hazanah et hakol.

נוֹדֶה לְעֵין הַחַיִּים
הַזָּנָה אֶת הַכֹּל.

Al ha'áretz hatovah v'har'ḥavah
nishmor na, v'hi t'kay'méynu,

עַל הָאָרֶץ הַטּוֹבָה וְהָרְחָבָה
נִשְׁמֹר נָא, וְהִיא תְּקַיְּמֵנוּ,

unvakeysh mazon l'hasbí'a bo
kol yosh'vey teyveyl.

וּנְבַקֵּשׁ מָזוֹן לְהַשְׂבִּיעַ בּוֹ
כָּל יוֹשְׁבֵי תֵּבֵל.

Blessings for the
End of the Day

בְּרָכוֹת לְסוֹפוֹ שֶׁל יוֹם

Sh'ma: *Personal Declaration of Faith*

*H*ear, O Israel—
The divine abounds everywhere
and dwells in everything;
the many are One.

————

Loving life
and its mysterious source
with all my heart
and all my spirit,
all my senses and strength,
I take upon myself
and into myself
these promises:
to care for the earth
and those who live upon it,
to pursue justice and peace,
to love kindness and compassion.
I will teach this to our children
throughout the passage of the day—
as I dwell in my home
and as I go on my journey,
from the time I rise
until I fall asleep.

Comm.
p. 431

קְרִיאַת שְׁמַע עַל הַמִּטָּה

K'ri'at Sh'ma Al Hamitah

Sh'ma, yisra'eyl—

la'elohut alfey panim,

m'lo olam sh'khinatah,

ribuy panéha eḥad.

שְׁמַע, יִשְׂרָאֵל—

לָאֱלֹהוּת אַלְפֵי פָנִים,

מְלֹא עוֹלָם שְׁכִינָתָה,

רִבּוּי פָּנֶיהָ אֶחָד.

Ohav et-haḥayim

v'eyt eyn haḥayim

b'khol-l'vavi uvkhol-nafshi

uvkhol-m'odi.

Yihyu had'varim ha'éyleh

bilvavi uvkirbi:

sh'mirat éretz v'yosh'véha,

r'difat tzédek v'shalom,

ahavat ḥésed v'raḥamim.

Ashan'neym

livnotéynu ulvanéynu

va'adabeyr bam

b'shivti b'veyti,

b'lekhti badérekh,

b'shokhbi uvkumi.

אֹהַב אֶת־הַחַיִּים

וְאֶת עֵין הַחַיִּים

בְּכָל־לְבָבִי וּבְכָל־נַפְשִׁי

וּבְכָל־מְאֹדִי.

יִהְיוּ הַדְּבָרִים הָאֵלֶּה

בִּלְבָבִי וּבְקִרְבִּי:

שְׁמִירַת אֶרֶץ וְיוֹשְׁבֶיהָ,

רְדִיפַת צֶדֶק וְשָׁלוֹם,

אַהֲבַת חֶסֶד וְרַחֲמִים.

אֲשַׁנְּנֵם

לִבְנוֹתֵינוּ וּלְבָנֵינוּ

וַאֲדַבֵּר בָּם

בְּשִׁבְתִּי בְּבֵיתִי,

בְּלֶכְתִּי בַּדֶּרֶךְ,

בְּשָׁכְבִּי וּבְקוּמִי.

And may my actions
be faithful to my words
that our children's children
may live to know:
Truth and kindness
have embraced,
peace and justice have kissed
and are one.

וְיִהְיוּ מַעֲשַׂי

נֶאֱמָנִים לִדְבָרַי,

לְמַעַן יֵדְעוּ דּוֹר אַחֲרוֹן,

בָּנוֹת וּבָנִים יִוָּלֵדוּ:

חֶסֶד וֶאֱמֶת נִפְגָּֽשׁוּ,

צֶֽדֶק וְשָׁלוֹם נָשָֽׁקוּ.

V'yihyu ma'asay

ne'emanim lidvaray,

l'má'an yeyd'u dor aḥaron,

banot uvanim yivaléydu:

Ḥésed ve'emet nifgáshu,

tzédek v'shalom nasháku.

Blessing Before Going to Sleep

Sleep descending
on my lids,
on my limbs,

I call to mind
the gifts
of the day—

the gift
of this day—
and give thanks.

B'rakhah Likrat Hasheynah   בְּרָכָה לִקְרַאת הַשֵּׁנָה

Ḥevley sheynah al eynay   חֶבְלֵי שֵׁנָה עַל עֵינַי

utnumah al af'apay,   וּתְנוּמָה עַל עַפְעַפַּי,

mal'ah nafshi hodayah   מָלְאָה נַפְשִׁי הוֹדָיָה

al mat'not hayom,   עַל מַתְּנוֹת הַיּוֹם,

mal'ah nafshi hodayah   מָלְאָה נַפְשִׁי הוֹדָיָה

al matat hayom.   עַל מַתַּת הַיּוֹם.

Daily Psalms

שִׁיר שֶׁל יוֹם

Introductory Recitation for the Daily Psalm

*T*oday is the _____ day of the week.
<small>(first, second . . .)</small>

We pause and notice
the desires and yearnings
that pulse through our daily lives,

and we call to mind
the sustaining ties
that infuse our lives with meaning.

הַקְדָּמָה לְשִׁיר שֶׁל יוֹם

Hakdamah L'shir Shel Yom

Hayom yom _____ bashabbat.
(day: rishon, sheyni, sh'lishi,
r'vi'i, ḥamishi, shishi)

הַ יוֹם יוֹם _____ בַּשַׁבָּת.
(ראשון, שני . . .)

Na'atzor l'réga. Niteyn da'téynu
נַעֲצֹר לְרֶגַע. נִתֵּן דַּעְתֵּנוּ

lama'avayim v'lakisufim
לַמַּאֲוַיִּים וְלַכִּסּוּפִים

ha'olim bimrutzat hayom,
הָעוֹלִים בִּמְרוּצַת הַיּוֹם,

un'ayeyn bak'sharim
וּנְעַיֵּן בַּקְשָׁרִים

hanot'nim l'ḥayéynu
הַנּוֹתְנִים לְחַיֵּינוּ

mashma'ut.
מַשְׁמָעוּת.

Psalm for Sunday   שִׁיר לְיוֹם רִאשׁוֹן

The Amphitheater

Here we are. We are here.

And why, when here, do we want more?

Here we are.

In a weedy patch of wood,

an empty arc proclaims dominion.

Moss-ridden, riddled with fungus and fern,

the soft disintegrations of the seasons,

it glows, inevitable, in the afternoon light.

We are here.

Who put it here? How long ago?

Who watched its pageants under darkening skies,

hoping for long, perhaps immortal life?

And why, when here, do we always want more?

Beneath mouldy stirrings, immobile stones.

Why has it gone so still?

What is left that we need to know?

Psalm for Monday   שִׁיר לְיוֹם שֵׁנִי

Clouds

Slow and white, they amble across pastures of sky.

On the other side of the horizon,

the prairie ripples like a pond.

Pinned at its corners to grass and sky,

the house stays down.

We are three-fourths water;

our bodies float across the earth

with an ease we are unaware of.

Gravity, old yearnings,

pin us down.

When the sky clears, the clouds leave

faint, indelible rubbings

on the mind.

You look up, close your eyes, and see them

gone.

Comm.
p. 438

Psalm for Tuesday   שִׁיר לְיוֹם שְׁלִישִׁי

The Rains

The rains have washed the ice away
and all over the woods, the birches

have dropped their scrolls
whose secret maps lead inside

to the tweet, tick, scritch, and gulp,
to the rumble of distant sky

and the muffled roar of sea,
sounds washed in rain like music

you have heard before,
you have not heard before,

the raw material of your life
abounding.

Psalm for Wednesday שִׁיר לְיוֹם רְבִיעִי

If You Sit Long Enough

If you sit long enough in the woods,
nothing happens.

Just the earth's breath rising and falling
up and down tree trunks

which go copper-green in the air
as if oxidized.

Just your own breath warming a spot of earth
while your heart beats

and you begin, like all the creatures,
to repeat yourself—

the same thoughts rasping in your head,
over and over,

the same yearnings rising, like the tails
of startled squirrels.

Psalm for Thursday   שִׁיר לְיוֹם חֲמִישִׁי

The Guests

Unsummoned,

they come to you:

the purple burdock with its hidden orange root,

the yellow birch shivering in the green light of ferns,

the deer disappearing into the clefts of the hills,

the soft hair of a lover's body, like starry moss—

Let them stay, stay in their bodies,

fragile and lovely,

stay past the winding of the slender thread,

the halted talk of the birds.

Psalm for Friday   שִׁיר לְיוֹם שִׁשִּׁי

The Feast

The laden arms of the oak, the elm,
and the agitated hunger of the small jays,

the fat globes of white sugarmum
where bees suck love,

and you, in the morning shade,
sipping hot coffee,

the taste of the new day sharp
and alive on your tongue,

are a chorus that says,
Indulge: the world is abundant—

this loving, dying world
to which we are given,

out of which we have come—
O body of the world,

eat with joy
the body of the world.

Comm.
p. 438

PART TWO

The Weekly Cycle

The Sabbath

מַחֲזוֹר הַשָּׁבוּעַ

שַׁבָּת

Introduction

Will

Three generations back
my family had only

to light a candle
and the world parted.

Today, Friday afternoon,
I disconnect clocks and phones.

When night fills my house
with passages,

I begin saving
my life.

In an ideal world, we might be aware of the potential for holiness at every moment of every day. Judaism reaches toward this ideal in the many opportunities it finds for blessing in daily life. Yet in the real world, the business of life—the busy-ness of life—often seems to distract us from our most profound connections. In truth, this is not the fault of dailiness, and it may not even be the fault of our work; rather, our own failure to be attentive to what matters is ultimately what gets in our way. Somehow we find, in the words of the poet, that the world is too much with us: getting and spending, we lay waste our powers. So, to return us to a sense of balance, to help us regain our perspective, we are given an opportunity to pause— a chance to step back from our occupation with the world and to appreciate instead our very being-in-the-world. This is the Sabbath, the day of rest, Judaism's magnificent invention. This is the day in which the routines of work are abandoned and time seems to become a different dimension. From sundown on Friday until the first stars of Saturday night, we disconnect the ordinary clocks that run our lives and dismantle the everyday systems of communication. In their absence, time flows like a balm, as we focus our awareness in solitude and celebrate in community, taking delight in the whole of creation.

How does one describe such a day? The metaphor of the Sabbath as "a palace in time" has become a definitive image in modern Jewish thought ever since the publication in 1951 of Abraham Joshua Heschel's now classic work *The Sabbath*.[11] In at least one way, the metaphor bears truth: the seven-day structure of the week, with the Sabbath as its pinnacle, *is* like a great piece of architecture—a brilliant human achievement, artfully conceived and (in the purest sense of the word) artificially created. For unlike the day, the month, and the year, the week is not determined by the natural world alone: the risings and settings of the sun, the phases of the moon, the seasons of the earth do not suffice to establish its domain. The cycle of the week is a human projection onto the natural flow of time, and the Sabbath gives this artifice its splendor.

But Heschel means to say more: "Technical civilization is [our] conquest of space. . . . Yet to have more does not mean to be more. The power we attain in the world of space terminates abruptly at the borderline of time. But time is the heart of existence."[12] Ultimately he uses his image of "the architecture of time" to define the Sabbath's very "essence" and "meaning": "Thus the essence of the Sabbath is completely detached from the world of space. The meaning of the Sabbath is to celebrate time rather than space."[13]

Who can fail to be moved by Heschel's eloquence, his passion? Yet at the same time I find myself troubled by his disparagement of the realm of space, and I am led to question: What does it mean to create a "palace in time"? Is not this "palace" (such an emphatically spatial image!) also a part of space? How do we consecrate time if not *in* space? The simple truth would seem to be that we cannot even know, much less celebrate or honor, the one without the other. The Sabbath is given life not in an abstract realm of time but in the embodied use of time within the physical world, by our whole physical-and-spiritual beings. The lighting of candles, with which we usher the Sabbath in and escort it out; the drinking of wine, with which we open Sabbath eve and close the Sabbath day; the sharing of feasts, through which we nurture both spirit and body; the enjoyment of sexual love, which is deemed especially fitting for this day—these are the real and symbolic acts that color and flavor Sabbath celebration. They mark and celebrate time *and* space—time in space and space in time.

In seeking to understand the meaning of the Sabbath, I would prefer a language that more clearly reflects the inseparability of these two domains. Rather than elevate time over space, I would claim the sacred potential of both, much as I claim the sacrality of both spirit and body, of our whole embodied-spirit-selves. Heschel's own argument suggests that the problem is not really with "space" but with the unbridled pursuit of its conquest, the pursuit of power in the world. So I would reword Heschel's statement that "time is the heart of existence" to say that "time is *at* the heart of existence"—in relation to, not to the exclusion of, space. I agree with him that "there is a realm of time where the goal is not to have but to be, not to own but to give, not to control but to share, not to subdue but to be in accord."[14] But even this realm exists in the physical world—in space that is shared rather than dominated, accepted and appreciated rather than manipulated and acted upon. When body and spirit join in the creation of such a domain, we have what might be called sacred time-space. In Jewish liturgical culture, the Sabbath is the quintessence of this experience.

Still, it is not hard to understand why Heschel's polarization of time and space has been embraced in modern Jewish thought, for such dichotomizing is prevalent in Jewish theology. Traditional rabbinic Judaism has typically conceptualized in oppositional, dualistic terms: space and time, body and soul, secular and holy, female and male, to name but a few obvious examples. The discernment of distinctions—especially oppositional distinctions—might be seen as core to rabbinic thinking, and there is no doubt it is often done brilliantly. Unfortunately, this conceptual approach sometimes underemphasizes or even ignores the connectedness out of which distinctions are formed. Distinctions are, after all, grounded in relation, and this relationality cries out for recognition. For many Jews today, especially feminist Jews, awareness of the connectedness—of the profound, underlying unity of all life—is at the heart of a monotheistic vision. And when we set out to draw boundaries—the distinctions that provide our lives with purpose and meaning—we seek to do so with a different vision from that which guided rabbinic thinking. We seek to distinguish without disparaging what is "other," to celebrate difference without necessarily presuming hierarchy.

In thinking about Heschel's metaphor and about the Sabbath and its place in the week, I keep coming back to these realizations: just as there is no human experience of time apart from space, there is no experience of rest without work, of Sabbath without weekday, of the extraordinary apart from the ordinary. I keep returning, in other words, to how we think about distinctions.

The issue of distinctions and differences is confronted nowhere more sharply than in the traditional ritual separating the Sabbath from the rest of the week, known as the *havdalah*—a word that means, literally, "separation." This ritual, which marks the Sabbath's departure, is also what establishes the context—the greater whole—in which all Sabbath celebration takes place. Thus, although relatively brief, it is pivotal to the Sabbath liturgy, the turning point of the weekly cycle. In re-creating the *havdalah*, I found myself rethinking the dichotomies associated with Sabbath observance: time and space, rest and work, holiness and ordinariness. As I did so, I reached for a conceptualization that would frame the distinction between Sabbath and weekdays in a new way, incorporating feminist insights into the process.

I began by reflecting on the traditional *havdalah* ritual, which contains four blessings:

over wine, spices, lights of fire, and the making of distinctions. While all of these have symbolic significance, it is in the fourth blessing (which I will take up shortly) that the rabbinic view of distinctions is explicit. Rabbinic theology is also implicitly conveyed in the ritual through an absence: the *havdalah* makes no reference to God's sanctifying the day that is about to begin. This is in clear contrast to the *kiddush* ritual over wine that is recited on Sabbath eve, in which the focus is on God's sanctification of the Sabbath. Indeed, the very word *kiddush* means "sanctification."

On first glance this distinction between the Sabbath and the rest of the week may not seem problematic; it may even seem unarguable. Yet the context of the whole *havdalah* ritual reveals what is at stake here: in the blessing over distinctions the hierarchy of Sabbath and weekday is explicitly connected to other hierarchies, at least one of which is more obviously troubling. This blessing is the liturgical heart and the conceptual core of the *havdalah*. In it God is praised for having distinguished between the parts (the implicitly oppositional poles) in each of the following pairs: the holy and the not-holy (translatable, in certain contexts, as "secular"), light and darkness, Israel and the (other) nations, the seventh day and the six days of work. What makes this blessing feel particularly inappropriate to many Jews today is its analogy between the categorical, value-laden dualism of holy and not-holy and the proposed dualism of Israel and the nations. In the process of distinguishing the Sabbath from the weekdays, the rabbis assume a hierarchical relationship not only between the Sabbath and all other days of the week but also between the people of Israel and all other human communities.[15] In this context, Sabbath and Israel are presumed to be holy, while the "others" mentioned are not. To many Jews today, this idea is unacceptable.

Yet our need for distinctions is real; indeed, the recognition of differences is part of our very appreciation of life. Just as the process of individual human growth involves learning to distinguish the self from other selves, so human cultures distinguish themselves from one another to emerge as discrete—though still interrelated—entities within the greater whole of human civilization. The differences between selves—both personal and communal—make for richness and diversity in the world. It seems apparent that the problem lies not in our perceiving a distinction between self and other but in our hierarchizing that distinction, turning it into a polarized dualism whose two halves are clearly unequal.

But if we do not wish to view the difference between self and other hierarchically, might we nonetheless want to maintain a hierarchical model when thinking about the difference between the Sabbath and the weekdays? Surely the Sabbath is uniquely precious. Yet precisely because the Sabbath is such an important symbol in Judaism, the way we distinguish it from the weekdays *itself models* how we make other distinctions—including those between self and other, between Israel and other nations, even between females and males.

My re-creation of the *havdalah* puts aside the hierarchical overview of the traditional ritual and considers the relationship between Sabbath and weekday in a new light. Viewing that relationship as one of mutual reference and support, I distinguish the Sabbath from the rest of the week by recognizing the special qualities of each. My formulation is based on the conviction that the potential for holiness is present in every aspect of our lives. To remind us of this potential, I believe it helpful to hallow *both* the Sabbath day *and* the entity of the week. This does not mean that we obliterate the differences between Sabbath and weekday; on the contrary, we highlight them. To put it in traditional terms, we might say that we distinguish *beyn kódesh l'kódesh,* "between holiness and holiness" (the language used in the traditional *havdalah* ritual when the Sabbath ends at the onset of a festival). As the Sabbath is precious for its *m'nuḥah,* "rest," and its *óneg,* "delight," the weekdays bear the hope of fruitfulness, of accomplishment and achievement. There is joy in this, too; indeed, there is no joy without it.

Thus the blessing over wine in my new *Havdalah:* **Parting Ritual for the Sabbath** is rendered as a *kiddush*—a sanctification—for the incoming week, parallel in its structure to the sanctifications over wine for the Sabbath. While the Sabbath sanctifications recall *creation*—our origins and the origin of all living things—the sanctification of the week honors our *journey*—our history, our generations. At the transitional moment of the Sabbath's departure, what leaves and what enters are connected. The sanctification of the latter recalls the sanctification of the former, reminding us that each depends on the other for its meaning, for its existence; reminding us that in each we may find fulfillment and that in the two together we may experience wholeness.

The *Havdalah:* **Parting Ritual for the Sabbath** also contains a new blessing of **Distinctions,** in which differences themselves are blessed, even as the unity of the whole is affirmed. New blessings for spices and for lights of fire are provided as well. In the blessing entitled **Spices,** individual identity—the uniqueness of every being—is celebrated; in **Lights of Fire,** the less visible aspects of identities are illuminated. The ritual starts with the **Opening Psalm,** which focuses on transitions—the passage from endings to beginnings—and it concludes with the **Blessing for the New Week,** which emphasizes the potential in beginnings. Thus, despite its brevity, the *Havdalah:* **Parting Ritual for the Sabbath** is a pivotal part of the Sabbath liturgy—the end that is also a beginning, giving THE WEEKLY CYCLE its genuinely cyclic shape. The *Havdalah* constitutes the third section of the cycle, **Departure of the Sabbath, Entrance of the Week.**

The other two sections of THE WEEKLY CYCLE, **Sabbath Eve** and **Sabbath Day,** are devoted to the entrance and ongoing celebration of the Sabbath itself. Because the Sabbath is observed in both the home and the community, liturgy is provided for both settings. Traditional Judaism offers several synagogue services on the Sabbath: *kabbalat shabbat*, which welcomes the Sabbath on Friday afternoon, followed by the evening prayers, called *ma'ariv*; the Saturday morning services of *shaharit* and *musaf*, the latter being a supplementary service recalling the Temple sacrifices; and the Saturday afternoon service, *minhah*, which leads into Saturday evening's *ma'ariv* and the *havdalah* ritual. Besides the **Havdalah: Parting Ritual for the Sabbath** (for use in either the communal setting or the home), I have created communal liturgy, in the form of two full-length prayer services, for those times of the Sabbath when Jewish communities today most often gather—Sabbath eve and Sabbath morning. I have also provided offerings for use in the home on Sabbath eve and at the meals of Sabbath day.

The first ceremony in **Sabbath Eve** is *Kabbalat Shabbat:* **Prayer Service Welcoming the Sabbath**, a community celebration based on the traditional *kabbalat shabbat* service. The **Opening** of *Kabbalat Shabbat* consists of a silent meditation followed by **Sabbath Candlelighting** and the **Psalm for Sabbath Candlelighting**. The core of the service is a selection of poems by Jewish women poets, taking the place of the biblical psalms in the traditional *kabbalat shabbat*. Entitled **Psalms of Creation**, this selection is presented in four parts: **Alone, and at One; The Healing of the Wind; The River and the Sea;** and **The Earth and Its Fullness**. Together these poems express the wonder of creation, a theme traditionally associated with Sabbath eve, as they explore our relationship to the whole of the natural world.

The climax of the service is the section called **Greeting the Sabbath,** which includes *L'khu, Rey'ot V'rey'im:* **Greeting the Sabbath Bride** (an adaptation of the popular kabbalistic hymn *l'khah, dodi*) and **Psalm for the Sabbath,** a new English poem. The service concludes with **Closing Prayers,** consisting of the *Kaddish:* **Mourners' Prayer** and the **Closing Blessing.**

Following *Kabbalat Shabbat* in the **Sabbath Eve** section of the cycle is *Kabbalat P'ney Shabbat:* **Home Ritual Welcoming the Sabbath,** which contains blessings and poetry to usher the Sabbath into the home. It begins with the **Opening Psalm,** leading the way for **Sabbath Candlelighting**. These are followed by two offerings focusing on personal relationships, **Blessing of the Children** and **Blessing the Beloved**; the latter takes the place of the traditional recitation from Proverbs known as *éyshet-hayil*, "a woman of valor." The focal point of the ritual is the **Sanctification over Wine for Sabbath Eve,** which begins the first of the three Sabbath feasts. Also provided are the three mealtime blessings—**Handwashing Before the Meal, Blessing Before the Meal,** and **Blessing After the Meal.**

Sabbath Day provides *Shaharit:* **Morning Service for the Sabbath,** a re-creation of the traditional *shaharit*. It begins with **Opening Blessings and Songs,** a sequence of six offerings. This sequence starts with two blessings said by the individual in preparation for communal prayer, **Putting on the Prayer Shawl** and **Morning Blessing** (the latter reprised from THE DAILY CYCLE). It continues with two biblical adaptations, **How Good the Dwellings** and *Hal'lu:* **Praise**, and an adaptation of a traditional rabbinic prayer, **The Breath of All Life**. It ends with the **Psalm for the Sabbath** (reprised from *Kabbalat Shabbat*). Like *Kabbalat Shabbat*, this first part of the Sabbath morning service emphasizes creation and our place in it.

The service proceeds with *Sh'ma* **and the Surrounding Blessings**, which opens with *Bar'khu:* **Call to Blessing**. The focal point of this section is the *Sh'ma:* **Communal Declaration of Faith** (a variation on the *Sh'ma:* **Personal Declaration of Faith**, found in THE DAILY CYCLE). The *Sh'ma* is framed here by three blessings—the **Blessing of Creation**, the **Blessing of Revelation**, and the **Blessing of Redemption**—which encapsulate the three overriding themes of both the Sabbath morning service and the Sabbath day as a whole.[16] (I will return in a moment to the themes of creation, revelation, and redemption as they relate to the structure of this *Shaḥarit.*)

The centerpiece of the service is the *Amidah:* **Sevenfold Prayer for the Sabbath**, comprising seven sections of blessings and meditations, supplemented with poems by Jewish women poets. In its multivocality, the *Amidah* resembles the **Psalms of Creation** in the new *Kabbalat Shabbat* service; the *Amidah* contains greater thematic scope, however, in that it reinterprets the seven discrete topics of the traditional *amidah* prayer. The seven sections of this new *Amidah* are: **Recalling Our Ancestors, Remembering Our Lives; Sustaining Life, Embracing Death; Hallowing Our Namings; Sanctifying the Sabbath Day; Restoring Shekhinah, Reclaiming Home; The Gift of Gratitude;** and **Blessing of Peace**.

Returning to the overarching themes of the day: as creation is the thematic focus of Sabbath eve, revelation (that is, the receiving of Torah, or sacred knowledge) may be thought of as the central focus of the daytime part of the Sabbath. And as creation is the theme of **Opening Blessings and Songs**, revelation is the focus of the section of the *Shaḥarit* entitled **Honoring Torah**, which is the high point of the service. Here, sacred texts are recited or studied and **Torah Blessings** are said. An extended meditation at the beginning of the section challenges the community to consider what it means by revelation, which texts it wishes to honor as sacred—as Torah—and what kind of relationship it will pursue with those texts. The liturgy for **Honoring Torah** begins with **Gates of Righteousness**, an adaptation of a biblical passage, and closes with **Tree of Life**, a biblical citation. Also included are special prayers for individuals under the rubric **As Those Who Came Before Us Were Blessed**. These prayers are said on behalf of those who have honored Torah and those in need of healing or support. On the Sabbath preceding Rosh Hodesh, the ritual of ***Birkat Haḥó-desh: Heralding the New Month***, found in THE MONTHLY CYCLE, is inserted at the conclusion of this section of the service.

The **Closing Prayers** of the *Shaḥarit* service include ***Aléynu L'shabéy'aḥ:* It Is Ours to Praise**, an adaptation of the traditional *aléynu* prayer. Here the third theme of the Sabbath—the theme of redemption—is explored, amplifying what was previously expressed in the **Blessing of Redemption**. The articulation of the theme of redemption at the close of the service finds a parallel in the larger structure of the Sabbath day, where redemption is associated with the close of the Sabbath. (Thus the traditional *havdalah* makes reference to messianic times, while the new *Havdalah* finds redemption in our ongoing commitment to seek holiness in each day.) The *Shaḥarit* service concludes with the ***Kaddish:* Mourners' Prayer** and the **Closing Blessing** (both reprised from *Kabbalat Shabbat*).

Appended to the *Shaḥarit* is the **Sanctification over Wine for Sabbath Day** (a variation of the **Sanctification over Wine for Sabbath Eve**). This may be recited in either the synagogue or the home following the *Shaḥarit* service. After the recitation of the **Sanctification over Wine**, the second feast of the Sabbath is eaten; mealtime blessings for this and for the third feast (eaten toward the end of the Sabbath day) are the same as those recited at the first feast and found in ***Kabbalat P'ney Shabbat***.

While themes of connectedness and connection thread through all these offerings for the home and the community, the Sabbath remains, in the end, a deeply personal experience, unique to each individual. "Everyone carries, within, a special image of the Sabbath," wrote the Israeli scholar of Hassidism Pinchas Peli. "Tell me what your Sabbath is like and I will tell you who you are."[17] We might expand these words to say, "Tell me what your Sabbath is like and that will tell me what your week is like; together, they will say who you are." THE WEEKLY CYCLE celebrates both the Sabbath and the week; users are encouraged to treat the offerings contained here as tools to make this most human of liturgical cycles personal, their own.

Sabbath Eve

לֵיל שַׁבָּת

KABBALAT SHABBAT

Prayer Service
Welcoming the Sabbath

קַבָּלַת שַׁבָּת

CONDUCTING THE *KABBALAT SHABBAT* SERVICE

This ceremony is intended primarily for group participation—ideally in a *minyan* (a quorum of ten). While communities should feel free to develop their own ways of using this liturgy, the following are some suggestions.

The person leading the service may read aloud the comments and meditations found on the opening pages to the major parts of the service (**Opening**, p. 59; **Psalms of Creation**, p. 65; **Greeting the Sabbath**, p. 99; and **Closing Prayers**, p. 103) and on the pages introducing the ***Kaddish:*** **Mourners' Prayer** (p. 105) and the **Closing Blessing** (p. 111). Alternatively, these pages may be read silently by the congregation.

Sabbath Candlelighting (pp. 60–61) may be recited by individuals or sung by the congregation as a whole, as each person present, or one member of each household, lights a candle. Placing the candles in the center of the room or around the periphery will allow many to be lit at once.

Individual congregants read aloud the **Psalm for Sabbath Candlelighting** (pp. 62–63), the **Psalms of Creation** (pp. 66–97), and the **Psalm for the Sabbath** (p. 102). If individuals remain in their places as they read their parts, the effect will be quite different from that of a leader chanting at the front of the synagogue.

The high point of the service is ***L'khu, Rey'ot V'rey'im*** (pp. 100–101). Like *l'khah, dodi,* the traditional hymn on which it is based, this poem is meant to be sung by the congregation rather than read, and dancing may accompany the singing. The Hebrew text of ***L'khu, Rey'ot V'rey'im*** will fit any of the hundreds of melodies that have been composed for *l'khah, dodi* (the English translation of ***L'khu, Rey'ot V'rey'im*** is not meant for singing but for reference).

Music may be used to enhance the service further; for example, the singing of *nigunim* (melodies without words) may be introduced at the beginning of each section of **Psalms of Creation** (pp. 66, 74, 82, and 90). To conclude the service, these *nigunim* may be reprised after the **Closing Blessing** (pp. 112–13), or the **Closing Blessing** itself may be sung.

Silence can be a powerful element of communal prayer services. There is a place for silence in the **Opening** (p. 59) and in the ***Kaddish:*** **Mourners' Prayer** (p. 105). Silence may also be encouraged after the **Psalm for the Sabbath** (p. 102).

In the *Kaddish:* **Mourners' Prayer,** the poem *Each of Us Has a Name* (pp. 106–9) may be read responsively: mourners may read in unison the opening line of each stanza, with the congregation as a whole reciting the remaining lines (these parts may also be reversed).

For those communities that include a sanctification over wine (*kiddush*) in their Friday evening service, the **Sanctification over Wine for Sabbath Eve** (found on pp. 128–29 in *Kabbalat P'ney Shabbat:* **Home Ritual Welcoming the Sabbath**) may be appended to the end of *Kabbalat Shabbat* or inserted before the **Closing Prayers** (p. 103).

Note that the celebration of this new *Kabbalat Shabbat* may take place either before or after the home ritual of *Kabbalat P'ney Shabbat,* depending on the custom of the community. (While Orthodox synagogues generally hold prayer services prior to the Sabbath meal in the home, Reform synagogues convene Sabbath evening services after dinnertime; among other non-Orthodox movements, a variety of practices exist.) In *ḥavurah*-style communities that meet in people's homes for prayer services and shared meals, *Kabbalat Shabbat* and *Kabbalat P'ney Shabbat* may be joined to form one continuous ritual.

Order of the Service

OPENING

Sabbath Candlelighting

Psalm for Sabbath Candlelighting

PSALMS OF CREATION

Alone, and at One

The Healing of the Wind

The River and the Sea

The Earth and Its Fullness

GREETING THE SABBATH

L'khu, Rey'ot V'rey'im: *Greeting the Sabbath Bride*

Psalm for the Sabbath

CLOSING PRAYERS

Kaddish: *Mourners' Prayer*

Closing Blessing

סֵדֶר קַבָּלַת שַׁבָּת

OPENING
פְּתִיחָה

As we light the Sabbath candles, we invite into our presence the memory of those who cannot be with us—friends and family in other places or from our past. We bring them into the community by holding their names in our thoughts, or by speaking their names aloud after the candles are lit.

Sabbath Candlelighting

*M*ay our hearts be lifted,
our spirits refreshed,
as we light the Sabbath candles.

Hadlakat Neyrot Shabbat   הַדְלָקַת נֵרוֹת שַׁבָּת

Yitromeym libéynu,

r'shovav nafshéynu,

b'hadlakat neyr shel shabbat.

יִתְרוֹמֵם לִבֵּנוּ,

תְּשׁוֹבַב נַפְשֵׁנוּ,

בְּהַדְלָקַת נֵר שֶׁל שַׁבָּת.

Psalm for Sabbath Candlelighting

When I Said the Blessing over the Candles

When I said the blessing over the candles,

my yearnings called out:

Good Sabbath to you, my dear ones.

But they had left the lands of the living

and did not respond to tenderness.

My trembling holiday said:

My roots are exposed.

I whispered:

Peace to you, Sabbath to you,

my soul.

Flames wander through my tears

and the wall shimmers gold.

So much light around me,

so great the pain—

one more moment, and my soul

will depart.

ZELDA
(*translation M. F.*)

מִזְמוֹר לְהַדְלָקַת נֵרוֹת שַׁבָּת

כַּאֲשֶׁר בֵּרַכְתִּי עַל הַנֵּרוֹת

כַּאֲשֶׁר בֵּרַכְתִּי עַל הַנֵּרוֹת

קָרְאוּ כְּסוּפַי בְּקוֹל:

שַׁבָּת שָׁלוֹם, יַקִּירִי—

אַךְ הֵמָּה נָטְשׁוּ אֶת אַרְצוֹת הַחַיִּים

וְלֹא עָנוּ לָךְ.

אָמַר חַגִּי הָרוֹעֶד: שָׁרָשַׁי לְמַעְלָה.

לָחַשְׁתִּי:

שָׁלוֹם לָךְ, שַׁבָּת לָךְ, נִשְׁמָתִי.

מִבַּעַד לְדִמְעוֹתַי שׁוֹטְטוּ שַׁלְהָבוֹת

וְהַקִּיר כֻּלּוֹ זָהָב מְנַצְנֵץ,

כָּל כָּךְ אוֹר מִסְּבִיבִי

וְכָל כָּךְ הַכְּאֵב—

עוֹד רֶגַע וְתֵצֵא נִשְׁמָתִי.

זלדה

PSALMS OF CREATION
מִזְמוֹרֵי הַבְּרִיאָה

These poems express our wonder and empathy in the face of the natural world. As we witness the beauty and the inevitable passing of all that lives in nature, poignant meaning accrues to the rabbinic idea that we are partners with divinity in creation. For, more than any other species, we affect the balance of the natural order; ultimately we are the ones who may determine whether the whole lives or dies. On Sabbath eve we celebrate the magnificence of the greater whole, affirming our place as a part of it.

Alone, and at One

The Golden Butterfly

When the golden butterfly wends its way

through a river of colors and scents

toward its flower-mate, and clings

as though this flower were the star

of its secret self—

an inexplicable clamor of hope

rises in every heart.

And when that beautiful flutterer

abandons the weary petals

and vanishes in space,

the lonely moment wakens in the world,

a soul vanishes in infinity.

ZELDA
(*translation M. F.*)

יַחַד וּלְבַד

הַפַּרְפַּר הַכָּתֹם

כַּאֲשֶׁר הַפַּרְפַּר הַכָּתֹם מְפַלֵּס דַּרְכּוֹ

בִּנְהַר שֶׁל צְבָעִים וְרֵיחוֹת

אֶל פֶּרַח בֶּן דְּמוּתוֹ וְדָבֵק בּוֹ

כְּמוֹ הָיָה פֶּרַח זֶה

כּוֹכַב הָאֲנִי הַסּוֹדִי שֶׁלּוֹ

מִתְעוֹרֶרֶת תִּקְוָה סוֹאֶנֶת וְחַסְרַת פֵּשֶׁר

בְּכָל הַלְּבָבוֹת.

וְכַאֲשֶׁר נוֹטֵשׁ אוֹתוֹ מְרַחֵף יָפֶה

אֶת עֲלֵי הַכּוֹתֶרֶת שֶׁעִיְּפוּ

וְנֶעְלָם בֶּחָלָל

מֵקִיץ בַּתֵּבֵל הָרֶגַע הַגַּלְמוּד,

נֶעְלֶמֶת נְשָׁמָה בָּאֵין־סוֹף.

זלדה

Humble Hour

My clear, humble hour—

when I carried a bundle of straw

for the newborn calf

and bent down

and spread the straw

beneath her quivering wetness,

my trembling hand playing

on the little chin

as I put two fingers

into her hot mouth

and cried

a sweet, satisfying cry

in the face of the calf

on Sheva's farm

in the village of Orot.

MALKA HEIFETZ TUSSMAN
(*translation M. F.*)

הכנעהדיקע שעה

מײַן לויטערע, הכנעהדיקע שעה,

ווען כ׳האָב אַ בינטל שטרוי געבראַכט צו טראָגן

פֿאַר אַ קעלבעלע אַ ניַי געבאָרן

און איַינגעבויגן זיך

און אויסגעשפּרייט דאָס שטרוי

אונטער קעלבלס צאַפּלדיקער נאַסקייט.

אַרום דער מאָרדעלע

האָט זיך אַרומגעשפּילט מײַן ציטערדיקע האַנט,

צוויי פֿינגער אים געגעבן אין זײַן הייסן מויל

און

איך האָב געוויינט,

געשמאַק אַזוי געוויינט אין פֿנים פֿונעם קעלבל

אין משק ״שבע״ פֿון מושבֿ ״אורות״.

מלכה חפֿץ טוזמאַן

The Bird

A small bird is making frantic moves—
of ecstasy? hunger?
You watch her shadow in the sun-lit mud
and wish you could see her round body
wherever it is, up there in the tree.

The woods are full of frustration:
emerging, half-finished sounds—
the snap of branch,
muffled stir of leaves
suddenly stopped—
as though creatures approaching the road
retreat when they see you there,
sitting, cold-lipped, cold-fingered,
offering your bread to invisible guests.

But here comes this half-mad bird,
out of place, out of season,
swooping down
in a flash of recognition
to take you up.

Company

The air is bathwater-warm,

the sky pale, its intensity drained,

as you walk together through the prairie,

up to your shoulders in grasses.

At your sides, the loosestrife flames up violet,

the cattails smolder brown.

You cannot see the distance at all.

You trust

the cool mud slosh of the path

and the sinking sun.

You talk

of what is absent in your lives.

By miracle or chance,

one may know something of the other,

but neither of you expects that.

It is enough

to walk together through deep grasses,

content with the landscape and the season.

Strange Plant

At midnight, a candle glowed

in the heart

of a blood-red flower.

At midnight, on the grief

of my face,

a strange plant's celebration

streamed like gold.

ZELDA
(*translation M. F.*)

צֶמַח זָר

בַּחֲצוֹת דָּלַק נֵר
בְּלִבּוֹ שֶׁל פֶּרַח
אָדֹם כַּדָּם.
בַּחֲצוֹת נִגֵּר כַּזָּהָב
עַל אֵבֶל פָּנַי
חַגּוֹ שֶׁל צֶמַח זָר.

זלדה

The Healing of the Wind

Awakening

High wind

and a blackbird

push the sky across the hills.

The windows shake. You pull

yourself out of the blankets,

a flash strikes the eastern walls

of houses.

　　　　　　Morning—

the city a cup full

of light, a bright

flask of wind

to rise to.

הָרוּחַ הַמְרַפְּאת

We Know Her

We see her in the shimmering blades,
their bright green waving on the hill,

and hear her through the cottonwoods, the birches,
flying free through their leafy crowns.

We breathe her as she lifts to the sky
the scents of the newly furrowed field,

and feel her touching our forehead
in our fevered dreams.

Only her taste is saved
for tomorrow—

the dark taste of her emptiness,
remembered honey of mother's milk—

manna of our longing,
wind.

Slender Ships

Slender ships drowse on swollen green water,

black shadows sleep on the cold heart of water.

All the winds are still.

Clouds shift like ghosts in the speechless night.

The earth, pale and calm, awaits lightning and thunder.

I will be still.

ANNA MARGOLIN
(*translation M. F.*)

שלאַנקע שיפֿן

שלאַנקע שיפֿן דרימלען אויפֿן געשוואָלן גרינעם וואַסער,
שוואַרצע שאָטנס שלאָפֿן אויפֿן קאַלטן האַרץ פֿון וואַסער.
אַלע ווינטן זײַנען שטיל.
כמאַרעס רוקן זיך געשפּענסטיק אין דער נאַכט דער שטומער.
בלייך און רויִק וואַרט די ערד אויף בליץ און דונער.
איך וועל זײַן שטיל.

אַנא מאַרגאָלין

All the Winds

All the winds have grown still

as though someone rocked them softly to sleep

between naked branches of the trees

on a rainy autumn night.

All the sorrows have made their home

at my doorstep, as though—in all the world—

they had no other harbor

but my eyes, my hands, my smile, my word.

RACHEL KORN
(*translation M. F.*)

אַלע ווינטן

אַלע ווינטן זענען שטיל געוואָרן,
ווי עס וואָלט זיי עמעץ איינגעוויגט באַזאַכט
צווישן נאָקעטדיקע צוויַיגן פֿון די ביימער
אין אַ חשוונדיקער רעגנדיקער נאַכט.

אַלע טרויערן האָבן זיך פֿאַראַנקערט
ביי מיַין שוועל, ווי ס׳וואָלט שוין נישט געווען קיין אָרט
אויף דער גאַנצער וועלט, אַחוץ אין מיַינע אויגן,
מיַינע העענט, מיַין שמייכל און מיַין וואָרט.

רחל קאָרן

Moon Is Teaching Bible

Moon is teaching Bible.

Cyclamen, Poppy, and Mountain

listen with joy.

Only the girl cries.

Poppy can't hear her crying—

Poppy is blazing in Torah,

Poppy is burning like the verse.

Cyclamen doesn't listen to the crying—

Cyclamen swoons

from the sweetness of the secret.

Mountain won't hear her crying—

Mountain is sunk

in thought.

But here comes Wind,

soft and fragrant,

to honor hope, to sing

the heart of each flying rider,

each ardent hunter

swept to the ends of the sea.

ZELDA
(*translation M. F.*)

הַיָּרֵחַ מְלַמֵּד תַּנַ״ךְ

הַיָּרֵחַ מְלַמֵּד תַּנַ״ךְ.
רַקֶּפֶת, כַּלָּנִית וָהָר
מַקְשִׁיבִים בְּשִׂמְחָה.
רַק הַיַּלְדָּה בּוֹכָה.
כַּלָּנִית אֶת בְּכִיָּהּ לֹא תִשְׁמַע,
כַּלָּנִית לוֹהֶטֶת בַּתּוֹרָה,
כַּלָּנִית בּוֹעֶרֶת כַּפָּסוּק.
רַקֶּפֶת לַבְּכִי לֹא תַקְשִׁיב,
רַקֶּפֶת מִתְעַלֶּפֶת
מִמְּתִיקוּת הַסּוֹד.
הָהָר אֶת בְּכִיָּהּ לֹא יִשְׁמַע,
הָהָר שָׁקַע
בְּמַחֲשָׁבוֹת.

אַךְ הִנֵּה בָּא
הָרוּחַ הָרַךְ, הַמְבֻשָּׂם,
לָתֵת כָּבוֹד לַתִּקְוָה,
לָשִׁיר כָּל לֵב פָּרָשׁ מְעוֹפֵף,
צַיָּד נִלְהָב,
הַנִּשָּׂא אֶל קְצֵי־יָם.

זלדה

The River and the Sea

Dead Sea

In the middle of July at the bottom of the middle of the world,

water turns to salt

and floats like frozen waves: a petrified ocean.

Below the white horizon lies a still and perfect blue;

above it, the same still blue;

for miles around, a blue dome stopping time.

Beneath yellow parasols, bathers lean into the flat blue air—

blue so hot it is almost yellow—

and their bodies soak up sky the way salt soaks up the sea,

soaks it dry as bones,

until the sea is a sea of white bones floating on sky.

You can walk into the sea and keep walking: you will not drown;

but if you cut your foot on a salt-rock, the sea will suck the wound,

turning it into a white flower of pain,

which, like desire, will be fickle and brief:

you fill desire like a wound with balm and the wound heals over

and the skin is new and needs nothing more until bruised again.

Sometimes the mind alone keeps alive pain or desire—

as when a gesture,

הַנַּחַל וְהַיָּם

such as the way a loved one throws back her hair,

embeds in the mind like a fossil

and the mind sucks the sweet imagined marrow—

the way birds skimming the salt-white water with their red-tipped wings

keep alive an ancient longing for wind.

Water Without Sound

The sea

tore a rib from its side

and said:

Go! Lie down there, be

a sign that I

am great and mighty.

Go

be a sign.

The canal

lies at my window,

speechless.

What can be sadder

than water

without sound?

MALKA HEIFETZ TUSSMAN
(*translation M. F.*)

וואַסער אָן לשון

דער ים

האָט פֿון זײַן זײַט

אַ ריף אַרויסגעריסן

און געזאָגט:

גיי,

לייג זיך דאָרטן,

זײַ מיר אַ סימן אַז איך בין

גרויס,

מעכטיק בין איך.

גיי,

זײַ מיר אַ סימן.

ליגט דער קאַנאַל ביי מײַנע פֿענצטער

שטום.

וואָס קען נאָר טרויעריקער זײַן

ווי וואַסער

אָן לשון.

מלכה חפֿץ טוזמאַן

The Blade of Grass Sings to the River

Even for the little ones like me,

one among the throng,

for the children of poverty

on disappointment's shores,

the river hums its song,

lovingly hums its song.

The sun's gentle caress

touches it now and then,

and I, too, am reflected

in waters that flow green,

and in the river's depths

each one of us is deep.

My ever-deepening image

streaming away to the sea

is swallowed up, erased

on the edge of vanishing.

And with the river's voice,

the ever-silent soul,

with the river's psalm,

sings praises of the world.

LEAH GOLDBERG
(*translation M. F.*)

גִּבְעוֹל הַדֶּשֶׁא שָׁר לַנַּחַל

גַּם לִקְטַנִּים כָּמוֹנִי,
אֶחָד מִנֵּי רְבָבָה,
גַּם לְיַלְדֵי הָעָנִי
עַל חוֹף הָאַכְזָבָה
הוֹמֶה, הוֹמֶה הַנַּחַל,
הוֹמֶה בְּאַהֲבָה.

הַשֶּׁמֶשׁ הַלּוֹטֶפֶת
תִּגַּע בּוֹ לִפְרָקִים,
וְגַם דְּמוּתִי נִשְׁקֶפֶת
בְּמַיִם יְרֻקִּים,
וּבִמְצוּלַת הַנַּחַל
כֻּלָּנוּ עֲמֻקִּים.

דְּמוּתִי הַמִּתְעַמֶּקֶת
בַּדֶּרֶךְ אֶל הַיָּם
נִבְלַעַת וְנִמְחֶקֶת
עַל סַף הַנֶּעְלָם.
וְעִם קוֹלוֹ שֶׁל נַחַל
הַנֶּפֶשׁ הַשּׁוֹתֶקֶת
עִם שִׁיר מִזְמוֹר הַנַּחַל
תַּגִּיד שִׁבְחֵי עוֹלָם.

לאה גולדברג

The River Sings to the Stone

I kissed the stone in the cold of her dream

for she is the silence and I am the psalm,

she is the riddle and I the riddler,

the two of us cut from one eternity.

I kissed the solitary flesh of the stone—

she, the sworn faithful, and I who betray,

she, the enduring, and I who pass on,

she, the earth's secrets, and I who tell all.

And I knew when I touched a speechless heart:

I am the poet and she is the world.

LEAH GOLDBERG
(*translation M. F.*)

הַנַּחַל שָׁר לָאֶבֶן

אֶת הָאֶבֶן נָשַׁקְתִּי בִּצְנַת חֲלוֹמָהּ,
כִּי אֲנִי הַמִּזְמוֹר וְהִיא הַדְּמָמָה,
כִּי הִיא הַחִידָה וַאֲנִי הֶחָד,
כִּי שְׁנֵינוּ קְרָעֲנוּ מִנֵּצַח אֶחָד.

אֶת הָאֶבֶן נָשַׁקְתִּי, אֶת בְּשָׂרָהּ הַבּוֹדֵד.
הִיא שְׁבוּעַת אֱמוּנִים וַאֲנִי הַבּוֹגֵד,
אֲנִי הַחוֹלֵף וְהִיא הַקַּיָּם,
הִיא סוֹדוֹת הַבְּרִיאָה, וַאֲנִי – גְּלוּיָם.

וָאֵדַע כִּי נָגַעְתִּי בְּלֵב נֶאֱלָם:
אֲנִי הַמְשׁוֹרֵר וְהִיא – הָעוֹלָם.

לאה גולדברג

The Earth and Its Fullness

Last Apple

"I am the last apple

that falls from the tree

and no one picks up."

I kneel to the fragrance

of the last apple

and I pick it up.

In my hands—the tree,

in my hands—the leaf,

in my hands—the blossom,

and in my hands—the earth

that kisses the apple

that no one picks up.

MALKA HEIFETZ TUSSMAN
(*translation M. F.*)

הָאָרֶץ וּמְלוֹאָה

לעצטער עפל

„כ׳בין דער לעצטער עפל

וואָס פֿאַלט אַראָפֿ פֿון בוים און

קיינער הייבט ניט אויף.

קיינער הייבט ניט אויף."

איך קני אַראָפֿ צום ריח

פֿון דעם לעצטן עפל

וואָס פֿאַלט אַראָפֿ פֿון בוים

און

איך הייב אויף.

איך הייב אויף!

אין מיינע הענט

דער בוים.

אין מיינע הענט

דער בלאַט.

אין מיינע הענט

דער צווייט

און

אין מיינע הענט די ערד

וואָס קושט דעם עפל

וואָס קיינער הייבט ניט אויף.

מלכה חפֿץ טוזמאַן

Nasturtiums

I planted nasturtiums in a garden—

colorful, fluttery thinness,

my bosom friends from the time when

I was a bashful little nobody in the village

and they smiled at all my child-play.

We meet again, sweet little nose-ticklers,

fineness from a common flower stock.

I take after you: sprouted

from the bread and earth of Volin.

MALKA HEIFETZ TUSSMAN
(*translation M. F.*)

נאַסטורציעס

איך האָב נאַסטורציעס פֿאַרפֿלאַנצט אין גערטל.

קאָליריק פֿלאַטערדיקע דינקייט —
בוזעם־פֿרײַנד מײַנע פֿון דעמאָלט ווען
כ׳בין געווען
אַ גאָרנישטל אַ שעמעווודיקס אין דאָרף,
און צוגעשמייכלט האָבן זיי
צו אַלע מײַנע קינדעריַיען.

מיר טרעפֿן זיך ווידער, זיסינקע נאָזיקצלערס,
איידלקייט פֿון פּראָסטן בלומענשטאַם.

איך בין אין אײַך גערֿאָטן:
אַ שפּראָצל
פֿון וואָלינער ערד און קאָרן־ברויט אַרויס.

מלכה חפֿץ טוזמאַן

With Teeth in the Earth

My cheek upon the earth
and I know mercy.

With lips to the earth
I know love.

My nose in the earth
and I know thievery.

With teeth in the earth
I know murder.

.   .   .

And I know why those
who dig their teeth into the earth

and why those
who tear themselves away from the earth

must always weep over themselves.

MALKA HEIFETZ TUSSMAN
(*translation M. F.*)

מיט צֵיין אין ערד

מײַן באַק אויף דער ערד
און איך ווייס פֿאַרוואָס גנאָד.

מיט ליפֿן צו דער ערד
און איך ווייס פֿאַרוואָס ליבע.

מיטן נאָז אין ערד
ווייס איך פֿאַרוואָס גנבֿה.

מיט צֵיין אין ערד
ווייס איך פֿאַרוואָס
מאָרד.

.   .   .

ווייס איך פֿאַרוואָס
דער מענטש
וואָס גראָבט מיט צֵיין די ערד
און דער
וואָס רַײַסט זיך פֿון דער ערד
וועט אַלע מאָל,
אוי אַלע מאָל,
דאַרפֿן וויינען איבער זיך.

מלכה חפֿץ טוזמאַן

The Pond

In a dense maze of wood, the sudden

stillness of a pond— And the body

is drawn to itself, remembering its home.

You sink to hug the huge earth,

fall into a bed of leaves.

Above, the birches shed their skins.

When you rise to leave, new veins stream,

roads spill into fields, water-green,

the silver pond retrieves the earth and sky.

Back

The woods are gone.

The snow on the cabin roof is gone.

The creatures in the woods and the unseen creatures

are gone.

The city birch is back in front of the study window,

the bare blue-red branches of the Japanese maple beside it,

and the gray and green and blue houses

with their hodge-podge of architecture, their oversprawling gardens,

are here.

And the cars—black, white, silver, red—

are lined up in the street

below the birch tree in front of the window.

The tiny birds in the snowy field are gone,

fading fast from the mind.

But the fat one at the feeder across from the kitchen window

greedily pecks at his food

as you walk through the rooms of the house,

the small domestic pleasures rising to greet you

from beds and tables and chairs.

GREETING THE SABBATH
לִקְרַאת שַׁבָּת

Lifting our voices in song, we greet the Sabbath bride.

Then we meet her again, in silence.

L'khu, Rey'ot V'rey'im: *Greeting the Sabbath Bride*

Refrain: Let us go, friends, to greet the bride,

let us welcome the Sabbath.

Let us go, friends, to greet the bride,

let us welcome the Sabbath.

Let us go out to greet the Sabbath

for she is the source of blessing,

from the very beginning spread above us,

the last thing created but the first conceived.

Awake, awake, your light is coming,

rise and share your light.

Arise, arise, sing a song,

Shekhinah's radiance is revealed in you.

Do not be embarrassed or ashamed.

Why are you saddened, why do you sigh?

You are a shelter for the poor of my people,

and Jerusalem will be rebuilt on its hill.

Come in peace, crown of Shekhinah,

in joy and in rejoicing,

among the faithful of those held dear,

come, bride, come, bride.

AFTER *L'KHAH, DODI,* BY SOLOMON ALKABETZ
(*adaptation M. F.*)

מחזור השבת

<h1>לְכוּ, רֵעוֹת וְרֵעִים</h1>

L'khu, Rey'ot V'rey'im

Refrain: L'khu, rey'ot, likrat kalah,

פִּזְמוֹן: לְכוּ, רֵעוֹת, לִקְרַאת כַּלָּה,

p'ney shabbat n'kab'lah,

פְּנֵי שַׁבָּת נְקַבְּלָה,

l'khu, rey'im, likrat kalah,

לְכוּ, רֵעִים, לִקְרַאת כַּלָּה,

p'ney shabbat n'kab'lah.

פְּנֵי שַׁבָּת נְקַבְּלָה.

Likrat shabbat l'khu v'neyl'khah

לִקְרַאת שַׁבָּת לְכוּ וְנֵלְכָה

ki hi m'kor hab'rakhah,

כִּי הִיא מְקוֹר הַבְּרָכָה,

meyrosh mikédem n'sukhah,

מֵראשׁ מִקֶּדֶם נְסוּכָה,

sof ma'aseh, b'mahashavah t'hilah.

סוֹף מַעֲשֶׂה, בְּמַחֲשָׁבָה תְּחִלָּה.

L'khu, rey'ot, likrat kalah . . .

לְכוּ, רֵעוֹת, לִקְרַאת כַּלָּה . . .

Hit'or'ri, hit'or'ri

הִתְעוֹרְרִי, הִתְעוֹרְרִי

ki va oreykh, kúmi, óri,

כִּי בָא אוֹרֵךְ, קוּמִי, אוֹרִי,

úri, úri, shir dabéyri,

עוּרִי, עוּרִי, שִׁיר דַּבֵּרִי,

ziv hash'khinah aláyikh niglah.

זִיו הַשְּׁכִינָה עָלַיִךְ נִגְלָה.

L'khu, rey'ot, likrat kalah . . .

לְכוּ, רֵעוֹת, לִקְרַאת כַּלָּה . . .

Lo teyvóshi v'lo tikal'mi,

לֹא תֵבְשִׁי וְלֹא תִכָּלְמִי,

mah tishtohahi umah tehemi,

מַה תִּשְׁתּוֹחֲחִי וּמַה תֶּהֱמִי,

bakh yehesu aniyey ami

בָּךְ יֶחֱסוּ עֲנִיֵּי עַמִּי

v'nivn'tah ir al tilah.

וְנִבְנְתָה עִיר עַל תִּלָּהּ.

L'khu, rey'ot, likrat kalah . . .

לְכוּ, רֵעוֹת, לִקְרַאת כַּלָּה . . .

Bó'i v'shalom, atéret sh'khinah,

בּוֹאִי בְשָׁלוֹם, עֲטֶרֶת שְׁכִינָה,

gam b'simhah uvtzoholah,

גַּם בְּשִׂמְחָה וּבְצָהֳלָה,

tokh emuney am s'gulah,

תּוֹךְ אֱמוּנֵי עַם סְגֻלָּה,

bó'i, khalah, bó'i, khalah.

בּוֹאִי, כַלָּה, בּוֹאִי, כַלָּה.

L'khu, rey'ot, likrat kalah . . .

לְכוּ, רֵעוֹת, לִקְרַאת כַּלָּה . . .

עַל־פִּי "לְכָה, דוֹדִי," מֵאֵת שְׁלֹמֹה אַלְקַבֵּץ

Psalm for the Sabbath   מִזְמוֹר שִׁיר לְיוֹם הַשַּׁבָּת

Listen

In the clearing, where the mind flowers

and the world sprouts up at every side,

listen

for the sound in the bushes

behind the grass.

CLOSING PRAYERS
סִיוּם

We have welcomed the Sabbath into our community. With the **Kaddish: Mourners' Prayer,** *we receive comfort from the community. And in the* **Closing Blessing,** *we reaffirm the connections on which we thrive.*

Kaddish: *Mourners' Prayer*
קַדִּישׁ

The traditional mourners' prayer, known as the kaddish, *magnifies and sanctifies the divine name. Tonight we sanctify life by expanding our namings, reflecting and honoring the diversity of our lives.*

We begin by silently calling to mind the names of all those whose absence we mourn.

————

We continue by saying aloud the names of loved ones who have died in the past year. Mourners and those observing the anniversary of the death of a loved one say the names of those they are mourning. Names may include lineage ("Rose, daughter of Pearl and Menakhem Mendl") and terms of relation ("my maternal grandmother"), as well as terms of endearment.

————

We conclude with the recitation of Each of Us Has a Name *(on the next page).*

Kaddish: *Mourners' Prayer*

Each of Us Has a Name

Each of us has a name
given by the source of life
and given by our parents

Each of us has a name
given by our stature and our smile
and given by what we wear

Each of us has a name
given by the mountains
and given by our walls

Each of us has a name
given by the stars
and given by our neighbors

Each of us has a name
given by our sins
and given by our longing

Each of us has a name
given by our enemies
and given by our love

Each of us has a name
given by our celebrations
and given by our work

קַדִּישׁ

L'khol B'riyah Yeysh Sheym   לְכָל בְּרִיָּה יֵשׁ שֵׁם

L'khol b'riyah yeysh sheym   לְכָל בְּרִיָּה יֵשׁ שֵׁם

shenat'nah lah eyn hahayim   שֶׁנָּתְנָה לָהּ עֵין הַחַיִּים

v'nat'nu lah avíha v'imah   וְנָתְנוּ לָהּ אָבִיהָ וְאִמָּהּ

L'khol b'riyah yeysh sheym   לְכָל בְּרִיָּה יֵשׁ שֵׁם

shenat'nu lah komatah v'ófen hiyukhah   שֶׁנָּתְנוּ לָהּ קוֹמָתָהּ וְאֹפֶן חִיּוּכָהּ

v'natan lah ha'arig   וְנָתַן לָהּ הָאָרִיג

L'khol b'riyah yeysh sheym   לְכָל בְּרִיָּה יֵשׁ שֵׁם

shenat'nu lah heharim   שֶׁנָּתְנוּ לָהּ הֶהָרִים

v'nat'nu lah k'taléha   וְנָתְנוּ לָהּ כְּתָלֶיהָ

L'khol b'riyah yeysh sheym   לְכָל בְּרִיָּה יֵשׁ שֵׁם

shenat'nu lah hamazalot   שֶׁנָּתְנוּ לָהּ הַמַּזָּלוֹת

v'nat'nu lah sh'kheynéha   וְנָתְנוּ לָהּ שְׁכֵנֶיהָ

L'khol b'riyah yeysh sheym   לְכָל בְּרִיָּה יֵשׁ שֵׁם

shenat'nu lah hata'éha   שֶׁנָּתְנוּ לָהּ חֲטָאֶיהָ

v'nat'nah lah k'mihatah   וְנָתְנָה לָהּ כְּמִיהָתָהּ

L'khol b'riyah yeysh sheym   לְכָל בְּרִיָּה יֵשׁ שֵׁם

shenat'nu lah son'éha   שֶׁנָּתְנוּ לָהּ שׂוֹנְאֶיהָ

v'nat'nah lah ahavatah   וְנָתְנָה לָהּ אַהֲבָתָהּ

L'khol b'riyah yeysh sheym   לְכָל בְּרִיָּה יֵשׁ שֵׁם

shenat'nu lah hagéha   שֶׁנָּתְנוּ לָהּ חַגֶּיהָ

v'nat'nah lah m'lakhtah   וְנָתְנָה לָהּ מְלַאכְתָּהּ

Each of us has a name

given by the seasons

and given by our blindness

Each of us has a name

given by the sea

and given by

our death.

AFTER A POEM BY ZELDA
(*adaptation M. F.*)

לְכָל בְּרִיָּה יֵשׁ שֵׁם

L'khol b'riyah yeysh sheym

שֶׁנָּתְנוּ לָהּ תְּקוּפוֹת הַשָּׁנָה

shenat'nu lah t'kufot hashanah

וְנָתַן לָהּ עִוְרוֹנָהּ

v'natan lah ivronah

לְכָל בְּרִיָּה יֵשׁ שֵׁם

L'khol b'riyah yeysh sheym

שֶׁנָּתַן לָהּ הַיָּם

shenatan lah hayam

וְנָתַן לָהּ

v'natan lah

מוֹתָהּ.

motah.

עַל־פִּי שִׁיר שֶׁל זֶלְדָּה

מוֹחֵר הַשַּׁבָּת אֵל מָלֵא קַדִּישׁ אַחֵר הַקִּדּוּשׁ מְנַחֵם

Closing Blessing
בִּרְכַּת סִיּוּם

As we began the service by welcoming into our midst individuals with whom we share connections, so we conclude by blessing the greater wholes to which we belong.

Closing Blessing

May the blessings of peace and kindness,
graciousness, goodness, and compassion
flow among us
and all the communities of Israel,
all the peoples of the world.

May this Sabbath bring peace and restoration.

בִּרְכַּת סִיוּם

Birkat Siyum

Yishru shalom, tovah uvrakhah,

יִשְׁרוּ שָׁלוֹם, טוֹבָה וּבְרָכָה,

ḥeyn vaḥéscd v'raḥamim

חֵן וָחֶסֶד וְרַחֲמִים

beynéynu,

בֵּינֵינוּ,

beyn kol adot yisra'eyl,

בֵּין כָּל עֲדוֹת יִשְׂרָאֵל,

uveyn kol yosh'vey teyveyl.

וּבֵין כָּל יוֹשְׁבֵי תֵבֵל.

Shabbat shalom umnuḥah.

שַׁבָּת שָׁלוֹם וּמְנוּחָה.

Comm. p. 448

KABBALAT P'NEY SHABBAT

Home Ritual
Welcoming the Sabbath

קַבָּלַת פְּנֵי שַׁבָּת

USHERING THE SABBATH INTO THE HOME

While prayer services are the focus of communal celebration of the Sabbath, mealtime ritual is the heart of home observance. The Sabbath is honored with three feasts, the first of which takes place on Sabbath eve. *Kabbalat P'ney Shabbat:* **Home Ritual Welcoming the Sabbath** provides blessings and poetry to accompany this feast and usher the Sabbath into the home. People should feel free to modify the ritual to suit their personal circumstances. The following suggestions for use are adaptations of traditional Ashkenazic practices.

Unlike other blessings, **Sabbath Candlelighting** (pp. 122–23) is recited after, not before, the act it accompanies; it may also be sung. It is traditional to light at least two candles for the Sabbath; some families light one candle for each family member. The custom is to cover one's eyes with one's hands, so as not to see the light until after the blessing is said; while the eyes are covered, some people add a personal prayer. Although historically women have performed the candlelighting ritual for their households, in many homes today the members of the household share in the ritual together.

At the time of candlelighting or at the start of the Sabbath feast, members of the household may choose to offer blessings for family members and friends. When children are present, the **Blessing of the Children** (pp. 124–25) may be recited to each child individually by parents or other adults. The Hebrew is provided in two forms, for a girl and for a boy. The dialogue **Blessing the Beloved** (pp. 126–27) is provided in three Hebrew forms: for a woman and a man, for two women, and for two men (one English version serves for all). *L'khu, Rey'ot V'rey'im:* **Greeting the Sabbath Bride,** found in *Kabbalat Shabbat:* Prayer Service Welcoming the Sabbath (pp. 100–101), also may be recited at this time as a way of embracing the Sabbath as a beloved friend.

The meal itself begins with the **Sanctification over Wine for Sabbath Eve** (pp. 128–29). One person at the table raises the ritual goblet of wine and all assembled recite or sing the blessing; traditions vary as to whether people are seated or standing for this part of the mealtime ritual. After the blessing, each person sips the wine. Then each individual performs the hand-washing ritual, using a cup to pour water over the hands and reciting **Handwashing Before the Meal** (pp. 130–31) as the hands are dried. When everyone is gathered back at the table, the **Blessing Before the Meal** (pp. 132–33) is recited as one person lifts two whole, uncut loaves of bread (representing the double portion of manna given to the Israelites in the desert on the sixth day of the week). After the recitation of this blessing, each person partakes of the bread. At the end of the meal, the **Blessing After the Meal** (pp. 134–35) is recited or sung by all.

On Sabbaths that coincide with Rosh Hodesh (approximately two Sabbaths a year), see *Kabbalat P'ney Haḥódesh:* **Welcoming the New Month** (pp. 351–83). Instructions found on pp. 352–53 and in footnotes throughout that ritual explain how to combine Sabbath eve home ritual with ritual for Rosh Hodesh eve.

Order of the Ritual

Opening Psalm

Sabbath Candlelighting

Blessing of the Children

Blessing the Beloved

Sanctification over Wine for Sabbath Eve

Handwashing Before the Meal

Blessing Before the Meal

Blessing After the Meal

סֵדֶר קַבָּלַת פְּנֵי שַׁבָּת

Opening Psalm   מִזְמוֹר פְּתִיחָה

Will

Three generations back
my family had only

to light a candle
and the world parted.

Today, Friday afternoon,
I disconnect clocks and phones.

When night fills my house
with passages,

I begin saving
my life.

Comm.
p. 449

Sabbath Candlelighting

May our hearts be lifted,
our spirits refreshed,
as we light the Sabbath candles.

הַדְלָקַת נֵרוֹת שַׁבָּת   Hadlakat Neyrot Shabbat

Yitromeym libéynu,

t'shovav nafshéynu,

b'hadlakat neyr shel shabbat.

יְ֫תְרוֹמֵם לִבֵּנוּ,

תְּשׁוֹבַב נַפְשֵׁנוּ,

בְּהַדְלָקַת נֵר שֶׁל שַׁבָּת.

Blessing of the Children

_____ ,
(the child's name)

*B*e who you are—
and may you be blessed
in all that you are.

בִּרְכַּת יַלְדָּה וְיֶלֶד   Birkat Yaldah V'yéled

To a girl: _____ ,
(the child's name)

לבת: _____ ,
(שם הילדה)

Hayi asher tihyi—
vahayi b'rukhah
ba'asher tihyi.

הֱיִי אֲשֶׁר תִּהְיִי־
וַהֲיִי בְּרוּכָה
בַּאֲשֶׁר תִּהְיִי.

To a boy: _____ ,
(the child's name)

לבן: _____ ,
(שם הילד)

Heyeyh asher tihyeh—
veheyeyh barukh
ba'asher tihyeh.

הֱיֵה אֲשֶׁר תִּהְיֶה־
וֶהֱיֵה בָּרוּךְ
בַּאֲשֶׁר תִּהְיֶה.

Blessing the Beloved

One partner: *H*ow fine
you are, my love,
how fine you are.

The other partner: *How fine*
are you, my love,
what joy is ours.

Together: *Of all pleasure,*
how sweet
is the taste of love.

AFTER SONG OF SONGS 1:15–16; 7:7

Couples may choose from the three Hebrew versions of this dialogue (for a woman and a man, for two women, and for two men). ***L'khu, Rey'ot V'rey'im: Greeting the Sabbath Bride*** (pp. 100–101) may be substituted or added here.

בִּרְכַּת אֲהוּבוֹת וַאֲהוּבִים

Birkat Ahuvot Va'ahuvim

To a woman:	Hinakh yafah, ra'yati, hin'akh yafah.	לאהובה:	הִנָּךְ יָפָה, רַעְיָתִי, הִנָּךְ יָפָה.
Response, to a man:	Hin'kha yafeh, dodi, af na'im.	לאהוב:	הִנְּךָ יָפֶה, דוֹדִי, אַף נָעִים.
Together:	Mah-yafit umah-na'amt, ahavah bata'anugim.	יחד:	מַה־יָּפִית וּמַה־נָּעַמְתְּ, אַהֲבָה בַּתַּעֲנוּגִים.

═══════════

To a woman:	Hinakh yafah, ra'yati, hinakh yafah.	לאהובה:	הִנָּךְ יָפָה, רַעְיָתִי, הִנָּךְ יָפָה.
Response, to a woman:	Hinakh yafah, ra'yati, af n'imah.	לאהובה:	הִנָּךְ יָפָה, רַעְיָתִי, אַף נְעִימָה.
Together:	Mah-yafit umah-na'amt ahavah bata'anugim.	יחד:	מַה־יָּפִית וּמַה־נָּעַמְתְּ אַהֲבָה בַּתַּעֲנוּגִים.

═══════════

To a man:	Hin'kha yafeh, dodi, hin'kha yafeh.	לאהוב:	הִנְּךָ יָפֶה, דוֹדִי, הִנָּךְ יָפָה.
Response, to a man:	Hin'kha yafeh, dodi, af na'im.	לאהוב:	הִנְּךָ יָפֶה, דוֹדִי, אַף נָעִים.
Together:	Mah-yafit umah-na'amt, ahavah bata'anugim.	יחד:	מַה־יָּפִית וּמַה־נָּעַמְתְּ, אַהֲבָה בַּתַּעֲנוּגִים.

על־פי שיר השירים א:טו–טז; ז:ז

Sanctification over Wine for Sabbath Eve

There was evening and there was morning, the sixth day.
The heavens and earth were complete, with all their host.

GENESIS 1:31–2:1

Let us bless the source of life
that ripens fruit on the vine
as we hallow the seventh day—
the Sabbath day—
in remembrance of creation,
for the Sabbath is first
among holy days,
recalling the exodus
and the covenant.

קִדּוּשׁ לְלֵיל שַׁבָּת Kiddush L'leyl Shabbat

Vayhi-érev vayhi-vóker, yom hashishi.
Vaykhulu hashamáyim v'ha'áretz v'khol-tz'va'am.

וַיְהִי־עֶרֶב וַיְהִי־בֹקֶר, יוֹם הַשִּׁשִּׁי.
וַיְכֻלּוּ הַשָּׁמַיִם וְהָאָרֶץ וְכָל־צְבָאָם.

בראשית א:לא–ב:א

N'vareykh et eyn hahayim
נְבָרֵךְ אֶת עֵין הַחַיִּים

matzmihat p'ri hagéfen
מַצְמִיחַת פְּרִי הַגֶּפֶן

unkadeysh et yom hash'vi'i—
וּנְקַדֵּשׁ אֶת יוֹם הַשְּׁבִיעִי—

yom hashabbat—
יוֹם הַשַּׁבָּת—

zikaron l'ma'aseyh v'reyshit
זִכָּרוֹן לְמַעֲשֵׂה בְרֵאשִׁית

ki hu yom t'hilah
כִּי הוּא יוֹם תְּחִלָּה

l'mikra'ey kódesh,
לְמִקְרָאֵי קֹדֶשׁ,

zéykher litzi'at mitzráyim.
זֵכֶר לִיצִיאַת מִצְרָיִם.

Handwashing Before the Meal

*Washing the hands, we call to mind
the holiness of body.*

נְטִילַת יָדַיִם לִפְנֵי הָאֲרוּחָה   N'tilat Yadáyim Lifney Ha'aruḥah

תִּזְכֹּר נַפְשֵׁנוּ אֶת קְדֻשַּׁת הַגּוּף בִּנְטִילַת יָדֵיִם.

Tizkor nafshéynu et k'dushat haguf
bintilat yadáyim.

Blessing Before the Meal

*Let us bless the source of life
that brings forth bread from the earth.*

הַמּוֹצִיאָה Hamotzi'ah

לְבָרֵךְ אֶת עֵין הַחַיִּים
הַמּוֹצִיאָה לֶחֶם מִן הָאָרֶץ.

N'vareykh et eyn haḥayim

hamotzi'ah léḥem min ha'áretz.

Blessing After the Meal

Let us acknowledge the source of life,
source of all nourishment.

May we protect the bountiful earth
that it may continue to sustain us,

and let us seek sustenance
for all who dwell in the world.

בִּרְכַּת הַמָּזוֹן   Birkat Hamazon

Nodeh l'eyn haḥayim
hazanah et hakol.

Al ha'áretz hatovah v'har'ḥavah
nishmor na, v'hi t'kay'méynu,

unvakéysh mazon l'hasbí'a bo
kol yosh'vey teyveyl.

נוֹדֶה לְעֵין הַחַיִּים
הַזָּנָה אֶת הַכֹּל.

עַל הָאָרֶץ הַטּוֹבָה וְהָרְחָבָה
נִשְׁמֹר נָא, וְהִיא תְּקַיְּמֶנוּ,

וּנְבַקֵּשׁ מָזוֹן לְהַשְׂבִּיעַ בּוֹ
כָּל יוֹשְׁבֵי תֵבֵל.

Comm.
p. 456

Sabbath Day

יוֹם שַׁבָּת

SHAḤARIT

Morning Service for the Sabbath

שַׁחֲרִית לְשַׁבָּת

CONDUCTING THE *SHAḤARIT* SERVICE

This new *Shaḥarit* closely parallels the structure and themes of the traditional Sabbath morning service, and it should therefore adapt readily to congregational customs. Like *Kabbalat Shabbat*, it is intended for group participation, and communities are encouraged to experiment with their own ideas for implementation. The following are some suggestions.

As in *Kabbalat Shabbat*, music and silence can play important roles in the dramatic ebb and flow of the *Shaḥarit*. Traditional melodies and liturgical chanting may be adapted to fit the offerings here; new melodies, too, may be introduced. Also as in *Kabbalat Shabbat*, the comments and meditations that introduce the major parts of the service (**Opening Blessings and Songs,** p. 151; *Sh'ma* **and the Surrounding Blessings,** p. 163; *Amidah:* **Sevenfold Prayer for the Sabbath,** p. 177; **Honoring Torah,** pp. 261–63; and **Closing Prayers,** p. 285) may be read aloud by a leader or by individual congregants, or read silently by the congregation.

The service begins with **Opening Blessings and Songs,** an introductory section intended to lead individuals from the personal realm to the communal setting and beyond that to a larger sense of connectedness. It includes **Putting on the Prayer Shawl** (pp. 152–53), to be recited by those individuals who choose to wear a *tallit* (the fringed prayer shawl traditionally worn for daytime services). This is followed by the **Morning Blessing** (pp. 154–55), reprised from the private daily ritual for awakening. Here, the **Morning Blessing** serves as a transition from individual to communal prayer; it is meant to be said privately by the individual upon taking her or his place in the gathering. The community begins to pray together with the recitation or singing of **How Good the Dwellings,** *Hal'lu:* **Praise,** and **The Breath of All Life** (pp. 156–61). The Hebrew version of *Hal'lu:* **Praise** is an adaptation of Psalm 150 and will fit melodies that have been composed for that psalm; the English version is not a translation of the Hebrew but a poetic complement to it. The Hebrew and English versions may be read responsively—a stanza of one followed by a stanza of the other—to create a bilingual psalm. **The Breath of All Life** is adapted from the traditional prayer known as *nishmat kol ḥay* and will fit traditional chanting associated with that prayer. The section concludes with the **Psalm for the Sabbath** (p. 162), which may be read aloud or silently, followed by silence.

In *Sh'ma* **and the Surrounding Blessings** the major themes of the Sabbath morning service are set forth and the central articulation of faith is declared. The person leading the prayer initiates a dialogue with the congregation in the *Bar'khu:* **Call to Blessing** (pp. 164–65), and the congregation as a whole recites the **Blessing of Creation**, the **Blessing of Revelation**, and the **Blessing of Redemption** (pp. 166–69, 174–75). Once again, traditional chanting may be adopted here. The focal point, *Sh'ma:* **Communal Declaration of Faith** (pp. 170–73), may be read silently, recited aloud, or chanted according to the biblical cantillation marks provided with the text.

The centerpiece of the service is the *Amidah:* **Sevenfold Prayer for the Sabbath**; here the individual has an opportunity to achieve personal focus (*kavanah*) within the context of the community. The *Amidah* contains blessings in Hebrew and in English, meditations in English, and poems in Hebrew, Yiddish, and English. Each of its seven sections opens with a meditation, continues with a blessing, and continues further with a selection of poems (except for the sixth section, in which silence replaces the poetry). At the conclusion of each section, the original blessing is repeated, followed by a blessing that is common to all sections.

There are many ways to implement this prayer in the *Shaharit* service. A dynamic effect can be created when the meditations and poems are read aloud by individual members of the congregation, with the congregation as a whole reciting, chanting, or singing the blessings. A more traditional approach is to have the whole prayer read silently by the congregation, while standing. The congregation is then seated and the prayer is repeated aloud by a leader.

Note that an abbreviated form of the *Amidah* may be constructed by omitting the selection of poems and the repetition of the blessing in each section (footnotes within the prayer indicate which pages to omit). The abbreviated form may be used for purposes of the leader's repetition; it may also be used by the congregation as an alternative to the complete prayer. Communities may wish to experiment with allowing silence and personal meditation to substitute for the poetry selections.

In **Honoring Torah**, the community celebrates, studies, and honors its sacred texts. The question of what constitutes our sacred texts—what is our Torah—is taken up at the beginning of the section (pp. 261–63). The comments and questions there are intended to open ongoing inquiries into our basic commitments and beliefs. The offerings in this section of the service may be adapted to different forms of Torah recitation and study, depending on the outcomes of these inquiries. For example, the **Torah Blessings** (pp. 266–69) may be recited or chanted before and after reading from the Torah scroll or before studying a portion of Torah; or they may frame other texts that the community chooses to treat as sacred teachings. Such texts may be chosen from other parts of Bible or other periods of Jewish history—including our own period, which offers literature by women as well as men. The passages that open and close this section of the service, **Gates of Righteousness** (pp. 264–65) and **Tree of Life** (pp. 280–81), may be sung as the Torah scroll is removed from and returned to its ark or as other texts are brought out and put away. These offerings will fit the many musical settings that have been composed for the biblical verses on which they are based. Because this service assumes a range of possible choices concerning what may constitute Torah, no ritual for *haftarah* (supplementary reading) is provided.

In accordance with the custom of offering blessings for individuals under a rubric commonly referred to as *mi shebeyrakh*, "[the One] who blessed," **Honoring Torah** provides three distinct blessings under the heading **As Those Who Came Before Us Were Blessed** (pp. 270–79). These blessings are for individuals who have participated in the reading or teaching of Torah, for people in need of healing, and for those gravely ill. Each blessing is presented in two English forms, for an individual and for more than one individual; in the Hebrew, three forms are provided: for a female, for a male, and for more than one individual. The forms for more than one individual may be particularly useful in larger congregations; when blessings are said on behalf of those who are ill, members of the congregation may simply call out names at the appropriate point.

Birkat Haḥódesh: **Heralding the New Month** is a special ritual recited on the Sabbath preceding Rosh Hodesh. It is found in THE MONTHLY CYCLE (pp. 335–47) and inserted in the *Shaḥarit* service after **Honoring Torah** (p. 283). Suggestions for its implementation are provided on p. 337.

The **Closing Prayers** include *Aléynu L'shabéy'aḥ:* **It Is Ours to Praise** (pp. 287–89), which recapitulates the themes of creation, revelation, and redemption. A leader may read aloud the meditation introducing the prayer (p. 287) or the congregation may read it silently; the prayer itself may be recited or sung by the congregation. Following it, the service draws to a close with the *Kaddish:* **Mourners' Prayer** (pp. 291–95) and the **Closing Blessing** (pp. 297–99). These may be performed as in *Kabbalat Shabbat* (see pp. 54–55 for suggestions).

Note that this *Shaḥarit* service may be used for communal celebration of Rosh Hodesh day (whether falling on a weekday or a Sabbath) by modifying the *Amidah:* **Sevenfold Prayer**. See specific instructions in THE MONTHLY CYCLE, on p. 389; directions are also provided on appropriate pages of the *Amidah* prayer itself. The **Psalm for the Sabbath** (p. 162) is deleted when Rosh Hodesh falls on a weekday.

CONVENING *KIDDUSH* ON SABBATH DAY

It is customary in many congregations to serve refreshments after the Sabbath morning service, particularly when a special event, like a baby naming or a bat/bar mitzvah, is being celebrated.

At such times, a sanctification over wine (*kiddush*) is recited, followed by blessings for the food (with the event as a whole also referred to as *kiddush*). It is equally customary to recite the sanctification over wine in the home, its original domain, at the start of the midday meal (the second feast of the Sabbath).

The **Sanctification over Wine for Sabbath Day** (pp. 300–301) may be recited following the *Shaḥarit* service in either the home or the communal setting. On Sabbaths coinciding with Rosh Hodesh, the **Sanctification over Wine for the Day of Sabbath Rosh Hodesh** (found on pp. 398–99, in THE MONTHLY CYCLE) is substituted for it. The blessings for eating—**Handwashing Before the Meal, Blessing Before the Meal,** and **Blessing After the Meal**—are found in *Kabbalat P'ney Shabbat:* Home Ritual Welcoming the Sabbath (pp. 130–35).

Order of the Service

OPENING BLESSINGS AND SONGS

Putting on the Prayer Shawl

Morning Blessing

How Good the Dwellings

Hal'lu: Praise

The Breath of All Life

Psalm for the Sabbath

SH'MA AND THE SURROUNDING BLESSINGS

Bar'khu: Call to Blessing

Blessing of Creation

Blessing of Revelation

Sh'ma: Communal Declaration of Faith

Blessing of Redemption

סֵדֶר תְּפִלַּת שַׁחֲרִית

AMIDAH: SEVENFOLD PRAYER FOR THE SABBATH

1. Recalling Our Ancestors, Remembering Our Lives

2. Sustaining Life, Embracing Death

3. Hallowing Our Namings

4. Sanctifying the Sabbath Day

5. Restoring Shekhinah, Reclaiming Home

6. The Gift of Gratitude

7. Blessing of Peace

HONORING TORAH

Gates of Righteousness
Upon taking out the Torah

Torah Blessings
Before and after the Torah reading

As Those Who Came Before Us Were Blessed
For one who has honored Torah

As Those Who Came Before Us Were Blessed
For one in need of healing

As Those Who Came Before Us Were Blessed
For one gravely ill

Tree of Life
Upon returning the Torah

עֲמִידָה: תְּפִלַּת שֶׁבַע לְיוֹם הַשַּׁבָּת

א. מָסֹרֶת הַדּוֹרוֹת

ב. מַעְגַּל הַחַיִּים

ג. נִשְׁמַת כָּל שֵׁם

ד. קְדֻשַּׁת יוֹם הַשַּׁבָּת

ה. הַחֲזָרַת הַשְּׁכִינָה

ו. בְּפֶה מָלֵא שִׁירָה

ז. בִּרְכַּת שָׁלוֹם

לִכְבוֹד תּוֹרָה

שַׁעֲרֵי־צֶדֶק
לְעֵת הוֹצָאַת הַתּוֹרָה

בִּרְכוֹת הַתּוֹרָה
לִפְנֵי וְאַחֲרֵי קְרִיאַת הַתּוֹרָה

כְּמוֹ שֶׁנִּתְבָּרְכוּ
לְעוֹלֶה לַתּוֹרָה

כְּמוֹ שֶׁנִּתְבָּרְכוּ
לְמַעַן חוֹלֶה

כְּמוֹ שֶׁנִּתְבָּרְכוּ
לְמַעַן חוֹלָה אֲנָשׁ/ה

עֵץ־חַיִּים הִיא
לְעֵת הַכְנָסַת הַתּוֹרָה

BIRKAT HAḤÓDESH: HERALDING THE NEW MONTH
For the Sabbath before Rosh Hodesh

בִּרְכַּת הַחֹדֶשׁ
לשבת מברכים

מַתְּנוֹת הַחֹדֶשׁ: הוֹדָיָה

הַכְרָזַת הַחֹדֶשׁ

תְּפִלַּת הַחֹדֶשׁ

סיום

עָלֵינוּ לְשַׁבֵּחַ

קַדִּישׁ

בִּרְכַּת סִיּוּם

_____

קִדּוּשׁ לְיוֹם שַׁבָּת

OPENING BLESSINGS AND SONGS
בִּרְכוֹת הַשַּׁחַר וּפְסוּקֵי זִמְרָה

These blessings and songs prepare us, as individuals and as a community, for the communal prayers to follow. With these offerings, we place ourselves in the realm of creation, affirming our sense of connectedness and belonging. The sequence moves in an outward progression, from the personal space enveloped by the prayer shawl, to the shared space of the community, to the whole of the natural world, whose beauty is ours to celebrate.

Putting on the Prayer Shawl

Recalling the generations,
I wrap myself
in the tallit.

May my mind be clear,
my spirit open,
as I envelop myself in prayer.

עֲטִיפַת טַלִּית   Atifat Tallit

Hin'ni mit'atéfet/mit'ateyf
(female)   (male)
b'tallit shel tzitzit

k'dey lizkor v'lishmor

et masóret hadorot

ukhdey l'khaveyn et libi.

Yipataḥ libi,

tizdakeykh nafshi,

b'hit'at'fi batallit.

הִנְנִי מִתְעַטֶּפֶת/מִתְעַטֵּף

בְּטַלִּית שֶׁל צִיצִית

כְּדֵי לִזְכּׂר וְלִשְׁמׂר

אֶת מָסֺרֶת הַדּוֹרוֹת

וּכְדֵי לְכַוֵּן אֶת לִבִּי.

יִפָּתַח לִבִּי,

תִּזְדַּכֶּךְ נַפְשִׁי,

בְּהִתְעַטְּפִי בַּטַלִּית.

Morning Blessing

The breath of my life
will bless,

the cells of my being
sing

in gratitude,
reawakening.

Birkat Hasháḥar   בִּרְכַּת הַשַּׁחַר

Nishmat ḥayay t'vareykh

v'kérev libi yashir:

Kol od n'shamah b'kirbi

modah/modeh ani.
(female)   *(male)*

נִשְׁמַת חַיַּי תְּבָרֵךְ

וְקֶֽרֶב לִבִּי יָשִׁיר:

כָּל עוֹד נְשָׁמָה בְּקִרְבִּי

מוֹדָה/מוֹדֶה אֲנִי.

How Good the Dwellings

How good the dwellings
where we gather—

serene and vibrant
as the gardens, the rivers,

the aloes
and the cedar trees.

How good to sit together
in peace.

AFTER NUMBERS 24:5–6; PSALM 133:1

Mah-Tóvu Mishk'notéynu — מַה־טֹּבוּ מִשְׁכְּנוֹתֶֽינוּ

Mah-tóvu ohaléynu,

mishk'notéynu, yisra'eyl,

kinḥalim nitáyu,

k'ganot aley nahar,

ka'ahalim n'tu'im,

ka'arazim aley-máyim.

Hineyh mah-tov umah-na'im

shévet kulánu yáḥad.

מַה־טֹּבוּ אֹהָלֶֽינוּ,

מִשְׁכְּנוֹתֶֽינוּ, יִשְׂרָאֵל,

כִּנְחָלִים נִטָּֽיוּ,

כְּגַנֹּת עֲלֵי נָהָר,

כַּאֲהָלִים נְטוּעִים,

כַּאֲרָזִים עֲלֵי־מָֽיִם.

הִנֵּה מַה־טּוֹב וּמַה־נָּעִים

שֶֽׁבֶת כֻּלָּֽנוּ יָֽחַד.

על־פי במדבר כד:ה–ו; תהילים קלג:א

Hal'lu: *Praise*

Praise the world—
praise its fullness
and its longing,
its beauty and its grief.

Praise stone and fire,
lilac and river,
and the solitary bird
at the window.

Praise the moment
when the whole
bursts through pain

and the moment
when the whole
bursts forth in joy.

Praise the dying beauty
with all your breath
and, praising, see

the beauty of the world
is your own.

Hal'lu הַלְלוּ

Hal'lu et hateyveyl,
hal'lu m'lo'ah,

הַלְלוּ אֶת הַתֵּבֵל,
הַלְלוּ מְלֹאָה,

hal'lu b'téyka shofar,
b'néyvel v'khinor.

הַלְלוּ בְּתֶקַע שׁוֹפָר,
בְּנֵבֶל וְכִנּוֹר.

Hal'lu b'tof umaḥol,
b'minim v'ugav,

הַלְלוּ בְּתֹף וּמָחוֹל,
בְּמִנִּים וְעֻגָב,

hal'lu b'tziltz'ley-sháma,
b'tziltz'ley t'ru'ah.

הַלְלוּ בְּצִלְצְלֵי־שָׁמַע,
בְּצִלְצְלֵי תְרוּעָה.

Kol han'shamah t'haleyl
et hateyveyl,

כֹּל הַנְּשָׁמָה תְּהַלֵּל
אֶת הַתֵּבֵל,

kol han'shamot t'haléylnah
yif'atah.

כֹּל הַנְּשָׁמוֹת תְּהַלֵּלְנָה
יִפְעָתָה.

עַל־פִּי תְהִילִים קנ

The Breath of All Life

The breath of all life will bless,
the body will exclaim:

Were our mouths filled with song as the sea
and our tongues lapping joy like the waves

and our lips singing praises broad as the sky
and our eyes like the sun and the moon

and our arms open wide as the eagle's wings
and our feet leaping light as the deer's,

it would not be enough to tell
the wonder.

נִשְׁמַת כָּל חַי   Nishmat Kol Ḥay

Nishmat kol ḥay t'vareykh

v'rú'aḥ kol basar t'fa'eyr:

נִשְׁמַת כָּל חַי תְּבָרֵךְ

וְרוּחַ כָּל בָּשָׂר תְּפָאֵר:

Ílu fínu maley shirah kayam

ulshonéynu rinah kahamon galav

אִלּוּ פִינוּ מָלֵא שִׁירָה כַּיָּם

וּלְשׁוֹנֵנוּ רִנָּה כַּהֲמוֹן גַּלָּיו

v'siftotéynu shévaḥ k'merḥavey raki'a

v'eynéynu m'irot kashémesh v'khayaréy'aḥ

וְשִׂפְתוֹתֵינוּ שֶׁבַח כְּמֶרְחֲבֵי רָקִיעַ

וְעֵינֵינוּ מְאִירוֹת כַּשֶּׁמֶשׁ וְכַיָּרֵחַ

v'yadéynu f'rusot k'nishrey shamáyim

v'ragléynu kalot ka'ayalot,

וְיָדֵינוּ פְרוּשׂוֹת כְּנִשְׁרֵי שָׁמָיִם

וְרַגְלֵינוּ קַלּוֹת כָּאַיָּלוֹת,

gam az, lo naspik l'hodot

v'lu al p'li'ah aḥat

גַּם אָז, לֹא נַסְפִּיק לְהוֹדוֹת

וְלוּ עַל פְּלִיאָה אַחַת

mini-élef alfey alafim

v'ribey r'vavot.

מִנִּי־אֶלֶף אַלְפֵי אֲלָפִים

וְרִבֵּי רְבָבוֹת.

Psalm for the Sabbath   מִזְמוֹר שִׁיר לְיוֹם הַשַּׁבָּת

Listen

In the clearing, where the mind flowers

and the world sprouts up at every side,

listen

for the sound in the bushes

behind the grass.

SH'MA
AND THE SURROUNDING BLESSINGS
קְרִיאַת שְׁמַע וּבִרְכוֹתֶיהָ

The **Sh'ma: Declaration of Faith** articulates our theological grounding and recalls our spiritual roots. In the context of this service, it is surrounded by three blessings—for creation, revelation, and redemption, central themes of the Sabbath liturgy.

If the theme of creation speaks to the magnificence of the whole of the natural world, revelation addresses our unique place within that whole. As beings with human awareness, capable of moral choice, we are the only species of creation that can act with righteousness—or without it. The possibility of redemption, then, lies in how we implement our choices, how we embody in our actions the values we hold as sacred.

מַחֲזוֹר הַשָּׁלֵם ליוֹם שַׁבָּת חוֹבֵר מִבָּרְכוֹתֶיהָ

Bar'khu: *Call to Blessing*

Leader: Let us bless the source of life.

Congregation: As we bless the source of life
so we are blessed.

Leader: As we bless the source of life
so may we be blessed.

Bar'khu בָּרְכוּ

Leader:	Bar'khu et eyn haḥayim.	שליח/ת הציבור: **בָּ**רְכוּ אֶת עֵין הַחַיִּים.
Congregation:	N'vareykh et eyn haḥayim v'khoh nitbareykh.	הקהל: נְבָרֵךְ אֶת עֵין הַחַיִּים וְכֹה נִתְבָּרֵךְ.
Leader:	N'vareykh et eyn haḥayim v'khoh nitbareykh.	שליח/ת הציבור: נְבָרֵךְ אֶת עֵין הַחַיִּים וְכֹה נִתְבָּרֵךְ.

Blessing of Creation

Let us bless the source of life,
source of darkness and light,
heart of harmony and chaos,
creativity and creation.

בִּרְכַּת יְצִירָה   Birkat Y'tzirah

נְבָרֵךְ אֶת עֵין הַחַיִּים,

מְקוֹר הַחְשֶׁךְ וְהָאוֹר,

מְקוֹר הַשְׁלֵמוּת וְהַתְּהוּ,

מְקוֹר הַטּוֹב וְהָרָע,

מְקוֹר כָּל יְצִירָה.

N'vareykh et eyn haḥayim,

m'kor haḥóshekh v'ha'or,

m'kor hash'leymut v'hatóhu,

m'kor hatov v'hara,

m'kor kol y'tzirah.

Blessing of Revelation

Let us bless the source of life,
source of the fullness of our knowing.

May we learn with humility and pleasure,
may we teach what we know with love,

and may we honor wisdom
in all its embodiments.

בִּרְכַּת תּוֹרָה   Birkat Torah

נְבָרֵךְ אֶת עֵין הַחַיִּים,
מְקוֹר הֲבָנָה וְהַבְחָנָה.

N'vareykh et eyn haḥayim,
m'kor havanah v'havḥanah.

נִזְכֶּה נָא לְהָבִין וּלְהַשְׂכִּיל,
לִשְׁמֹעַ, לִלְמֹד וּלְלַמֵּד,
לִשְׁמֹר וְלַעֲשׂוֹת וּלְקַיֵּם
דִּבְרֵי תוֹרָה בְּאַהֲבָה.

Nizkeh na l'havin ulhaskil,
lishmó'a, lilmod ul'lameyd,
lishmor v'la'asot ulkayeym
divrey torah b'ahavah.

Comm. p. 465

Sh'ma: *Communal Declaration of Faith*

*H*ear, O Israel—
The divine abounds everywhere
and dwells in everything;
the many are One.

———

Loving life
and its mysterious source
with all our heart
and all our spirit,
all our senses and strength,
we take upon ourselves
and into ourselves
these promises:
to care for the earth
and those who live upon it,
to pursue justice and peace,
to love kindness and compassion.
We will teach this to our children
throughout the passage of the day—
as we dwell in our homes
and as we go on our journeys,
from the time we rise
until we fall asleep.

קְרִיאַת שְׁמַע בַּקְּהִלָה

K'ri'at Sh'ma Bak'hilah

Sh'ma, yisra'eyl—	שְׁמַע, יִשְׂרָאֵל –
la'elohut alfey panim,	לָאֱלֹהוּת אַלְפֵּי פָּנִים,
m'lo olam sh'khinatah,	מְלֹא עוֹלָם שְׁכִינָתָהּ,
ribuy panéha eḥad.	רִבּוּי פָּנֶיהָ אֶחָד.

___

Nohav et-haḥayim	נֹאהַב אֶת־הַחַיִּים
v'eyt eyn haḥayim	וְאֶת עֵין הַחַיִּים
b'khol-l'vavéynu uvkhol-nafshéynu	בְּכָל־לְבָבֵנוּ וּבְכָל־נַפְשֵׁנוּ
uvkhol-m'odéynu.	וּבְכָל־מְאֹדֵנוּ.
Yihyu had'varim ha'éyleh	יִהְיוּ הַדְּבָרִים הָאֵלֶּה
bilvavéynu uvkirbéynu:	בִּלְבָבֵנוּ וּבְקִרְבֵּנוּ:
sh'mirat éretz v'yosh'véha,	שְׁמִירַת אֶרֶץ וְיוֹשְׁבֶיהָ,
r'difat tzédek v'shalom,	רְדִיפַת צֶדֶק וְשָׁלוֹם,
ahavat ḥésed v'raḥamim.	אַהֲבַת חֶסֶד וְרַחֲמִים.
N'shan'nam	נְשַׁנְּנָם
livnotéynu ulvanéynu	לִבְנוֹתֵינוּ וּלְבָנֵינוּ
undabeyr bam	וּנְדַבֵּר בָּם
b'shivtéynu b'veytéynu,	בְּשִׁבְתֵּנוּ בְּבֵיתֵנוּ,
b'lekhtéynu badérekh,	בְּלֶכְתֵּנוּ בַּדֶּרֶךְ,
b'shokhbéynu uvkuméynu.	בְּשָׁכְבֵּנוּ וּבְקוּמֵנוּ.

Comm.
p. 466

And may our actions
be faithful to our words
that our children's children
may live to know:
Truth and kindness
have embraced,
peace and justice have kissed
and are one.

V'yihyu ma'aséynu
ne'emanim lidvaréynu,
l'má'an yeyd'u dor aḥaron,
banot uvanim yivaléydu:
Ḥésed ve'emet nifgáshu,
tzédek v'shalom nasháku.

וְיִהְיוּ מַעֲשֵׂינוּ
נֶאֱמָנִים לִדְבָרֵינוּ,
לְמַעַן יֵדְעוּ דּוֹר אַחֲרוֹן,
בָּנוֹת וּבָנִים יִוָּלֵדוּ:
חֶסֶד וֶאֱמֶת נִפְגָּשׁוּ,
צֶדֶק וְשָׁלוֹם נָשָׁקוּ.

Blessing of Redemption

Let us bless the source of life,
source of faith and daring,
wellspring of new song
and the courage to mend.

בִּרְכַּת גְּאֻלָּה   Birkat G'ulah

N'vareykh et eyn haḥayim,

m'kor emunah v'tikvah,

ma'yan shirah ḥadashah,

m'kor tikun olam.

נְבָרֵךְ אֶת עֵין הַחַיִּים,

מְקוֹר אֱמוּנָה וְתִקְוָה,

מַעְיַן שִׁירָה חֲדָשָׁה,

מְקוֹר תִּקּוּן עוֹלָם.

AMIDAH: SEVENFOLD PRAYER
FOR THE SABBATH
עֲמִידָה: תְּפִלַּת שֶׁבַע לְיוֹם הַשַּׁבָּת

With the **Amidah**, *we stand as individuals in community to pray the prayer of the heart. For the rabbis, another name for the amidah was the word for prayer itself,* t'filah. *This new* **Amidah** *is unlike anything else in this service in that it presents the words of a number of Jewish women, poets whose names appear with their poems. Why this multivocal chorus? Why the names? Because the words of a single tradition—a single school or a single liturgist—cannot always speak for every heart. The collage of poems offered here only begins to suggest the diversity of our voices, reclaiming some of the many that have been forgotten or lost in the mainstream of tradition. And because the reclaiming of voices leads to the recovering of identities, we recall the names of the women whose words move us today. Above all, this compilation encourages us to contribute our own voices to the tradition.*

THE SEVEN SECTIONS OF THE PRAYER
שִׁבְעָה חֶלְקֵי הַתְּפִלָה

1 . Recalling Our Ancestors, Remembering Our Lives

א. מָסְרֶת הַדּוֹרוֹת

2 . Sustaining Life, Embracing Death

ב. מַעְגַּל הַחַיִּים

3 . Hallowing Our Namings

ג. נִשְׁמַת כָּל שֵׁם

4 . Sanctifying the Sabbath Day

ד. קְדֻשַּׁת יוֹם הַשַּׁבָּת

5 . Restoring Shekhinah, Reclaiming Home

ה. הַחֲזָרַת הַשְּׁכִינָה

6 . The Gift of Gratitude

ו. בְּפֶה מָלֵא שִׁירָה

7 . Blessing of Peace

ז. בִּרְכַּת שָׁלוֹם

I
Recalling Our Ancestors,
Remembering Our Lives
מָסֹרֶת הַדּוֹרוֹת

*Looking back can illumine; origins reveal meanings. Tradition—
from the verb "deliver, hand over"; masóret—from "hand over,"
also perhaps "tie." Tradition is not just what we receive; it is what
we create with our own hands and then hand over, the ties we make
with past and future. Recalling our past, we remember our selves,
making the branches part of the whole again.*

For an abbreviated form of this prayer, continue after this page on pp. 190–91.

Recalling Our Ancestors, Remembering Our Lives

*R*ecalling the generations,
we weave our lives
into the tradition.

מָסֹרֶת הַדּוֹרוֹת   Masóret Hadorot

Nizkor et masóret hadorot

v'nishzor bah et sarigey ḥayéynu.

נִזְכֹּר אֶת מָסֹרֶת הַדּוֹרוֹת
וְנִשְׁזֹר בָּהּ אֶת שָׂרִיגֵי חַיֵּינוּ.

From My Mother's House

My mother's mother died
in the spring of her years,
and her daughter forgot her face.
Her portrait, engraved
on my grandfather's heart,
was erased from the world of images
when he died.

In the house, just her mirror remained,
sunk with age in its silver frame.
And I, the pale grandchild
who does not resemble her,
peer into it today as into a lake
that hides its treasures underwater.

Deep behind my face,
I see a young woman—
pink-cheeked, smiling,
a wig on her head—
threading a long-looped earring
through the tender flesh of her lobe.
Deep behind my face,
shines the bright gold of her eyes.
And the mirror passes on
the family lore:
She was very beautiful.

LEAH GOLDBERG
(*translation M. F.*)

מִבֵּית אִמִּי

מֵתָה אִמָּהּ שֶׁל אִמִּי
בַּאֲבִיב יָמֶיהָ. וּבִתָּהּ
לֹא זָכְרָה אֶת פָּנֶיהָ. דְּיוֹקְנָהּ הֶחָרוּט
עַל לִבּוֹ שֶׁל סָבִי
נִמְחָה מֵעוֹלַם הַדְּמֻיּוֹת
אַחֲרֵי מוֹתוֹ.

רַק הָרְאִי שֶׁלָּהּ נִשְׁתַּיֵּר בַּבַּיִת.
הֶעֱמִיק מֵרֹב שָׁנִים בְּמִשְׁבֶּצֶת הַכֶּסֶף.
וַאֲנִי, נֶכְדָּתָהּ הַחִוֶּרֶת, שֶׁאֵינֶנִּי דּוֹמָה לָהּ,
מַבִּיטָה הַיּוֹם אֶל תּוֹכוֹ כְּאֶל תּוֹךְ
אֲגַם הַטּוֹמֵן אוֹצְרוֹתָיו
מִתַּחַת לַמַּיִם.

עָמֹק מְאֹד, מֵאֲחוֹרֵי פָּנַי,
אֲנִי רוֹאָה אִשָּׁה צְעִירָה
וְרַדַּת לְחָיַיִם מְחַיֶּכֶת.
וּפֵאָה נָכְרִית לְרֹאשָׁהּ.
הִיא עוֹנֶדֶת
עָגִיל מָאֳרָךְ אֶל תְּנוּךְ אָזְנָהּ. מַשְׁחִילַתְהוּ
בִּנְקֵב זָעִיר בַּבָּשָׂר הֶעָנֹג
שֶׁל הָאֹזֶן.
עָמֹק מְאֹד, מֵאֲחוֹרֵי פָּנַי, קוֹרֶנֶת
זְהוּבִית בְּהִירָה שֶׁל עֵינֶיהָ.
וְהָרְאִי מַמְשִׁיךְ אֶת מָסֹרֶת
הַמִּשְׁפָּחָה:
שֶׁהִיא הָיְתָה יָפָה מְאֹד.

לאה גולדברג

Eating an Apple

The little paring knife

with the cool, round, ivory handle

took pride in being

in my grandpa's Sabbath hand

when

he would peel an apple,

and slowly lift to his lips

the thin, ripe, fragrant slices,

and say the blessing over the fruit of the tree.

He was a fine and proper grandpa, and behaved

as a proper grandpa should.

I'm a kid with an apple in my hand.

I dig my teeth in, greedily.

MALKA HEIFETZ TUSSMAN
(*translation M. F.*)

אַ ייִנגלינג מיט אַן עפל אין האַנט

דאָס קליין מעסערל מיטן ווײַסן,

קילן, קײַלעכדיקן העלפֿאַנטביין העניטל

האָט זיך געגרויסט

אין מײַן זיידנס שבתדיקער האַנט

בשעת

ער האָט אַן עפל געשיילט

און דינינקע רײַף־שמעקעדיקע ריפֿטעלעך

פֿאַמעלעבקע צום מויל געטראָגן

און זײַנע ליפֿן האָבן אַ ברכה געמאַכט

אויף פֿרי פֿון בוים.

ער איז געווען אַן איידעלער זיידע־ייִד.

און האָט געטאָן

ווי אַן איידעלער זיידע־ייִד.

איך בין

אַ ייִנגלינג מיט אַן עפל אין האַנט.

איך בײַס די ציין אַרײַן

פֿאַרשייַט.

מלכה חפֿץ טוזמאַן

I Am Woman

I am the exalted Rachel

whose love lit the way for Rabbi Akiba.

I am the small, bashful village girl

who grew up among the tall poplars

and blushed at the "Good morning" of her brother's tutor.

I am the pious girl

who paled as her mother raised her hands to her eyes

for the blessing over the Sabbath candles.

I am the obedient bride

who humbly bent her head beneath the shears

the night before the wedding.

I am the rabbi's daughter

who offered her chaste body to save a Jewish town

and afterwards set fire to herself.

I am the woman of valor

who bore and fed children

for a promised bit of paradise.

I am the mother

who, in great hardship,

raised sons to be righteous men.

איך בין פֿרוי

איך בין די עקזולטירטע רחל
וועמעס ליבע האָט באלויכטן דעם וועג פֿון די רבי עקיבאס.

איך בין דאָס קליינע, שעמעוודיקע דאָרף־מיידל
וואָס איז צווישן הויכע טאָפּאָלן געוואקסן
און זיד גערוויטלט ביַים ״גוט מאָרגן״ פֿון ברודערס מלמד.

איך בין דאָס פֿרומע מיידל
וואָס האָט זיך געבלייקט ביַי דער מאַמעס ציטערדיקע פֿינגער אויף די אויגן
אַנטקעגן די בענטשליכט.

איך בין דאָס געהאָרכזאַם כלה־מיידל
וואָס האָט הכנעהדיק דאָס קעפל אונטערגעטראָגן צום שער ערב חופה.

איך בין די אויסגעאיידלטע בת תלמיד חכם
וואָס האָט מיט איר אָפּגעהיט לייב אַ שטאָט אַ ייִדישע מציל געווען
און נאָכדעם מיט אייגענע הענט זיך אונטערגעצונדן.

איך בין די אשת־חיל
וואָס האָט זיך אונטערגענומען געבערן און שפּיַיזן
פֿאַר אַ ביסעלע צוגעזאָגט גן עדן־ליכט.

איך בין די מאַמע
וואָס האָט אונטער ענוויים קשים
בנים מגדל געווען צו מעשים טובים.

I am the Hassid's daughter,

infused with her father's fervor,

who went out defiant, with her hair cropped,

to educate the people.

I am the barrier-breaker

who freed love from the wedding canopy.

I am the pampered girl

who set herself behind a plow

to force the gray desert into green life.

I am the one whose fingers

tightened around the hoe,

on guard for the steps of the enemy.

I am the one who stubbornly

carries around a strange alphabet

to impart to children's ears.

I am all these and many more.

And everywhere, always, I am woman.

MALKA HEIFETZ TUSSMAN
(*translation M. F.*)

איך בין די חסידישע טאַכטער

וואָס האָט מיטן טאַטנס התלהבות געטראָגן

דאָס געשווירן קעפל אין פֿאָלק אַריַין.

איך בין די צוימען־ברעכערין

וואָס האָט "ברויט און פֿרייַהייט" געטיילט

און די ליבע באַפֿרייַט פֿון אונטער חופּה־שטאַנגען.

איך בין דאָס פֿאַרצערטלט מיידל

וואָס האָט זיך הינטערן אַקער געשטעלט

גרוויען מדבר צו גרין לעבן באַצווינגען.

איך בין די וועמעס פֿינגער שטײַפֿן אַרום רידל

אין לויער פֿון טריט פֿון פֿאַרווייסטער.

איך בין די וואָס טראָגט פֿאַרעקשנט אַרום אַן אלף־בית אַ מאָדנעם

און רוים אים אין קינדערשע אויערלעך איַין.

איך בין אָט די אַלע און נאָך אַ סך, אַ סך ניט דערמאָנטע.

און אומעטום,

און אַלעמאָל

בין איך

פֿרוי.

מלכּה חפֿץ טוזמאַן

Recalling Our Ancestors, Remembering Our Lives

Recalling the generations,
we weave our lives
into the tradition.

———

As we bless the source of life
so we are blessed.

מָסֹרֶת הַדּוֹרוֹת Masóret Hadorot

נִזְכֹּר אֶת מָסֹרֶת הַדּוֹרוֹת
וְנִשְׁזֹר בָּהּ אֶת שָׂרִיגֵי חַיֵּינוּ.

Nizkor et masóret hadorot
v'nishzor bah et sarigey hayéynu.

נְבָרֵךְ אֶת עֵין הַחַיִּים
וְכֹה נִתְבָּרֵךְ.

N'vareykh et eyn hahayim
v'khoh nitbareykh.

2
Sustaining Life, Embracing Death
מַעְגַּל הַחַיִּים

*To celebrate life is to acknowledge the ongoing dying, and ulti-
mately to embrace death. For although all life travels toward its
death, death is not a destination: it too is a journey to beginnings:
all death leads to life again. From peelings to mulch to new pota-
toes, the world is ever renewing, ever renewed.*

For an abbreviated form of this prayer, continue after this page on pp. 202–3.

Comm.
p. 471

Sustaining Life, Embracing Death

Let us bless the well
eternally giving—
the circle of life
ever-dying, ever-living.

מַעְגַּל הַחַיִּים   Ma'gal Haḥayim

נְבָרֶךְ אֶת הַמַּעְיָן   N'vareykh et hama'yan

עֲדֵי־עַד מְפַכֶּה —   adey-ad m'fakeh—

מַעְגַּל הַחַיִּים   ma'gal haḥayim

הַמֵּמִית וּמְחַיֶּה.   hameymit umḥayeh.

In Everything

In everything, there is at least an eighth

of death. It doesn't weigh much.

With what hidden, peaceful charm

we carry it everywhere we go.

In sweet awakenings,

in our travels,

in our love talk,

when we are unaware,

forgotten in all the corners of our being—

always with us.

And never heavy.

LEAH GOLDBERG
(*translation M. F.*)

בְּכָל דָּבָר יֵשׁ לְפָחוֹת שְׁמִינִית

בְּכָל דָּבָר יֵשׁ לְפָחוֹת שְׁמִינִית
שֶׁל מָוֶת. מִשְׁקָלוֹ אֵינוֹ גָּדוֹל.
בְּאֵיזֶה חֵן טָמִיר וְשַׁאֲנָן
נִשָּׂא אוֹתוֹ אֶל כָּל אֲשֶׁר נֵלֵךְ.
בִּיקִיצוֹת יָפוֹת, בְּטִיּוּלִים,
בְּשִׂיחַ אוֹהֲבִים, בְּהֶסַח־דַּעַת
נִשְׁכָּח בְּיַרְכְּתֵי הַוָּיָתֵנוּ
תָּמִיד אִתָּנוּ. וְאֵינוֹ מַכְבִּיד.

לאה גולדברג

Leaves

Leaves don't fall. They descend.

Longing for earth, they come winging.

In their time, they'll come again,

For leaves don't fall. They descend.

On the branches, they will be again

Green and fragrant, cradle-swinging,

For leaves don't fall. They descend.

Longing for earth, they come winging.

MALKA HEIFETZ TUSSMAN
(*translation M. F.*)

בלעטער

בלעטער פֿאַלן ניט. זיי נידערן.

ערד־פֿאַרבענקטע זיי קומען פֿליגלדיק.

אין זייער צײַט זיי וועלן ווידער ווידערן,

ווײַל בלעטער פֿאַלן ניט. זיי נידערן.

זיי וועלן ווידער מיט די צווייַגן גלידערן

גרין און שמעקנדיק און ווייגלדיק

ווײַל בלעטער פֿאַלן ניט. זיי נידערן.

ערד־פֿאַרבענקטע זיי קומען פֿליגלדיק.

מלכה חפֿץ טוזמאַן

The Weekly Cycle   SABBATH DAY   *Shaḥarit*   *Amidah: Sevenfold Prayer*

Winter Solstice 1

Here you are, back
in the blue-white woods—

how tall the birches,
how delicate the pines!

Standing on the frozen plot of snow,
you suddenly know these trees

will be your gravestone.
Nothing stirs—but what

are those sounds?
You balance on the crusty edge

while all around you ice
invisibly thaws,

beneath the snow
the mushrooms smolder,

and under your feet the unborn grass
hums in its bed.

Winter Solstice 2

Warm breeze across the winter sky,

the birch trunk shedding its skin,

ice beginning to give beneath your feet—

It's alive, alive beneath the stillness,

under the frozen surface of the pond,

in the moss-webbed rock, alive!

In the unseen hoof of the deer

whose quick track lightly pierced the snow,

and in all the unnamed footprints

and in all the longed-for music

of the last dead leaves

and the still-twittering birds, alive!

And in the bronze of the inert star

that melts the snow

and erases the deer tracks

and turns wet skin to parchment,

flesh to fossil, water to stone

again—

Sustaining Life, Embracing Death

Let us bless the well
eternally giving—
the circle of life
ever-dying, ever-living.

———

As we bless the wellspring of life
so we are blessed.

מַעְגַּל הַחַיִּים Ma'gal Haḥayim

נְבָרֵךְ אֶת הַמַּעְיָן
עֲדֵי־עַד מְפַכֶּה —
מַעְגַּל הַחַיִּים
הַמֵּמִית וּמְחַיֶּה.

N'vareykh et hama'yan
adey-ad m'fakeh—
ma'gal haḥayim
hameymit umḥayeh.

נְבָרֵךְ אֶת עֵין הַחַיִּים
וְכֹה נִתְבָּרֵךְ.

N'vareykh et eyn haḥayim
v'khoh nitbareykh.

3
Hallowing Our Namings
נִשְׁמַת כָּל שֵׁם

Naming—our most human act. With words and images, we name the world, name toward the divine. As tradition repeatedly tells us, the more we recount and name, the more we increase the presence of holiness in the world. The more names with which we mark and claim experience, the more inclusive our vision of the One.

For an abbreviated form of this prayer, continue after this page on pp. 212–13.

Hallowing Our Namings

Let us sing the soul in every name
and the name of every soul,
let us sing the soul in every name,
the sacred name of every soul.

Nishmat Kol Sheym — נִשְׁמַת כָּל שֵׁם

Nashir l'nishmat kol sheym

ulsheym kol n'shamah,

nashir l'nishmat kol sheym

v'likdushat kol n'shamah.

נָשִׁיר לְנִשְׁמַת כָּל שֵׁם
וּלְשֵׁם כָּל נְשָׁמָה,
נָשִׁיר לְנִשְׁמַת כָּל שֵׁם
וְלִקְדֻשַׁת כָּל נְשָׁמָה.

Each of Us Has a Name

Each of us has a name

given by the source of life

and given by our parents

Each of us has a name

given by our stature and our smile

and given by what we wear

Each of us has a name

given by the mountains

and given by our walls

Each of us has a name

given by the stars

and given by our neighbors

Each of us has a name

given by our sins

and given by our longing

Each of us has a name

given by our enemies

and given by our love

Each of us has a name

given by our celebrations

and given by our work

לְכָל בְּרִיָּה יֵשׁ שֵׁם

לְכָל בְּרִיָּה יֵשׁ שֵׁם
שֶׁנָּתְנָה לָהּ עֵין הַחַיִּים
וְנָתְנוּ לָהּ אָבִיהָ וְאִמָּהּ

לְכָל בְּרִיָּה יֵשׁ שֵׁם
שֶׁנָּתְנוּ לָהּ קוֹמָתָהּ וְאֹפֶן חִיּוּכָהּ
וְנָתַן לָהּ הָאָרִיג

לְכָל בְּרִיָּה יֵשׁ שֵׁם
שֶׁנָּתְנוּ לָהּ הֶהָרִים
וְנָתְנוּ לָהּ כְּתָלֶיהָ

לְכָל בְּרִיָּה יֵשׁ שֵׁם
שֶׁנָּתְנוּ לָהּ הַמַּזָּלוֹת
וְנָתְנוּ לָהּ שְׁכֵנֶיהָ

לְכָל בְּרִיָּה יֵשׁ שֵׁם
שֶׁנָּתְנוּ לָהּ חֲטָאֶיהָ
וְנָתְנָה לָהּ כְּמִיהָתָהּ

לְכָל בְּרִיָּה יֵשׁ שֵׁם
שֶׁנָּתְנוּ לָהּ שׂוֹנְאֶיהָ
וְנָתְנָה לָהּ אַהֲבָתָהּ

לְכָל בְּרִיָּה יֵשׁ שֵׁם
שֶׁנָּתְנוּ לָהּ חַגֶּיהָ
וְנָתְנָה לָהּ מְלַאכְתָּהּ

Each of us has a name

given by the seasons

and given by our blindness

Each of us has a name

given by the sea

and given by

our death.

AFTER A POEM BY ZELDA
(*adaptation M. F.*)

לְכָל בְּרִיָּה יֵשׁ שֵׁם

שֶׁנָּתְנוּ לָהּ תְּקוּפוֹת הַשָּׁנָה

וְנָתַן לָהּ עֶזְרוֹנָהּ

לְכָל בְּרִיָּה יֵשׁ שֵׁם

שֶׁנָּתַן לָהּ הַיָּם

וְנָתַן לָהּ

מוֹתָהּ.

עַל־פִּי שִׁיר שֶׁל זֶלְדָּה

Hallowing Our Namings

Let us sing the soul in every name
and the name of every soul,
let us sing the soul in every name,
the sacred name of every soul.

———————

As we bless the source of life
so we are blessed.

נִשְׁמַת כָּל שֵׁם   Nishmat Kol Sheym

Nashir l'nishmat kol sheym

ulsheym kol n'shamah,

nashir l'nishmat kol sheym

v'likdushat kol n'shamah.

———————

N'vareykh et eyn haḥayim

v'khoh nitbareykh.

נָשִׁיר לְנִשְׁמַת כָּל שֵׁם

וּלְשֵׁם כָּל נְשָׁמָה,

נָשִׁיר לְנִשְׁמַת כָּל שֵׁם

וְלִקְדֻשַׁת כָּל נְשָׁמָה.

———————

נְבָרֵךְ אֶת עֵין הַחַיִּים

וְכֹה נִתְבָּרֵךְ.

When this *Amidah* is being used on Rosh Hodesh occurring on a weekday, omit pp. 215–25 and substitute pp. 391–95.

4
Sanctifying the Sabbath Day
קְדֻשַּׁת יוֹם הַשַּׁבָּת

Sabbath: There is what we make happen through our acts of will, our conscious choices to keep the Sabbath day. And then there is the miracle, which we can only receive: when it happens, releasing us from time, all of creation is one, and we are one with it. Though momentary, it is a recollection of our earliest origins, and a glimpse of time to come.

For an abbreviated form of this prayer, continue after this page on pp. 224–25.

Sanctifying the Sabbath Day

Let us hallow the Sabbath day
and let us keep it—
in remembrance of creation
and the covenant.

קְדֻשַּׁת יוֹם הַשַּׁבָּת

K'dushat Yom Hashabbat

נְקַדֵּשׁ אֶת יוֹם הַשַּׁבָּת
וְנִשְׁמֹר אוֹתוֹ –
זִכָּרוֹן לְמַעֲשֵׂה בְרֵאשִׁית,
זֵכֶר לִיצִיאַת מִצְרָיִם.

N'kadeysh et yom hashabbat
v'nishmor oto—
zikaron l'ma'aseyh v'reyshit,
zéykher litzi'at mitzráyim.

Sabbath Morning

In the green and yellow grass of the broad field

fringed by greening trees,

leaves flapping,

birds talking and flapping,

a young girl disappears.

She lies down in her bright shirt

into the soft green grass

and disappears.

Later, the girl rises from her bed in the grass,

lifting her head above the white-topped stalks of clover.

She rises and walks off,

wading down into the field,

which waves around her like a lake—

so that soon she imagines she is sailing on a summer lake,

her body light as a sail in the fresh cold breeze.

All this is seen by the woman who sits on the roof.

She sits on the sun-warmed roof

and watches the tree-ringed field rock and sway

around the bobbing head of a girl wading through the weeds.

This is the picture the woman sees:

field, girl, bluejay, trees.

No matter what happens outside of this,

the girl will always be part of this.

Then, for a tiny instant,

the woman is weightless in the galaxy

which floats around her, blue and indifferent

and fierce as a winter sea.

Today Is Forever

I stroll in a nearby park—

old trees wildly overgrown,

bushes, flowers blooming all four seasons,

a creek babbling childishly over stones,

a bridge with railings, rough-hewn—

.　　.　　.

Leaning on the railing,

looking at myself

in clear water,

I ask: Little creek,

will you tumble and flow here forever?

The stream babbles back, laughing:

Today is forever. Forever is now.

I smile, a spark's-worth believing,

a sigh's-worth not believing:

Today is forever. Forever is now.

Under a leafy twig on a bush,

a bird is scratching the dirt,

digging, scraping,

bracing himself with his feet,

until there's a little trough

היינט איז אייביק

אָפֿט איך שפּאַציר אין נאָענטן פּאַרקל:

אַלטע ביימער מגושמדיק צעוואָקסן,

קוסטן, בלומען אין צעעבלי פֿאַר אַלע פֿיר סעזאָנען,

אַ וואַסערל וואָס בולבולט קינדיש איבער שטיינדלער,

אַ בריקל מיט ניט־געהוביבלטע פּאַרענטשן —

. . .

אָנגעלענט אָן פּלויט,

זיך שפּיגלענדיק אין וואַסער־לויטער,

איך פֿרעג:

וועסטו, ריטשקעלע, דאָ בייכלען, טייכלען

אייביק?

בולבולט לאַכנדיק דאָס טייכל:

‏„היינט איז אייביק.

אייביק איז אָט איצט".

שמייכל איך אַ פֿונקל גלייביק

און אַ זיפֿצעלע ניט גלייביק:

היינט איז אייביק.

אייביק איז אָט איצט.

אונטער אַ צעוואָקסן קוסטנצווייַיגל

אַ פֿויגל

שאַרט די ערד פֿון אונטער זיך,

ריִעט, שאַרט מיט אָנגעשפּאַנטע פֿיסלעך

ביז

ס׳איז אַ מולטערל אַ טיפֿס געוואָרן

just the size of his body—

a cradle.

Carefully he fits himself in,

spreads his left wing,

puts his head sideways down.

A transparent film settles over him—

rest.

A calm slips between the trees,

the leaves move barely a breath,

the grasses ever-so-slightly bow,

and I, steeped in silence,

walk slowly home,

a spark's-worth believing,

a sigh's-worth not believing:

Today is forever. Forever is now.

MALKA HEIFETZ TUSSMAN
(*translation M. F.*)

פּונקט די גרייס ווי

ס׳איז דאָס גופֿל זיינס —

אַ וויגל.

ער האָט פֿאַמעלעכקע אַריינגעמאָסטעט זיך אַהין,

אויסגעשפּרייט דעם לינקן פֿליגל,

זייטיק

דאָס קעפּעלע אויף דעם אַוועקגעלייגט.

צוגעדעקט האָט אים

אַ לייכטער דורכזיכטיקער פֿילם —

רו.

אַ שטילקייט האָט זיך פֿרום אַריינגעשאַרט

צווישן ביימער,

די בלעטער קוים-קוים זיך באַוועגט,

די גראָזן קוים-קוים זיך געניגט

און איך

אַן אַריינגעשוויגטע,

מיט פֿאַמעלעכן טראָט

האָב געשפּאַנט אַהיים —

אַ פֿונקל גלייביק,

אַ זיפֿצעלע ניט גלייביק:

היינט איז אייביק.

אייביק איז אָט איצט.

מלכה חפץ טוזמאַן

Sanctifying the Sabbath Day

Let us hallow the Sabbath day
and let us keep it—
in remembrance of creation
and the covenant.

———

As we bless the source of life
so we are blessed.

K'dushat Yom Hashabbat   קְדֻשַּׁת יוֹם הַשַּׁבָּת

N'kadeysh et yom hashabbat

v'nishmor oto—

zikaron l'ma'aseyh v'reyshit,

zéykher litzi'at mitzráyim.

נְקַדֵּשׁ אֶת יוֹם הַשַּׁבָּת

וְנִשְׁמֹר אוֹתוֹ—

זִכָּרוֹן לְמַעֲשֵׂה בְרֵאשִׁית,

זֵכֶר לִיצִיאַת מִצְרָיִם.

N'vareykh et eyn haḥayim

v'khoh nitbareykh.

נְבָרֵךְ אֶת עֵין הַחַיִּים

וְכֹה נִתְבָּרֵךְ.

When the Sabbath coincides with Rosh Hodesh, insert pp. 391–95 here before going on to the next section of the *Amidah* on p. 227.

5
Restoring Shekhinah, Reclaiming Home
הַחֲזָרַת הַשְּׁכִינָה

Shekhinah (in Hebrew, a feminine noun) is a traditional name for the divine presence. Although the word itself means "indwelling"—the very embodiment of home—the Shekhinah has been depicted as homeless, exiled, abandoned. Is it coincidence that so many Jewish women identify with this image? Today, as we claim our rightful places in the tradition, we honor the Shekhinah that dwells in all our lives. And as women and men, members of a fully inclusive community, we aspire to make a place for holiness everywhere we make our homes.

For an abbreviated form of this prayer, continue after this page on pp. 238–39.

Restoring Shekhinah, Reclaiming Home

*L*et us restore Shekhinah to her place
in Israel and throughout the world,
and let us infuse all places
with her presence.

הַחֲזָרַת הַשְּׁכִינָה

Haḥazarat Hash'khinah

נַחֲזִיר אֶת הַשְּׁכִינָה לִמְקוֹמָה
בְּצִיּוֹן וּבַתֵּבֵל כֻּלָּהּ.

Naḥazir et hash'khinah limkomah
b'tziyon uvateyveyl kulah.

To My Land

I have not sung of you

or glorified your name

with tales of bravery

and spoils of war.

I've only walked a trail

across your furrowed fields

to plant a tree

beside the Jordan's shore.

And so, of course, I know

how modest are my gifts,

how poor the offerings, Mother,

of your child—

a clarion of joy

on a sun-washed day,

and silent weeping

for your poverty.

RACHEL
(*translation M. F.*)

אֶל אַרְצִי

לֹא שַׁרְתִּי לָךְ, אַרְצִי,
וְלֹא פֵּאַרְתִּי שְׁמֵךְ
בַּעֲלִילוֹת גְּבוּרָה,
בִּשְׁלַל קְרָבוֹת;
רַק עֵץ–יָדַי נָטְעוּ
חוֹפֵי יַרְדֵּן שׁוֹקְטִים.
רַק שְׁבִיל–כָּבְשׁוּ רַגְלַי
עַל פְּנֵי שָׂדוֹת.

אָכֵן דַּלָּה מְאֹד–
יָדַעְתִּי זֹאת, הָאֵם,
אָכֵן דַּלָּה מְאֹד
מִנְחַת בִּתֵּךְ;
רַק קוֹל תְּרוּעַת הַגִּיל
בְּיוֹם יִגַּהּ הָאוֹר,
רַק בְּכִי בַּמִּסְתָּרִים
עֲלֵי עָנְיֵךְ.

רחל

Holy Quiet

Quietly you utter

the word "quiet"

and already you have marred

the quiet.

I was in a holy quiet

only once.

Once—

Once I had an orchard—

apples, pears, cherries, plums,

and at the fringes, by the fences,

raspberries, gooseberries, currants,

and all kinds of flowers.

Summer dusk. Alone in my orchard.

A moment, an eternity:

the owl held back its poo-hoo,

the cuckoo forgot its cuckoo—

a wild berry by the path in the weeds

fixed in its gaze.

And I—

quiet multiplied by quiet—

did not interrupt my quiet prayer

with even a quiver

when the Shekhinah

הייליקע שטילקייט

זאָגסטו שטיל אַרויס דאָס וואָרט "שטיל"
און שוין
דו האָסט געמאַכט אַ מום אין שטילקייט.

איך בין אין אַ הייליקער שטילקייט געווען –
נאָר איין מאָל געווען.

אמאָל, אמאָל,
איך האָב אַ סאָד געהאַט אמאָל –
עפל, באַרן, וויַינשל, פֿלוימען,
און ביַי די זיַיטן, ביַי די פֿלויטן,
וויַינפערלרלרעך, אַגדעסן, מאָלינעס, און בלומען אַלע סאָרטן.

זומער פֿאַרנאַכט. אַליין אין מיַין סאָד.
אַ וויַילינקע – אַן אייביקייט:
די סאָװע האָט איר פֿוהו פֿאָרהאַלטן,
קוקאַווקע איר קוקו פֿאַרגעסן,
אַ פֿאָזעמקע ביַים זיַיטיקן שטעענגל אין ווילדגראָז
פֿאַרשטאָרט אין איר בליקל געבליבן.
און איך – שטיל מאָל שטיל –
אַ תפֿילה אַ שטילע
ניט מפֿסיק געווען מיט אַ ציטער אַפֿילו
ווען שכינה

kissed a leaf down from a pear tree,

carried it away,

and let it fall onto the brook

at the orchard's edge.

MALKA HEIFETZ TUSSMAN
(*translation M. F.*)

האָט אַראָפּגעקושט אַ בלעטל פֿון אַ באַרנבוים,

אַוועקגעטראָגן

און אַראָפּגעלאָזט דאָס בלעטל

אויף דער ריטשקעלע

צופֿוסנס מײַן סאָד.

מלכּה חפֿץ טוזמאַן

Comm.
p. 474

The New Colossus

Not like the brazen giant of Greek fame,

With conquering limbs astride from land to land;

Here at our sea-washed, sunset gates shall stand

A mighty woman with a torch, whose flame

Is the imprisoned lightning, and her name

Mother of Exiles. From her beacon-hand

Glows world-wide welcome; her mild eyes command

The air-bridged harbor that twin cities frame.

"Keep, ancient lands, your storied pomp!" cries she

With silent lips. "Give me your tired, your poor,

Your huddled masses yearning to breathe free,

The wretched refuse of your teeming shore.

Send these, the homeless, tempest-tost to me,

I lift my lamp beside the golden door!"

EMMA LAZARUS

Recovery

The sky is soft as a grandmother's quilt, fleecy as sheep—

sheep as you imagine them to be, not as they are.

The leaves and grass are soft, too.

They seem to heal you with their green fingers,

their heady perfumes rising.

The wind will open its arms, the field will catch you in its lap,

they will rock you, rock you like a baby

as you dreamed in your deepest longing,

not as it happens when you wish for it

but as it's told in an old old story,

a story you were born knowing and later forgot.

Restoring Shekhinah, Reclaiming Home

*Let us restore Shekhinah to her place
in Israel and throughout the world,
and let us infuse all places
with her presence.*

――――――――

*As we bless the source of life
so we are blessed.*

הַחֲזָרַת הַשְּׁכִינָה

Haḥazarat Hash'khinah

Naḥazir et hash'khinah limkomah
b'tziyon uvateyveyl kulah.

נַחֲזִיר אֶת הַשְּׁכִינָה לִמְקוֹמָה
בְּצִיּוֹן וּבַתֵּבֵל כֻּלָּה.

N'vareykh et eyn haḥayim
v'khoh nitbareykh.

נְבָרֵךְ אֶת עֵין הַחַיִּים
וְכֹה נִתְבָּרֵךְ.

6
The Gift of Gratitude
בְּפֶה מָלֵא שִׁירָה

Out of silence, in the opened space, the song of gratitude is born.

For an abbreviated form of this prayer, continue after this page on pp. 246–47.

The Gift of Gratitude

*O*ur mouths filled with song,
our tongues overflowing with joy—

בְּפֶה מָלֵא שִׁירָה

B'feh Maley Shirah

B'feh maley shirah

uvlashon shofá'at rinah—

בְּפֶה מָלֵא שִׁירָה

וּבְלָשׁוֹן שׁוֹפַעַת רִנָּה—

Silence: personal meditation.

תפילה אישית.

The Gift of Gratitude

*O*ur mouths filled with song,
our tongues overflowing with joy—

————

We bless the source of life
and so we are blessed.

בְּפֶה מָלֵא שִׁירָה

B'feh Maley Shirah

בְּפֶה מָלֵא שִׁירָה
וּבְלָשׁוֹן שׁוֹפַעַת רִנָּה—

B'feh maley shirah

uvlashon shofá'at rinah—

_____

_____

נְבָרֵךְ אֶת עֵין הַחַיִּים
וְכֹה נִתְבָּרֵךְ.

N'vareykh et eyn haḥayim

v'khoh nitbareykh.

7
Blessing of Peace
בִּרְכַּת שָׁלוֹם

For millennia, the flood has been a symbol of world destruction; yet today it is fire that we must fear. So water may be redeemed as a saving image, becoming again the water of redemption. We are told that our bodies are composed mostly of water—water and breath. It is time to reclaim the power of our bodies—the power of our physical acts—and save the fragile body of the world. But to do so, we must first imagine the possibility and give voice to the vision of a world at peace.

For an abbreviated form of this prayer, continue after this page on pp. 258–59.

Blessing of Peace

*E*ternal wellspring of peace—
may we be drenched with the longing for peace
that we may give ourselves over
as the earth to the rain, to the dew,
until peace overflows our lives
as living waters overflow the seas.

Birkat Shalom · בִּרְכַּת שָׁלוֹם

Nish'al mey'eyn hashalom:

Yizal katal,

ya'arof kamatar hashalom,

v'timla ha'áretz shalom

kamáyim layam m'khasim.

נִשְׁאַל מֵעֵין הַשָּׁלוֹם:

יִזַּל כַּטַּל,

יַעֲרֹף כַּמָּטָר הַשָּׁלוֹם,

וְתִמְלָא הָאָרֶץ שָׁלוֹם

כַּמַּיִם לַיָּם מְכַסִּים.

Pause

For the terrorist who saved an Israeli prisoner
from the hands of the other terrorists
who wanted to torture him

A gesture of the hand

wipes out the fantasies of torture—

a gesture

by one of the wolves of suicide,

an eager youth who suddenly

set hate aside

because his soul revealed to him:

hatred lies,

hatred lies,

hatred lies.

And the force of his imaginings

burst upon a new path

with the sounds of childhood

and of miracles.

When the primordial good

awoke in him,

he saved the prisoner.

When a river flowed from his inner Eden,

he gave him water

to revive him in the desert.

Slowly the monster of vengeance

retreated,

הַפּוּגָה

למחבל שהציל שבוי ישראלי
מידי המחבלים
כאשר רצו לעשות בו שפטים.

תְּנוּעַת יָד מְבַטֶּלֶת

אֶת הַהֲזָיוֹת עַל עֲנָוִיִּים,

תְּנוּעַת יָדוֹ

שֶׁל אֶחָד מִזְּאֵבֵי הַהִתְאַבְּדוּת –

נַעַר שׁוֹקֵק

שֶׁבָּחַל פִּתְאֹם בַּשִּׂנְאָה

כִּי נַפְשׁוֹ גָּלְתָה לוֹ:

הַשִּׂנְאָה מְשַׁקֶּרֶת

הַשִּׂנְאָה מְשַׁקֶּרֶת

הַשִּׂנְאָה מְשַׁקֶּרֶת –

וְכֹחַ דִּמְיוֹנוֹ פָּרַץ

אֶל שְׁבִיל חָדָשׁ

עִם קוֹלוֹת הַיַּלְדוּת וְהַמּוֹפְתִים.

כַּאֲשֶׁר הֵקִיץ בּוֹ הַטּוֹב הַהִיּוּלִי

הִצִּיל אֶת הַשָּׁבוּי,

כַּאֲשֶׁר יָצָא נָהָר מֵעֵדֶן פְּנִימִיּוּתוֹ

נָתַן לוֹ מַיִם

לְחַיּוֹתוֹ בַּמִּדְבָּר.

אַט אַט נָסוֹגָה לְאָחוֹר

מִפְלֶצֶת הַנְּקָמָה

and fresh worlds of hope

and the joy of wells rich with water

were revealed.

Oh! Both of them knew—

this was not the whole truth,

this was a pause

on a green island,

the island beyond all nations,

beyond all outlets.

On this island, in one of the caves,

peace opened its eyes.

ZELDA
(*translation M. F.*)

וְנִגְלוּ עוֹלָמוֹת רַעֲנַנִּים שֶׁל תִּקְוָה

וְשִׂמְחַת מַעְיָנוֹת נִכְבְּדֵי־מַיִם.

אוֹיָה!

שְׁנֵיהֶם יָדְעוּ:

אֵין זוֹ כָּל הָאֱמֶת,

זוֹ הֲפוּגָה

בְּאִי יָרֹק,

הָאִי שֶׁהוּא מִחוּץ לְכָל לְאֹם

וּלְכָל מוֹצָא.

בָּאִי הַזֶּה בְּאַחַת הַמְּעָרוֹת

פָּקַח אֶת עֵינָיו הַשָּׁלוֹם.

זלדה

First Rain

The first rain—

a plenitude of freshness

with no sign of Cain.

And agony will no longer

whisper to my soul:

I am the king.

No longer will it say:

I am the ruler.

Each drop is a link

between me and things,

a link

between me and the world.

And when night

conjures up the abyss,

the abyss conjures up

fields and gardens.

ZELDA
(*translation M. F.*)

הַגֶּשֶׁם הָרִאשׁוֹן

הַגֶּשֶׁם הָרִאשׁוֹן
אַלְפֵי רְבָבָה רַעֲנַנּוּת
בְּלִי אוֹת שֶׁל קַיִן.
וְהַדְוַי לֹא יִלְחַשׁ עוֹד
לְנַפְשִׁי
אֲנִי הַמֶּלֶךְ,
לֹא יַגִּיד עוֹד
אֲנִי הַשַּׁלִּיט.
כָּל טִפָּה וְטִפָּה
הִיא זִקָּה
בֵּינִי וּבֵין הַדְּבָרִים,
זִקָּה
בֵּינִי וּבֵין הָעוֹלָם.
וְכַאֲשֶׁר הַלַּיְלָה
מַעֲלֶה אֶת הַתְּהוֹם
הַתְּהוֹם מַעֲלֶה
שָׂדוֹת וְגַנִּים.

זלדה

Blessing of Peace

*E*ternal wellspring of peace—
may we be drenched with the longing for peace
that we may give ourselves over
as the earth to the rain, to the dew,
until peace overflows our lives
as living waters overflow the seas.

———

As we bless the source of life
so we are blessed.

בִּרְכַּת שָׁלוֹם · Birkat Shalom

Nish'al mey'eyn hashalom:

Yizal katal,

ya'arof kamatar hashalom,

v'timla ha'áretz shalom

kamáyim layam m'khasim.

———————

N'vareykh et eyn haḥayim

v'khoh nitbareykh.

נִשְׁאַל מֵעֵין הַשָּׁלוֹם:

יִזַּל כַּטַּל,

יַעֲרֹף כַּמָּטָר הַשָּׁלוֹם,

וְתִמְלָא הָאָרֶץ שָׁלוֹם

כַּמַּיִם לַיָּם מְכַסִּים.

———————

נְבָרֵךְ אֶת עֵין הַחַיִּים

וְכֹה נִתְבָּרֵךְ.

HONORING TORAH
לִכְבוֹד תּוֹרָה

עֲשָׂרָה שֶׁיּוֹשְׁבִין וְעוֹסְקִין בַּתּוֹרָה שְׁכִינָה שְׁרוּיָה בֵּינֵיהֶם.
פרקי אבות ג:ז

When ten sit together and study Torah, Shekhinah is in their midst.

PIRKEY AVOT 3:7

אֵלּוּ דְבָרִים שֶׁאָדָם אוֹכֵל פֵּרוֹתֵיהֶם בָּעוֹלָם הַזֶּה וְהַקֶּרֶן קַיֶּמֶת לוֹ לָעוֹלָם
הַבָּא, וְאֵלּוּ הֵן: כִּבּוּד אָב וָאֵם, וּגְמִילוּת חֲסָדִים, וְהַשְׁכָּמַת בֵּית הַמִּדְרָשׁ שַׁחֲרִית
וְעַרְבִית, וְהַכְנָסַת אוֹרְחִים, וּבִקּוּר חוֹלִים, וְהַכְנָסַת כַּלָּה, וְהַלְוָיַת הַמֵּת, וְעִיּוּן
תְּפִלָּה, וַהֲבָאַת שָׁלוֹם בֵּין אָדָם לַחֲבֵרוֹ; וְתַלְמוּד תּוֹרָה כְּנֶגֶד כֻּלָּם.
מתפילת שחרית המסורתית (מבוסס על תלמוד בבלי, שבת קכז:א)

These are the things of which a person enjoys the fruits in this world and that continue to yield rewards in the world to come: honoring one's father and one's mother, practicing lovingkindness, arriving early at the house of study in the morning and in the evening, welcoming guests, visiting the sick, bringing the bride to the wedding canopy, accompanying the dead to the grave, being thoughtful in prayer, bringing peace between human beings. And the study of Torah outweighs them all.

FROM THE TRADITIONAL MORNING SERVICE (BASED ON TALMUD, B. SHABBAT 127A)

In a tradition that views Torah as sacred and values the study of Torah beyond all else, we consider with utmost care what is Torah and what it means to honor it.

Torah has many meanings in our history: the Five Books of Moses (or the Pentateuch, the first third of the Hebrew Bible, found in the Torah scroll); all of Hebrew Bible (including the Pentateuch, the Prophets, and the Writings); "the written Torah" together with "the oral Torah" (that is, Bible with rabbinic commentaries). Above all, Torah means "teaching": our central teachings, our sacred texts.

So we ask ourselves: What, for us, are the sacred texts? Which are the stories we choose to tell and retell; what are the readings we give to them? What myths instruct us about where we have been, and which ones help us go where we are headed? What teachings do we preserve because they explain our history; which do we embrace as wise today?

Torah is also revelation. So we ask not only: What do we know? but also: How do we know it? How do we know *we know? What are our sources of authority?*

And what does it mean to honor a text as sacred? Can one read reverentially yet openly—without predetermining meaning? What is the effect of a worshipful stance? Does it open the doors to wisdom—or close the doors to some of our truths?

When is the honoring of Torah the dishonoring of self or others? What do we do about the limitations—even the harmfulness—of words that have long been honored and embraced? What does it mean that our honoring has turned text into icon, icon into sine qua non?

We must keep asking: Whose text is it? For whom does it speak, whom does it represent? Whose story does it tell, and whose does it erase? Whose values does it convey, whose power preserve? How do we feel—indeed what shall we do—about the patriarchal portrayals of divinity that are so pervasive in the Bible? About the ethnocentricity so profoundly embedded there? About the sweeping erasures of women as full human agents from our history? Can this be our *Torah?*

We are told that this Torah is ours, our people's. But to which of our people has it been taught? Which of our people teach it? How much of it did our mothers and grandmothers—and the mothers before them—learn? How much did these women participate in handing it on, *contributing their own insights to the tradition? Did any of them gain entrance to the community we call* rabbéynu, *our most esteemed teachers of Torah?*

Still, can we entirely abandon what has become emblematic of our people's identity, even of our people's survival? If it is not all we wish it were, it remains what history has bequeathed us; it is, for the most part, what we have. Where, then, is its proper place today?

The rabbis said, "Turn it, turn it, for all is contained in it." We turn, and we turn—but not *all is in it. We find we have more to add. We cannot read all our truths into a place where they have never been. So we invent and inscribe, and we ask: Can new texts, too, become sacred? Can our own voices become Torah?*

And throughout the process, we ask what it means to us to keep on wrestling with tradition—with what is difficult and causes us pain. How do we know when we have wrestled enough? How do we know when it is time to let go, time to free ourselves for something new?

We ask these questions here today, in the context of our service, because questioning—in pursuit of our deepest truths—is itself a form of Torah. We ask our questions, fully realizing that well-meaning people among us may differ—perhaps vehemently—in their answers. It is not our purpose to be divisive. But we are already of many minds. Silencing the concerns will not diminish them; it will not make them go away.

Dare we ask these questions? Dare we not ask them? If not now, when?

Gates of Righteousness

Upon taking out the Torah

*M*ay the gates of righteousness open
that I may enter, grateful.

*H*ere is the way before us—
let us enter, let us bless.

AFTER PSALM 118:19–20

שַׁעֲרֵי־צֶדֶק Sha'arey-Tzédek

לְעֵת הוֹצָאַת הַתּוֹרָה

פִּתְחוּ־לִי שַׁעֲרֵי־צֶדֶק,
אָבֹא בָם וְאוֹדֶה.

Pitḥu-li sha'arey-tzédek,
avo vam v'odeh.

זֶה הַשַּׁעַר לַתּוֹרָה,
נָבֹא בוֹ וּנְבָרֵךְ.

Zeh hashá'ar latorah,
navo vo unvareykh.

עַל־פִּי תְהִילִים קיח:יט

Torah Blessings

Before the Torah reading

The individual: Let us bless the source of life.

The congregation: As we bless the source of life
so we are blessed.

The individual: As we bless the source of life
so may we be blessed.

May our hearts be lifted,
our spirits refreshed,
our understanding deepened
by the study of Torah.

בִּרְכוֹת הַתּוֹרָה
Birkhot Hatorah

לִפְנֵי קְרִיאַת הַתּוֹרָה

The individual:	Bar'khu et eyn haḥayim.

הָעוֹלֶה לַתּוֹרָה: בָּרְכוּ אֶת עֵין הַחַיִּים.

The congregation: N'vareykh et eyn haḥayim
v'khoh nitbareykh.

הַקָּהָל: נְבָרֵךְ אֶת עֵין הַחַיִּים
וְכֹה נִתְבָּרֵךְ.

The individual: N'vareykh et eyn haḥayim
v'khoh nitbareykh.

הָעוֹלֶה לַתּוֹרָה: נְבָרֵךְ אֶת עֵין הַחַיִּים
וְכֹה נִתְבָּרֵךְ.

Yitromeym libéynu,
t'shovav nafshéynu,
ta'amik havanatéynu
b'oskéynu b'divrey torah.

יִתְרוֹמֵם לִבֵּנוּ,
תְּשׁוֹבַב נַפְשֵׁנוּ,
תַּעֲמִיק הֲבָנָתֵנוּ
בְּעָסְקֵנוּ בְּדִבְרֵי תּוֹרָה.

Torah Blessings

After the Torah reading

The individual: **M**ay our hearts be lifted,
our spirits refreshed,
our understanding deepened
by the study of Torah.

And may the words of Torah be sweet
to us and to our offspring
and to all the offspring of Israel.

The congregation: As we bless the source of life
so we are blessed.

בִּרְכוֹת הַתּוֹרָה   Birkhot Hatorah

אַחֲרֵי קְרִיאַת הַתּוֹרָה

הָעוֹלֶה לַתּוֹרָה:

The individual:

Yitromeym libéynu,   יִתְרוֹמֵם לִבֵּנוּ,

t'shovav nafshéynu,   תְּשׁוֹבֵב נַפְשֵׁנוּ,

ta'amik havanatéynu   תַּעֲמִיק הֲבָנָתֵנוּ

b'oskéynu b'divrey torah.   בְּעָסְקֵנוּ בְּדִבְרֵי תוֹרָה.

V'ye'ervu divrey torah b'fínu   וְיֶעֱרְבוּ דִבְרֵי תוֹרָה בְּפִינוּ

uvfi tze'etza'éynu   וּבְפִי צֶאֱצָאֵינוּ

uvfi kol tze'etza'ey yisra'eyl.   וּבְפִי כָּל צֶאֱצָאֵי יִשְׂרָאֵל.

הַקָּהָל:

The congregation:

N'vareykh et eyn haḥayim   נְבָרֵךְ אֶת עֵין הַחַיִּים

v'khoh nitbareykh.   וְכֹה נִתְבָּרֵךְ.

As Those Who Came Before Us Were Blessed

For one who has honored Torah

For an individual:

*A*s those who came before us were blessed
in the presence of the communities that sustained them,

so we offer our blessings to _____ ,
(name)
who has risen to Torah.

For more than one individual:

*A*s those who came before us were blessed
in the presence of the communities that sustained them,

so we offer our blessings to _____ ,
(names)
who have risen to Torah.

A blessing may be said for each individual (see the first two versions of the Hebrew, first version of the English), or individuals may be named together in a single blessing (third version of the Hebrew, second version of the English).

כְּמוֹ שֶׁנִּתְבָּרְכוּ   K'mo Shenitbar'khu

לְעוֹלָה וּלְעוֹלֶה לַתּוֹרָה

For a female: לְאִשָּׁה אוֹ יַלְדָּה:

K'mo shenitbar'khu imotéynu va'avotéynu,   כְּמוֹ שֶׁנִּתְבָּרְכוּ אִמּוֹתֵינוּ וַאֲבוֹתֵינוּ,

keyn titbareykh _____   כֵּן תִּתְבָּרֵךְ _____
                (name)   (שם)

she'al'tah likhvod torah   שֶׁעָלְתָה לִכְבוֹד תּוֹרָה

v'likhvod k'hilatéynu.   וְלִכְבוֹד קְהִלָּתֵנוּ.

For a male: לְגֶבֶר אוֹ יֶלֶד:

K'mo shenitbar'khu imotéynu va'avotéynu,   כְּמוֹ שֶׁנִּתְבָּרְכוּ אִמּוֹתֵינוּ וַאֲבוֹתֵינוּ,

keyn yitbareykh _____   כֵּן יִתְבָּרֵךְ _____
                (name)   (שם)

she'alah likhvod torah   שֶׁעָלָה לִכְבוֹד תּוֹרָה

v'likhvod k'hilatéynu.   וְלִכְבוֹד קְהִלָּתֵנוּ.

For more than one individual: לִקְבוּצָה:

K'mo shenitbar'khu imotéynu va'avotéynu,   כְּמוֹ שֶׁנִּתְבָּרְכוּ אִמּוֹתֵינוּ וַאֲבוֹתֵינוּ,

keyn yitbar'khu _____   כֵּן יִתְבָּרְכוּ _____
                (names)   (שמות)

she'alu likhvod torah   שֶׁעָלוּ לִכְבוֹד תּוֹרָה

v'likhvod k'hilatéynu.   וְלִכְבוֹד קְהִלָּתֵנוּ.

As Those Who Came Before Us Were Blessed

For one in need of healing

For an individual:

*A*s those who came before us were blessed
in the presence of the communities that sustained them,

so we offer our blessings
for one among us in need of healing.

_____ ,
   (name)
may you have comfort and relief
in the healing of body and mind,

and may you return in time
to health and wholeness and strength.

A blessing may be said for each individual (see the first version of the English, first two versions of the Hebrew), or individuals may be named together in a single blessing (second version of the English, on p. 274; third version of the Hebrew, on p. 275).

כְּמוֹ שֶׁנִּתְבָּרְכוּ K'mo Shenitbar'khu

לְמַעַן חוֹלָה וְחוֹלֶה

For a female:

לְאִשָּׁה אוֹ לְיַלְדָּה:

K'mo shenitbar'khu imotéynu va'avotéynu,

כְּמוֹ שֶׁנִּתְבָּרְכוּ אִמוֹתֵינוּ וַאֲבוֹתֵינוּ,

keyn titbareykh v'teyrafey _____
(name)

כֵּן תִּתְבָּרֵךְ וְתֵרָפֵא _____
(שם)

Y'hi ratzon shetahlim uvimheyrah tizkeh

יְהִי רָצוֹן שֶׁתַּחֲלִים וּבִמְהֵרָה תִּזְכֶּה

lirfu'at hanéfesh v'lirfu'at haguf,

לִרְפוּאַת הַנֶּפֶשׁ וְלִרְפוּאַת הַגּוּף,

r'fu'ah sh'leymah.

רְפוּאָה שְׁלֵמָה.

For a male:

לְגֶבֶר אוֹ לְיֶלֶד:

K'mo shenitbar'khu imotéynu va'avotéynu,

כְּמוֹ שֶׁנִּתְבָּרְכוּ אִמוֹתֵינוּ וַאֲבוֹתֵינוּ,

keyn yitbareykh v'yeyrafey _____
(name)

כֵּן יִתְבָּרֵךְ וְיֵרָפֵא _____
(שם)

Y'hi ratzon sheyahlim uvimheyrah yizkeh

יְהִי רָצוֹן שֶׁיַּחֲלִים וּבִמְהֵרָה יִזְכֶּה

lirfu'at hanéfesh v'lirfu'at haguf,

לִרְפוּאַת הַנֶּפֶשׁ וְלִרְפוּאַת הַגּוּף,

r'fu'ah sh'leymah.

רְפוּאָה שְׁלֵמָה.

Comm.
p. 481

For more than one individual:

*A*s those who came before us were blessed
in the presence of the communities that sustained them,

so we offer our blessings
for those among us in need of healing.

——————————— ,
      (names)
may you have comfort and relief
in the healing of body and mind,

and may you return in time
to health and wholeness and strength.

For more than one individual:

לִקְבוּצָה:

K'mo shenitbar'khu imotéynu va'avotéynu,

כְּמוֹ שֶׁנִּתְבָּרְכוּ אִמוֹתֵינוּ וַאֲבוֹתֵינוּ,

keyn yitbar'khu v'yeyraf'u _____
(names)

כֵּן יִתְבָּרְכוּ וְיֵרָפְאוּ _____ . _____
(שמות)

Y'hi ratzon sheyaḥlímu uvimheyrah yizku

יְהִי רָצוֹן שֶׁיַּחְלִימוּ וּבִמְהֵרָה יִזְכּוּ

lirfu'at hanéfesh v'lirfu'at haguf,

לִרְפוּאַת הַנֶּפֶשׁ וְלִרְפוּאַת הַגּוּף,

r'fu'ah sh'leymah.

רְפוּאָה שְׁלֵמָה.

As Those Who Came Before Us Were Blessed

For one gravely ill

For an individual:

*A*s those who came before us were blessed
in the presence of the communities that sustained them,

so we offer our blessings
for one among us needing support.

_____ ,
　　　(name)
may your spirit be calmed
and your pain be eased,

may you receive comfort
from those who care for you,

and may you drink from the waters
of the ever-giving well.

A blessing may be said for each individual (see the first version of the English, first two versions of the Hebrew), or individuals may be named together in a single blessing (second version of the English, on p. 278; third version of the Hebrew, on p. 279).

כְּמוֹ שֶׁנִּתְבָּרְכוּ

K'mo Shenitbar'khu

לְמַעַן חוֹלָה אֲנוּשָׁה וְחוֹלֶה אָנוּשׁ

For a female:

לאשה או לילדה:

K'mo shenitbar'khu imotéynu va'avotéynu,

כְּמוֹ שֶׁנִּתְבָּרְכוּ אִמּוֹתֵינוּ וַאֲבוֹתֵינוּ,

keyn titbareykh _____ .
        (name)

כֵּן תִּתְבָּרֵךְ _____ .
        (שם)

Y'hi ratzon sheyeyḥal'shu k'eyvéha

יְהִי רָצוֹן שֶׁיֵּחָלְשׁוּ כְּאֵבֶיהָ

v'yafúgu yisuréha,

וְיָפוּגוּ יִסּוּרֶיהָ,

yishkot libah v'teyraga nafshah.

יִשְׁקֹט לִבָּהּ וְתֵרָגַע נַפְשָׁהּ.

Y'hi ratzon shetishteh

יְהִי רָצוֹן שֶׁתִּשְׁתֶּה

mimey hama'yan

מִמֵּי הַמַּעְיָן

adey-ad m'fakeh.

עֲדֵי־עַד מְפַכֶּה.

═══════════════════

For a male:

לגבר או לילד:

K'mo shenitbar'khu imotéynu va'avotéynu,

כְּמוֹ שֶׁנִּתְבָּרְכוּ אִמּוֹתֵינוּ וַאֲבוֹתֵינוּ,

keyn yitbareykh _____ .
        (name)

כֵּן יִתְבָּרֵךְ _____ .
        (שם)

Y'hi ratzon sheyeyḥal'shu k'eyvav

יְהִי רָצוֹן שֶׁיֵּחָלְשׁוּ כְּאֵבָיו

v'yafúgu yisurav,

וְיָפוּגוּ יִסּוּרָיו,

yishkot libo v'teyraga nafsho.

יִשְׁקֹט לִבּוֹ וְתֵרָגַע נַפְשׁוֹ.

Y'hi ratzon sheyishteh

יְהִי רָצוֹן שֶׁיִּשְׁתֶּה

mimey hama'yan

מִמֵּי הַמַּעְיָן

adey-ad m'fakeh.

עֲדֵי־עַד מְפַכֶּה.

═══════════════════

Comm. p. 481

For more than one individual:

*A*s those who came before us were blessed
in the presence of the communities that sustained them,

so we offer our blessings
for those among us needing support.

_____ ,
(names)

may your spirit be calmed
and your pain be eased,

may you receive comfort
from those who care for you,

and may you drink from the waters
of the ever-giving well.

For more than one individual:

לִקְבוּצָה:

K'mo shenitbar'khu imotéynu va'avotéynu,

כְּמוֹ שֶׁנִּתְבָּרְכוּ אִמוֹתֵינוּ וַאֲבוֹתֵינוּ,

keyn yitbar'khu _____ .
      (names)

כֵּן יִתְבָּרְכוּ _____ .
      (שמות)

Y'hi ratzon sheyeyḥal'shu hak'eyvim

יְהִי רָצוֹן שֶׁיֶּחָלְשׁוּ הַכְּאֵבִים

v'yafúgu hayisurim,

וְיָפוּגוּ הַיִּסּוּרִים,

yishkot haleyv v'teyraga hanéfesh.

יִשְׁקֹט הַלֵּב וְתֵרָגַע הַנֶּפֶשׁ.

Y'hi ratzon sheyishtu

יְהִי רָצוֹן שֶׁיִּשְׁתּוּ

mimey hama'yan

מִמֵּי הַמַּעְיָן

adey-ad m'fakeh.

עֲדֵי־עַד מְפַכֶּה.

Tree of Life

Upon returning the Torah

*It is a tree of life
for those who grasp it*

*and all who reach for it
are blessed.*

*Its ways are sweet
and its paths are peace.*

PROVERBS 3:18, 17

עֵץ־חַיִּים הִיא   Eytz-Ḥayim Hi

לְעֵת הַכְנָסַת הַתּוֹרָה

Eytz-ḥayim hi

lamaḥazikim bah

v'tom'khéha m'ushar.

D'rakhéha darkhey-nó'am

v'khol-n'tivotéha shalom.

עֵץ־חַיִּים הִיא

לַמַּחֲזִיקִים בָּהּ

וְתֹמְכֶיהָ מְאֻשָּׁר.

דְּרָכֶיהָ דַרְכֵי־נֹעַם

וְכָל־נְתִיבוֹתֶיהָ שָׁלוֹם.

משלי ג:יח,יז

BIRKAT HAHÓDESH: HERALDING THE NEW MONTH
בִּרְכַּת הַחֹדֶשׁ

On *shabbat m'var'khim* (the Sabbath before Rosh Hodesh), turn to p. 335 for:

Gifts of the Month: A Thanksgiving
מַתְּנוֹת הַחֹדֶשׁ: הוֹדָיָה

Announcing the New Month
הַכְרָזַת הַחֹדֶשׁ

Prayer for the New Month
תְּפִלַּת הַחֹדֶשׁ

The **Shaharit** service continues on p. 285.

CLOSING PRAYERS
סִיוּם

In this Sabbath service, we have celebrated creation and opened ourselves to revelation and redemption. We now recall these themes with **Aléynu L'shabéy'aḥ:** *It Is Ours to Praise. Then, with the* **Kaddish:** *Mourners' Prayer and the* **Closing Blessing,** *we embrace community, through which we keep these themes alive.*

Aléynu L'shabéy'aḥ: *It Is Ours to Praise*
עָלֵינוּ לְשַׁבֵּחַ

With **Aléynu L'shabéy'aḥ** *we reaffirm these commitments: to honor creation—the natural world in its fullness, its beauty and wonder; to be open to revelation—our capacity for awareness, our experience of truth; and to help bring about redemption—a world in which justice is pursued and peace is lived.*

Aléynu L'shabéy'aḥ: *It Is Ours to Praise*

*It is ours to praise
the beauty of the world*

*even as we discern
the torn world.*

*For nothing is whole
that is not first rent*

*and out of the torn
we make whole again.*

*May we live with promise
in creation's lap,*

*redemption budding
in our hands.*

עָלֵינוּ לְשַׁבֵּחַ   Aléynu L'shabéy'aḥ

Aléynu l'shabéy'aḥ l'yif'at teyveyl,

lif'ol v'la'amol l'tikun olam,

ki b'khoḥéynu livnot ultakeyn,

uvyadéynu l'hatzmí'aḥ g'ulah.

Bayom hahu yishk'nu lavétaḥ

kol ba'ey olam.

עָלֵינוּ לְשַׁבֵּחַ לְיִפְעַת תֵּבֵל,

לִפְעֹל וְלַעֲמֹל לְתִקּוּן עוֹלָם,

כִּי בְכֹחֵנוּ לִבְנוֹת וּלְתַקֵּן,

וּבְיָדֵינוּ לְהַצְמִיחַ גְּאֻלָּה.

בַּיּוֹם הַהוּא יִשְׁכְּנוּ לָבֶטַח

כָּל בָּאֵי עוֹלָם.

Kaddish: *Mourners' Prayer*
קַדִּישׁ

The traditional mourners' prayer, known as the kaddish, *magnifies and sanctifies the divine name. Today we sanctify life by expanding our namings, reflecting and honoring the diversity of our lives.*

We begin by silently calling to mind the names of all those whose absence we mourn.

—————

We continue by saying aloud the names of loved ones who have died in the past year. Mourners and those observing the anniversary of the death of a loved one say the names of those they are mourning. Names may include lineage ("Rose, daughter of Pearl and Menakhem Mendl") and terms of relation ("my maternal grandmother"), as well as terms of endearment.

—————

We conclude with the recitation of Each of Us Has a Name *(on the next page).*

Kaddish: *Mourners' Prayer*

Each of Us Has a Name

Each of us has a name

given by the source of life

and given by our parents

Each of us has a name

given by our stature and our smile

and given by what we wear

Each of us has a name

given by the mountains

and given by our walls

Each of us has a name

given by the stars

and given by our neighbors

Each of us has a name

given by our sins

and given by our longing

Each of us has a name

given by our enemies

and given by our love

Each of us has a name

given by our celebrations

and given by our work

קַדִּישׁ

L'khol B'riyah Yeysh Sheym

לְכָל בְּרִיָּה יֵשׁ שֵׁם

L'khol b'riyah yeysh sheym

shenat'nah lah eyn hahayim

v'nat'nu lah avîha v'imah

לְכָל בְּרִיָּה יֵשׁ שֵׁם
שֶׁנָּתְנָה לָהּ עֵין הַחַיִּים
וְנָתְנוּ לָהּ אָבִיהָ וְאִמָּהּ

L'khol b'riyah yeysh sheym

shenat'nu lah komatah v'ófen hiyukhah

v'natan lah ha'arig

לְכָל בְּרִיָּה יֵשׁ שֵׁם
שֶׁנָּתְנוּ לָהּ קוֹמָתָהּ וְאֹפֶן חִיּוּכָהּ
וְנָתַן לָהּ הָאָרִיג

L'khol b'riyah yeysh sheym

shenat'nu lah heharim

v'nat'nu lah k'taléha

לְכָל בְּרִיָּה יֵשׁ שֵׁם
שֶׁנָּתְנוּ לָהּ הֶהָרִים
וְנָתְנוּ לָהּ כְּתָלֶיהָ

L'khol b'riyah yeysh sheym

shenat'nu lah hamazalot

v'nat'nu lah sh'kheynéha

לְכָל בְּרִיָּה יֵשׁ שֵׁם
שֶׁנָּתְנוּ לָהּ הַמַּזָּלוֹת
וְנָתְנוּ לָהּ שְׁכֵנֶיהָ

L'khol b'riyah yeysh sheym

shenat'nu lah hata'éha

v'nat'nah lah k'mihatah

לְכָל בְּרִיָּה יֵשׁ שֵׁם
שֶׁנָּתְנוּ לָהּ חֲטָאֶיהָ
וְנָתְנָה לָהּ כְּמִיהָתָהּ

L'khol b'riyah yeysh sheym

shenat'nu lah son'éha

v'nat'nah lah ahavatah

לְכָל בְּרִיָּה יֵשׁ שֵׁם
שֶׁנָּתְנוּ לָהּ שׂוֹנְאֶיהָ
וְנָתְנָה לָהּ אַהֲבָתָהּ

L'khol b'riyah yeysh sheym

shenat'nu lah hagéha

v'nat'nah lah m'lakhtah

לְכָל בְּרִיָּה יֵשׁ שֵׁם
שֶׁנָּתְנוּ לָהּ חַגֶּיהָ
וְנָתְנָה לָהּ מְלַאכְתָּהּ

Comm.
p. 486

Each of us has a name

given by the seasons

and given by our blindness

Each of us has a name

given by the sea

and given by

our death.

AFTER A POEM BY ZELDA
(*adaptation M. F.*)

לְכָל בְּרִיָּה יֵשׁ שֵׁם

שֶׁנָּתְנוּ לָהּ תְּקוּפוֹת הַשָּׁנָה

וְנָתַן לָהּ עִוְרוֹנָהּ

לְכָל בְּרִיָּה יֵשׁ שֵׁם

שֶׁנָּתַן לָהּ הַיָּם

וְנָתַן לָהּ

מוֹתָהּ.

עַל־פִּי שִׁיר שֶׁל זֶלְדָּה

L'khol b'riyah yeysh sheym

shenat'nu lah t'kufot hashanah

v'natan lah ivronah

L'khol b'riyah yeysh sheym

shenatan lah hayam

v'natan lah

motah.

Closing Blessing
בִּרְכַּת סִיּוּם

We have come full circle. As we began the service seeking connections, we conclude by affirming the greater wholes to which we belong.

Closing Blessing

May the blessings of peace and kindness,
graciousness, goodness, and compassion
flow among us
and all the communities of Israel,
all the peoples of the world.

———————

*As we bless the source of life
so we are blessed.*

May this Sabbath bring peace and restoration.

בִּרְכַּת סִיּוּם

Birkat Siyum

יִשְׁרוּ שָׁלוֹם, טוֹבָה וּבְרָכָה,

Yishru shalom, tovah uvrakhah,

חֵן וָחֶסֶד וְרַחֲמִים

ḥeyn vaḥésed v'raḥamim

בֵּינֵינוּ,

beynéynu,

בֵּין כָּל עֲדוֹת יִשְׂרָאֵל,

beyn kol adot yisra'eyl,

וּבֵין כָּל יוֹשְׁבֵי תֵבֵל.

uveyn kol yosh'vey teyveyl.

נְבָרֵךְ אֶת עֵין הַחַיִּים

N'vareykh et eyn haḥayim

וְכֹה נִתְבָּרֵךְ.

v'khoh nitbareykh.

שַׁבָּת שָׁלוֹם וּמְנוּחָה.

Shabbat shalom umnuḥah.

Sanctification over Wine for Sabbath Day

The people of Israel shall keep the Sabbath,
making it an enduring covenant for generations to come.

AFTER EXODUS 31:16

Let us bless the source of life
that ripens fruit on the vine
as we hallow the seventh day—
the Sabbath day—
in remembrance of creation,
for the Sabbath is first
among holy days,
recalling the exodus
and the covenant.

קִדּוּשׁ לְיוֹם שַׁבָּת

Kiddush L'yom Shabbat

V'sham'ru veyt-yisra'eyl et-hashabbat,
la'asot et-hashabbat l'dorotam b'rit olam.

וְשָׁמְרוּ בֵית־יִשְׂרָאֵל אֶת־הַשַּׁבָּת,
לַעֲשׂוֹת אֶת־הַשַּׁבָּת לְדֹרֹתָם בְּרִית עוֹלָם.

על־פי שמות לא:טז

N'vareykh et eyn haḥayim

matzmiḥat p'ri hagéfen

unkadeysh et yom hash'vi'i—

yom hashabbat—

zikaron l'ma'aseyh v'reyshit;

ki hu yom t'ḥilah

l'mikra'ey kódesh,

zéykher litzi'at mitzráyim.

נְבָרֵךְ אֶת עֵין הַחַיִּים

מַצְמִיחַת פְּרִי הַגֶּפֶן

וּנְקַדֵּשׁ אֶת יוֹם הַשְּׁבִיעִי—

יוֹם הַשַּׁבָּת—

זִכָּרוֹן לְמַעֲשֵׂה בְרֵאשִׁית;

כִּי הוּא יוֹם תְּחִלָּה

לְמִקְרָאֵי קֹדֶשׁ,

זֵכֶר לִיצִיאַת מִצְרָיִם.

Departure of the Sabbath, Entrance of the Week

מוֹצָאֵי שַׁבָּת וּכְנִיסַת הַשָּׁבוּעַ

HAVDALAH
Parting Ritual for the Sabbath

הַבְדָּלָה לְמוֹצָאֵי שַׁבָּת

Comm.
p. 487

PERFORMING THE *HAVDALAH* RITUAL

The *Havdalah:* **Parting Ritual for the Sabbath** contains four core blessings based on the traditional *havdalah* ritual, framed by the **Opening Psalm** and a closing prayer, **Blessing for the New Week**. Numerous folk customs have arisen around the *havdalah*, and new ones are continually emerging. In the following suggestions for implementation of this new *Havdalah* ritual, the customs of several cultures are described.

The **Opening Psalm** (p. 311) is read aloud or silently. A cup of wine is raised for the recitation of the first blessing, **Sanctification over Wine for the Week** (pp. 312–13), but the wine is not yet sipped. It is customary to fill the goblet to the brim, even allowing the wine to overflow, symbolizing the blessing anticipated for the coming week. In Moroccan tradition, one looks into the goblet, sees one's reflection, and laughs, so that the week will be filled with laughter and joy. After the recitation of the second blessing, **Spices** (pp. 314–15), sweet scents are inhaled. Moroccan Jews sometimes use rosewater for this purpose, as do Persian Jews; Judeo-Spanish Jews use fresh lemons, myrtle, or mint; still others use citron pomanders. To enact the third blessing, **Lights of Fire** (pp. 316–17), one lifts one's hands before the flame of a candle, so that light may be seen reflecting off one's fingernails. Some people cup the hands, observing the shadow cast by the fingers upon the palm, to see the difference between darkness and light. Ashkenazic Jews use a special candle made of two or more braided wicks; if such is not available, two ordinary candles are held together so that their flames merge. After the fourth blessing, **Distinctions** (pp. 318–19), the wine is sipped and the flame of the candle is extinguished in the remaining wine. In some Ashkenazic practices, one touches wine to one's eyelids before extinguishing the candle, so that a remnant of the Sabbath will be carried over into the new week; in Moroccan tradition, one dabs the wine on the nape of the neck and in one's pockets, as signs for health and prosperity. The *Havdalah:* **Parting Ritual for the Sabbath** concludes with the recitation or singing of the **Blessing for the New Week** (pp. 322–23).

WHEN *HAVDALAH* COINCIDES WITH THE ONSET OF A HOLIDAY

When the Sabbath ends at the onset of a holiday, the *Havdalah* ritual is modified and incorporated into the sanctification over wine for the holiday in the following manner: The **Opening Psalm** is omitted. In place of the **Sanctification over Wine for the Week**, the sanctification over wine for the appropriate holiday is recited; the wine is not yet sipped. The blessing for **Spices** is omitted. **Lights of Fire** is recited and enacted as described above, using the light of the holiday candles (which are lit prior to the sanctification over wine) rather than a special candle for the *Havdalah*. Following this, **Distinctions** (the variation for the onset of a holiday, pp. 320–21) is recited. At its conclusion, the wine is sipped (note that the flames of the candles are not extinguished). The **Blessing for the New Week** may be recited or sung before continuing with further holiday ritual. (Holiday rituals containing sanctifications over wine will be included in forthcoming volumes of *The Book of Blessings*.)

Order of the Ritual

Opening Psalm

Sanctification over Wine for the Week

Spices

Lights of Fire

Distinctions

Blessing for the New Week

סֵדֶר הַהַבְדָּלָה

מִזְמוֹר פְּתִיחָה

קִדּוּשׁ לַשָּׁבְוּעַ

בְּשָׂמִים

מְאוֹרֵי הָאֵשׁ

הַבְדָּלוֹת

בִּרְכַּת הַשָּׁבְוּעַ

Opening Psalm מִזְמוֹר פְּתִיחָה

Open Gate

The arc of evening
slowly turning,

the sun's blue shadows
washed away,

the gate still open
as three stars wait

to pierce the sky—
In the corridor

where night
bares its maze

you begin
to begin again.

Sanctification over Wine for the Week

Light and joy, happiness and honor—
as they have been ours in the past,
may they be ours today.

AFTER ESTHER 8:16

Let us bless the source of life
that ripens fruit on the vine
as we hallow the week,
calling to mind our history.

Kiddush Lashavú'a · קִדוּשׁ לַשָּׁבוּעַ

Lay'hudim hay'tah orah v'simḥah
v'sason vikar—
keyn tihyeh lánu.

לַיְּהוּדִים הָיְתָה אוֹרָה וְשִׂמְחָה
וְשָׂשׂוֹן וִיקָר–
כֵּן תִּהְיֶה לָנוּ.

על־פִּי אסתר ח:טז

N'vareykh et eyn haḥayim
matzmiḥat p'ri hagéfen
unkadeysh et shéyshet y'mey hama'aseh
zéykher l'toldotéynu.

נְבָרֵךְ אֶת עֵין הַחַיִּים
מַצְמִיחַת פְּרִי הַגֶּפֶן
וּנְקַדֵּשׁ אֶת שֵׁשֶׁת יְמֵי הַמַּעֲשֶׂה
זֵכֶר לְתוֹלְדוֹתֵינוּ.

Spices

---

*Let us celebrate the breath
of all living things
and praise all essences.*

בְּשָׂמִים B'samim

N'haleyl et nishmat kol ḥay

unvareykh al miney b'samim.

נְהַלֵּל אֶת נִשְׁמַת כָּל חַי

וּנְבָרֵךְ עַל מִינֵי בְשָׂמִים.

Comm.
p. 489

Lights of Fire

Let us seek the unseen sparks
that kindle the greater lights.

מְאוֹרֵי הָאֵשׁ   M'orey Ha'eysh

לְבַקֵּשׁ אֶת נִיצוֹצוֹת הַנֶּפֶשׁ

מַצִּיתֵי מְאוֹרֵי הָאֵשׁ.

N'vakeysh et nitzotzot hanéfesh

matzitey m'orey ha'eysh.

Distinctions

Let us distinguish parts within the whole
and bless their differences.

Like the Sabbath and the six days of creation,
may our lives be made whole through relation.

As rest makes the Sabbath precious,
may our work give meaning to the week.

Let us separate the Sabbath
from other days of the week,

seeking holiness in each.

הַבְדָּלוֹת Havdalot

Navḥin beyn ḥelkey hashaleym
v'al hahevdeylim n'vareykh.

נַבְחִין בֵּין חֶלְקֵי הַשָּׁלֵם
וְעַל הַהֶבְדֵּלִים נְבָרֵךְ.

Navdil beyn yom hash'vi'i
l'shéyshet y'mey hama'aseh,

נַבְדִּיל בֵּין יוֹם הַשְּׁבִיעִי
לְשֵׁשֶׁת יְמֵי הַמַּעֲשֶׂה,

ukdushah b'khol yom n'vakeysh.

וּקְדֻשָׁה בְּכָל יוֹם נְבַקֵּשׁ.

Distinctions

For the onset of a holiday

*Let us distinguish parts within the whole
and bless their differences,*

*as we separate the Sabbath
from this holiday,*

seeking holiness in each.

הַבְדָלוֹת Havdalot

לְלֵיל חַג

Navḥin beyn ḥelkey hashaleym
v'al hahevdeylim n'vareykh.

נַבְחִין בֵּין חֶלְקֵי הַשָּׁלֵם
וְעַל הַהֶבְדֵּלִים נְבָרֵךְ.

Navdil beyn yom hashabbat
l'veyn yom tov,

נַבְדִּיל בֵּין יוֹם הַשַּׁבָּת
לְבֵין יוֹם טוֹב,

ukdushah b'khol yom n'vakeysh.

וּקְדֻשָּׁה בְּכָל יוֹם נְבַקֵּשׁ.

Blessing for the New Week

May blessing abound
in the city and in the field,

in the home
and on the journey.

Blessed be the vessel
and the work of the hands,

the fruit of the body
and the fruit of the land.

May it be
a fruitful week.

Birkat Hashavú'a   בִּרְכַּת הַשָּׁבוּעַ

Tishreh hab'rakhah
ba'ir uvasadeh,
tishreh babáyit uvadérekh.

תִּשְׁרֶה הַבְּרָכָה
בָּעִיר וּבַשָּׂדֶה,
תִּשְׁרֶה בַּבַּיִת וּבַדֶּרֶךְ.

Y'vorakh haténe
vivorakh hap'ri—
p'ri habéten ufri ha'adamah.

יְבֹרַךְ הַטֶּנֶא
וִיבֹרַךְ הַפְּרִי—
פְּרִי הַבֶּטֶן וּפְרִי הָאֲדָמָה.

Y'vor'khu hayadáyim
v'khol ma'aseyhen.
Y'hi shavú'a tov umvorakh.

יְבֹרְכוּ הַיָּדַיִם
וְכָל מַעֲשֵׂיהֶן.
יְהִי שָׁבוּעַ טוֹב וּמְבֹרָךְ.

The Monthly Cycle

The New Moon Festival and Surrounding Rituals

מַחֲזוֹר הַחֹדֶשׁ

רֹאשׁ חֹדֶשׁ וּטְקָסִים הַקְּשׁוּרִים בּוֹ

Introduction

Leisure

We had a hidden treasure of leisure
gentle as the morning air,
leisure of stories, kisses, tears,
leisure of holidays,
leisure of mama, grandma, and the aunts
gliding in a boat of light,
slowly floating
in the small boat of peace
with the moon and the heavenly bodies.

ZELDA
(*translation M. F.*)

The New Moon holiday has charted an unlikely course through Jewish history. A significant festival in biblical times, it dipped in importance over the millennia only to ascend unexpectedly—boosted by a gently rising wind—in our own era. It was but a few decades ago that the festival of the New Moon, or Rosh Hodesh—literally, "the head of the month"— was revived by feminists who saw in it a hidden treasure of potential for Jewish women.[18]

Of course, Rosh Hodesh has, since its inception, always been part of the Jewish calendar, a calendar based on cycles of both the sun and the moon; the festival of the New Moon liturgically marks the lunar cycle. Although in recent centuries Rosh Hodesh has not been attended with elaborate festivities, the lunar cycle has nonetheless been an important aspect of the Jewish sense of time. Thus while the Rosh Hodesh festival today has entered new waters, there is much in past and even present-day practice to give it direction and moorings.

Rosh Hodesh was established as a holiday in the Torah, where it was on a par with the major festivals. Numbers 10:10 decrees, "On the day of your rejoicing, and on your festive days, and at the beginnings of your months, you shall blow the trumpets over your burnt offerings and over the sacrifices of your peace offerings"; in Numbers 28:11–15, a special sacrifice for the holiday is ordained. In ancient times, the date of Rosh Hodesh was determined by direct observation of the new (crescent) moon by two witnesses, who had to testify to its appearance in the Great Court in Jerusalem. After the court proclaimed the day, beacons were lit on the Mount of Olives to announce the news; when these fires were seen, other bonfires were lit on the hills to spread the word across the land. Eventually this method gave way to reliance on a precalculated calendar, but traces of the original practices of witnessing the crescent moon and announcing the New Moon festival have persisted until today.

Predominant among early customs that have survived to modern times is the practice of announcing the day of the forthcoming Rosh Hodesh on the Sabbath preceding it, a Sabbath referred to as *shabbat m'var'khim*, "Sabbath [during which] we bless." This announcement is surrounded by prayers to form a ritual known as *birkat haḥódesh*, "blessing of the month." On the day of Rosh Hodesh itself, synagogue services are embellished with biblical readings and special prayers. Among these is a prayer referred to as *ya'aleh v'yavo*, "may it ascend and come," in which the congregation asks to be remembered and blessed along with Israel's ancestors.

Among some communities—in particular, in Yemen—candles are lit for Rosh Hodesh in both the synagogue and the home; this practice has been explained as a way of recalling the ancient fires on the hills. It was once also customary to partake of a festive meal, but this custom has fallen out of practice. It remains to be seen whether the Rosh Hodesh feast will be revived either as part of family observance of the holiday or as the locus of new communal ceremonies.

By far the most striking ritual associated with the lunar cycle—one with poignant potential for new creativity—has traditionally taken place not on Rosh Hodesh itself but some time after the holiday, during the moon's waxing phase. *Birkat hal'vanah*, "blessing of the moon," also known as *kiddush hal'vanah*, "sanctification of the moon," is a uniquely dramatic ceremony in which the moon is gazed upon and addressed; in its enactment, ancient practices seem to come alive.

Despite the fact that Rosh Hodesh has for centuries been given less weight than other festivals prescribed in the Torah, it has had a long tradition of special significance for Jewish women. Although work was not prohibited on Rosh Hodesh, women refrained from it; and they may have done so, originally, at their own initiative. The abstention from work was clearly sanctioned by the rabbis (see, for example, the Talmud, y. Ta'anit 1:6; also Rashi on b. Megillah 22b), but that seems to be a justification after the fact. Some rabbinic sources (see, especially, Pirkey de-Rabbi Eliezer, chap. 45) explain Rosh Hodesh as a reward to Jewish women for not having contributed to the building of the idol of the golden calf (in Exod. 32). This inventive bit of midrashic exegesis, however, bears little relation to the biblical story itself. Once again, it is possible that women originated the explanation, with the rabbis adopting it later as a rationale.

Notwithstanding the textual justification for women's celebration of the New Moon, it is likely that the adoption of Rosh Hodesh by women was rooted, at least in part, in a generally perceived connection between lunar cycles and menstrual cycles. While this may have been the original link between women and Rosh Hodesh, it need not be the basis today for Jewish women's embracing of the holiday; there are other, more feminist possibilities to explore.[19] Consider, for example, the talmudic story about the relationship of the moon to the sun (b. Hullin 60b). According to it, the two great lights were originally created equal, but when the moon questioned "whether it is possible for two kings to share a single crown," God told her to go and make herself smaller. The moon then argued the unfairness of this judgment—"Because I have raised a proper point, should I be diminished?"—and eventually convinced God to atone for reducing her. This midrash was used to support a belief expressed in Isaiah 30:26, later rearticulated in the traditional *birkat hal'vanah*, that the moon and the sun would be made equal again in the world to come.

A curious feature of this story is that, although it uses grammatically masculine words—*yaréy'ah* and *ma'or*—to refer to the moon, it gives the related pronoun and verbs in the feminine gender. While grammatical incongruities are not uncommon in the Talmud, the consistent reversal here of grammatical gender from the masculine to the feminine would seem to be deliberate—the result of the rabbis' desire to emphasize a correlation between women and the moon. If we understand this as a projection of "femaleness" onto the moon, it surely becomes problematic. But if we read the story as an allegorical commentary on human society, its analogy bears truth: like the moon in this fable, women in patriarchal cultures have been unfairly subjugated. The implicit comparison of *the status of the moon* (in relation to the sun) and *the status of women* (in relation to men) speaks well to a feminist point of view. If the moon was not always smaller than the sun, its inferiority cannot be innate and, therefore, it need not be a permanent condition; similarly, if systems of patriarchal domination did not always exist on earth, they cannot be inevitable and, one may hope, they too may not be here forever.

Whether or not one draws some symbolic connection between women and the moon, it is hard not to see an analogy between the moon's diminished status in the midrash and the diminished status of the New Moon holiday in Jewish tradition. The potential inherent in the exploration of what was once an important festival makes Rosh Hodesh a true treasure for Jews interested in restoring value to that which has been underappreciated or neglected in the mainstream of tradition. It does not, finally, seem surprising that Jewish women of all denominations have turned to the festival of Rosh Hodesh as an opportunity to reclaim their places within Judaism, using the holiday as an occasion to create new, woman-centered ceremonies and spiritual communities known as Rosh Hodesh groups.

THE MONTHLY CYCLE of this book offers a variety of liturgical materials intended to connect new practices with layers of the historical tradition. The first section of the cycle, **Awaiting the New Moon,** offers a ritual entitled *Birkat Haḥódesh:* **Heralding the New Month,** which, like the traditional *birkat haḥódesh* ritual, consists of prayers surrounding an announcement of the upcoming Rosh Hodesh holiday. It is intended for use in synagogue (or wherever the community gathers) during the morning service on the Sabbath preceding Rosh Hodesh. Its contents include **Gifts of the Month: A Thanksgiving,** which offers an opportunity to appreciate the month that is drawing to a close; **Announcing the New Month,** which states the day of the upcoming Rosh Hodesh festival; and **Prayer for the New Month,** a petition for blessings in the month to come.

The last section of the cycle, **In the Presence of the Moon,** provides the ritual of *Birkat Hal'vanah:* **Blessing of the Moon,** which is based on the traditional *birkat hal'vanah*. It consists of a meditative prayer, **Renewal of the Moon,** preceded by poems in English and Hebrew that serve as the **Opening Psalms.** *Birkat Hal'vanah* may be performed by the community or by the individual on any evening during the first half of the month (that is, after the eve of Rosh Hodesh and before the full moon).

Between **Awaiting the New Moon** and **In the Presence of the Moon** is the liturgy for the main event of the lunar cycle—Rosh Hodesh, the festival of the New Moon. **Eve of the New Moon Festival** presents a new ceremony for the holiday, *Kabbalat P'ney Haḥódesh:* **Welcoming the New Month.** Because Rosh Hodesh ceremonies today often take place in people's homes, this new celebration is built on the model of home ritual for the eve of Sabbaths and holidays, the structure of which is represented in the following offerings: **Rosh Hodesh Candlelighting** (an original blessing not based on the blessing for Sabbath candlelighting), **Blessing of the Children** (the same blessing found after Sabbath candlelighting in THE WEEKLY CYCLE), **Sanctification over Wine for Rosh Hodesh** (which is parallel to the sanctifications over wine for the Sabbath and for the week, found in THE WEEKLY CYCLE), **Blessing for the New and for Renewal** (which is based on the traditional *sheheḥeyánu* blessing recited on major holidays), and the three mealtime blessings—**Handwashing Before the Meal, Blessing Before the Meal,** and **Blessing After the Meal.** To this core, a layer of embellishments has been added, consisting of a new English poem that serves as the **Opening Psalm,** the **Meditation for the Sanctification over Wine for Rosh Hodesh,** the **Prayer for the New Month** accompanied by **Personal Prayers,** and a modern Hebrew poem that serves as the **Closing Psalm.** Note that the **Prayer for the New Month** is reprised from *Birkat Haḥódesh:* **Heralding the New Month** but that here, in the *Kabbalat P'ney Haḥódesh* ceremony, the communal prayer is extended with personal contributions from individual participants. In addition, a set of instructions for adapting the liturgy is provided for those dates (approximately two a year) when Rosh Hodesh coincides with the Sabbath, a day traditionally referred to as Sabbath Rosh Hodesh. An extended blessing over wine, **Sanctification over Wine for the Eve of Sabbath Rosh Hodesh,** is included for these occasions.

While Rosh Hodesh groups usually meet in the evening, some groups gather for prayer services on the morning of Rosh Hodesh day. **Day of the New Moon Festival** provides instructions for adapting the prayer service for Sabbath morning (found in THE WEEKLY CYCLE) into a morning service for Rosh Hodesh, with versions for both the weekday and the Sabbath. The liturgy provided for this adaptation includes a meditation and blessings under the heading **Sanctifying Rosh Hodesh** as well as a special blessing, **May We Be Remembered,** based on the traditional *ya'aleh v'yavo* prayer. Also included are two forms of the blessing over wine for use following the service: the **Sanctification over Wine for Rosh Hodesh** (reprised from the *Kabbalat P'ney Haḥódesh* ceremony) and the **Sanctification over Wine for the Day of Sabbath Rosh Hodesh** (a variant of the **Sanctification over Wine for the Eve of Sabbath Rosh Hodesh,** found in the *Kabbalat P'ney Haḥódesh* ceremony).

As a reemerging festival, Rosh Hodesh is still very much in flux; both its structure and liturgical content are likely to evolve further over time. And with the ongoing influence of feminism on the Jewish community at large, we may one day see men joining women in greater numbers to celebrate Rosh Hodesh and other lunar rituals. We might speculate what forms these evolving ceremonies will take; for example, will they be centered in the home or in the synagogue? Or perhaps the boundaries between home observance and communal celebration will become less significant. With the growing participation of women in all aspects of synagogue life and the increasing involvement of men in home life, the two domains, once divided along gender lines, are already today more closely and fluidly interrelated. Overall, Rosh Hodesh may become a testing ground for broader changes in Jewish religious practice. In creating liturgy for Rosh Hodesh and other events of the lunar cycle, I have assumed that my offerings will be approached with a sense of experimentation, a sense of continuing the voyage.

Awaiting the New Moon

לִקְרַאת רֹאשׁ חֹדֶשׁ

BIRKAT HAḤÓDESH
Heralding the New Month

בִּרְכַּת הַחֹֽדֶשׁ

PERFORMING THE *BIRKAT HAHÓDESH* RITUAL

The ritual heralding the upcoming festival of the New Moon takes place during the morning service on *shabbat m'var'khim*, the Sabbath before Rosh Hodesh (see p. 283). It opens with **Gifts of the Month: A Thanksgiving** (pp. 340–41), which provides an opportunity to reflect on the month drawing to a close. This may be followed by time for silent meditation. The ritual continues with **Announcing the New Month** (pp. 342–43), which is its focal point. It concludes with the **Prayer for the New Month** (pp. 344–47), in which the community expresses its wishes for the month about to begin.

Order of the Prayers

Gifts of the Month: A Thanksgiving

Announcing the New Month

Prayer for the New Month

סֵדֶר הַתְּפִלּוֹת

מַתְּנוֹת הַחְדֶשׁ: הוֹדָיָה

הַכְרָזַת הַחְדֶשׁ

תְּפִלַּת הַחְדֶשׁ

Gifts of the Month: A Thanksgiving

*A*s the new month approaches
we call to mind the gifts of _____
(name of the current month)
and give thanks.

מַתְּנוֹת הַחֹדֶשׁ: הוֹדָיָה
Mat'not Haḥódesh: Hodayah

Likrat haḥódesh haba

mal'ah nafshéynu hodayah

al mat'not ḥódesh _____
(name of the current month)

לִקְרַאת הַחֹדֶשׁ הַבָּא

מָלְאָה נַפְשֵׁנוּ הוֹדָיָה

עַל מַתְּנוֹת חֹדֶשׁ _____ .
(שם החודש החולף)

Announcing the New Month

*T*his _____
(day of the week)
will be Rosh Hodesh _____ ,
(name of the new month)
a festival for us and all Israel.

May it be a day of blessings,

goodness, and joy.

הַכְרָזַת הַחֹדֶשׁ   Hakhrazat Haḥódesh

Rosh ḥódesh _____
(name of the new month)

yihyeh b'yom _____
(day of the week)

haba aléynu

v'al kol yisra'eyl

l'tovah.

רֹאשׁ חֹדֶשׁ _____
(שם החודש הבא)

יִהְיֶה בְּיוֹם _____
(ראשון, שני . . .)

הַבָּא עָלֵינוּ

וְעַל כָּל יִשְׂרָאֵל

לְטוֹבָה.

Prayer for the New Month

$\mathcal{M}$ay the month of ＿＿＿＿＿＿
(name of the new month)
be a month of blessings:

blessings of goodness,
blessings of joy,

peace and kindness,
friendship and love,

creativity, strength,
serenity,

fulfilling work
and dignity,

satisfaction, success,
and sustenance,

physical health
and radiance.

May truth and justice
guide our acts,

תְּפִלַּת הַחֹדֶשׁ   T'filat Haḥódesh

Y'hi ratzon sheyithadeysh aléynu

ḥódesh ‒‒‒‒‒‒‒
(name of the new month)

יְהִי רָצוֹן שֶׁיִּתְחַדֵּשׁ עָלֵינוּ

חֹדֶשׁ ‒‒‒‒‒‒‒
(שם החודש הבא)

l'tovah v'livrakhah,

l'sason ulsimḥah,

לְטוֹבָה וְלִבְרָכָה,

לְשָׂשׂוֹן וּלְשִׂמְחָה,

l'shalom v'aḥavah,

rey'ut v'ahavah,

לְשָׁלוֹם וְאַחֲוָה,

רֵעוּת וְאַהֲבָה,

la'avodah vitzirah,

parnasah v'khalkalah,

לַעֲבוֹדָה וִיצִירָה,

פַּרְנָסָה וְכַלְכָּלָה,

l'shalvat hanéfesh

uvri'ut haguf,

לְשַׁלְוַת הַנֶּפֶשׁ

וּבְרִיאוּת הַגּוּף,

l'ḥayim shel dérekh éretz

v'ahavat torah,

לְחַיִּים שֶׁל דֶּרֶךְ אֶרֶץ

וְאַהֲבַת תּוֹרָה,

and compassion
temper our lives

that we may blossom
as we age

and become
our sweetest selves.

May it be so.

At the conclusion of this prayer, return to p. 285 for the continuation of the **Shaḥarit** service.

l'ḥayim sheyimal'u bam

mish'alot libéynu l'tovah.

לְחַיִּים שֶׁיִּמָּלְאוּ בָם
מִשְׁאֲלוֹת לִבֵּנוּ לְטוֹבָה.

Keyn y'hi ratzon.

כֵּן יְהִי רָצוֹן.

Eve of the New Moon Festival

לֵיל רֹאשׁ חֹדֶשׁ

KABBALAT P'NEY HAḤÓDESH
Welcoming the New Month

קַבָּלַת פְּנֵי הַחֹדֶשׁ

USHERING IN THE NEW MONTH

Kabbalat P'ney Haḥódesh: **Welcoming the New Month** is based on mealtime ritual for the eve of holidays and is designed to be used as a family or community celebration. The meal around which it is centered—the Rosh Hodesh feast—may be a full repast or a symbolic sharing (as of seasonal fruit). The focal point of the feast is the discussion of a subject related to upcoming holidays, historical events, or other associations with the month or the season. The following are some suggestions for implementation of this ritual.

Rosh Hodesh Candlelighting (pp. 358–59) is recited by each person present while lighting a candle; once all candles are lit, the group may repeat these words with melody. When children are present, the **Blessing of the Children** (pp. 360–61) is recited to each child individually by parents or other adults. The **Meditation for the Sanctification over Wine for Rosh Hodesh** (p. 363) may be read silently or aloud, followed by the recitation or singing of the **Sanctification over Wine for Rosh Hodesh** (pp. 364–65). The cup of wine is lifted for the recitation of this blessing; following it, the **Blessing for the New and for Renewal** (pp. 368–69) is recited or sung, after which the wine is sipped. The **Prayer for the New Month** (pp. 370–73) is then recited aloud by the family or community. At its conclusion, individuals add their own words to the opening lines provided in **Personal Prayers** (pp. 374–75), and the community affirms each participant's contribution with the line of response. **Handwashing Before the Meal** and **Blessing Before the Meal** (pp. 376–79) then take place, and the Rosh Hodesh feast is shared. The discussion occurs during or after the meal, and the feast concludes with the recitation or singing of the **Blessing After the Meal** (pp. 380–81). The **Closing Psalm** (pp. 382–83) may be read silently or aloud before the group disperses.

WHEN ROSH HODESH COINCIDES WITH THE SABBATH

When Rosh Hodesh falls on a Sabbath (a day referred to as *shabbat rosh ḥódesh*, "Sabbath Rosh Hodesh"), *Kabbalat P'ney Haḥódesh* may be integrated with *Kabbalat P'ney Shabbat:* **Home Ritual Welcoming the Sabbath** (found on pp. 115–35) to create a combined ceremony for use by individual households or by communities. The order of the complete offerings for this ceremony is as follows: **Opening Psalm** for Sabbath eve (replacing the **Opening Psalm** for Rosh Hodesh), **Sabbath Candlelighting** followed by **Rosh Hodesh Candlelighting** (candles are lit once, then each blessing is recited), **Blessing of the Children, Blessing the Beloved, Meditation for the Sanctification over Wine for Rosh Hodesh, Sanctification over Wine for the Eve of Sabbath Rosh Hodesh, Blessing for the New and for Renewal, Prayer for the New Month, Personal Prayers, Handwashing Before the Meal, Blessing Before the Meal, Blessing After the Meal, Closing Psalm.** Page numbers and directions for combining *Kabbalat P'ney Haḥódesh* with *Kabbalat P'ney Shabbat* appear in footnotes throughout the *Kabbalat P'ney Haḥódesh* ceremony.

Order of the Ceremony

Opening Psalm

Rosh Hodesh Candlelighting

Blessing of the Children

Meditation for the Sanctification over Wine for Rosh Hodesh

Sanctification over Wine for Rosh Hodesh

Blessing for the New and for Renewal

Prayer for the New Month

Personal Prayers

Handwashing Before the Meal

Blessing Before the Meal

Blessing After the Meal

Closing Psalm

סֵדֶר קַבָּלַת פְּנֵי הַחֹדֶשׁ

מִזְמוֹר פְּתִיחָה

הַדְלָקַת נֵרוֹת רֹאשׁ חֹדֶשׁ

בִּרְכַּת יַלְדָּה וָיֶלֶד

כַּוָּנַת הַלֵּב לְקִדּוּשׁ לְרֹאשׁ חֹדֶשׁ

קִדּוּשׁ לְרֹאשׁ חֹדֶשׁ

שֶׁהֶחֱיָנוּ

תְּפִלַּת הַחֹדֶשׁ

תְּפִלּוֹת אִישִׁיּוֹת

נְטִילַת יָדַיִם לִפְנֵי הָאֲרוּחָה

הַמּוֹצִיאָה

בִּרְכַּת הַמָּזוֹן

מִזְמוֹר סִיּוּם

Opening Psalm   מִזְמוֹר פְּתִיחָה

Witnessing

Cypresses point to the night,

through clouds and beyond them.

We follow them up the mountain

to stake our site.

We wait. The air is still.

The leaf, the branch, the bark—

our signposts in the darkness

of the hill.

And now the blade of night

gleams through the briars.

We gather twigs for the fires:

New Moon, old light.

On the eve of Sabbath Rosh Hodesh, substitute for this psalm the **Opening Psalm** of *Kabbalat P'ney Shabbat* (p. 121).

Rosh Hodesh Candlelighting

New moon, ancient light—
may my spirit rise to you,
in _____'s sky.
_(name of the new month)

On the eve of Sabbath Rosh Hodesh, perform **Sabbath Candlelighting** (pp. 122–23) and follow it with this blessing.

הַדְלָקַת נֵרוֹת רֹאשׁ חֹֽדֶשׁ

Hadlakat Neyrot Rosh Ḥódesh

אוֹר חָדָשׁ, מָאוֹר קַדְמוֹן –

Or ḥadash, ma'or kadmon—

תִּנָּשֵׂא נַפְשִׁי אֵלֶֽיךָ

tinasey nafshi eylékha

בְּשָׁמֵי חֹֽדֶשׁ _____.
(שם החודש)

bishmey ḥódesh _____.
(*name of the new month*)

Blessing of the Children

_____ ,
(the child's name)

*B*e who you are—
and may you be blessed
in all that you are.

On the eve of Sabbath Rosh Hodesh, **Blessing the Beloved** (pp. 126–27) may be added after this blessing.

Birkat Yaldah V'yéled · בִּרְכַּת יַלְדָּה וְיֶלֶד

To a girl: ———————,
(the child's name)

לבת: ———————,
(שם הילדה)

Hayi asher tihyi—
vahayi b'rukhah
ba'asher tihyi.

הָיִי אֲשֶׁר תִּהְיִי—
וַהֲיִי בְּרוּכָה
בַּאֲשֶׁר תִּהְיִי.

====

To a boy: ———————,
(the child's name)

לבן: ———————,
(שם הילד)

Heyeyh asher tihyeh—
veheyeyh barukh
ba'asher tihyeh.

הֱיֵה אֲשֶׁר תִּהְיֶה—
וֶהֱיֵה בָּרוּךְ
בַּאֲשֶׁר תִּהְיֶה.

Comm.
p. 498

Meditation
for the Sanctification over Wine
for Rosh Hodesh

כַּוָּנַת הַלֵּב
לְקִדּוּשׁ לְרֹאשׁ חְׂדֶשׁ

The vine is courageous and tenacious, as each of us is called upon to be. Growing toward light, it twists without knowing what may lie beyond. In its journey, the vine intertwines with other vines. We might think of community this way, as an interweaving of the paths of many vines.

Our history, then, is the tapestry of interwoven vines. To it, we continually add new weaving. And tonight we unroll our tapestries, holding them up to the light, where their colors and intricate patterns—each perfect and imperfect stitch—may shine.

Comm.
p. 499

Sanctification over Wine for Rosh Hodesh

It shall come to be from one month to the next
that your hearts will rejoice
and your bones will flower like young grass.

AFTER ISAIAH 66:23, 14

Let us bless the source of life
that ripens fruit on the vine,
as we hallow the Rosh Hodesh festival,
weaving new threads
into the tapestry of tradition.

On the eve of Sabbath Rosh Hodesh, substitute for this blessing the **Sanctification over Wine for the Eve of Sabbath Rosh Hodesh** (pp. 366–67).

קִדּוּשׁ לְרֹאשׁ חֹדֶשׁ

Kiddush L'rosh Ḥodesh

וְהָיָה מִדֵּי־חֹדֶשׁ בְּחָדְשׁוֹ

V'hayah midey-ḥódesh b'ḥodsho

וְשָׂשׂ לִבְּכֶם

v'sas lib'khem

וְעַצְמוֹתֵיכֶם כַּדֶּשֶׁא תִפְרַחְנָה.

v'atzmoteykhem kadéshe tifráḥnah.

עַל־פִּי יְשַׁעְיָה סו:כג, יד

נְבָרֵךְ אֶת עֵין הַחַיִּים

N'vareykh et eyn haḥayim

מַצְמִיחַת פְּרִי הַגֶּפֶן

matzmiḥat p'ri hagéfen

וּנְקַדֵּשׁ אֶת רֹאשׁ הַחֹדֶשׁ

unkadeysh et rosh haḥódesh

בַּאֲרִיגַת פְּתִילֵי חַיֵּינוּ

ba'arigat p'tiley ḥayéynu

לְתוֹךְ מַסֶּכֶת הַדּוֹרוֹת.

l'tokh masékhet hadorot.

Sanctification over Wine
for the Eve of Sabbath Rosh Hodesh

There was evening and there was morning, the sixth day.
The heavens and earth were complete, with all their host.

GENESIS 1:31—2:1

Let us bless the source of life

that ripens fruit on the vine,

as we hallow the seventh day—

the Sabbath day—

in remembrance of creation,

for the Sabbath is first

among holy days,

recalling the exodus

and the covenant.

It shall come to be from one month to the next
and from one Sabbath to the next
that your hearts will rejoice
and your bones will flower like young grass.

AFTER ISAIAH 66:23, 14

And let us hallow the Rosh Hodesh festival,

weaving new threads

into the tapestry of tradition.

Kiddush L'leyl

Shabbat Rosh Ḥódesh

קִדּוּשׁ לְלֵיל
שַׁבָּת רֹאשׁ חֹדֶשׁ

Vayhi-érev vayhi-vóker, yom hashishi.
Vaykhulu hashamáyim v'ha'áretz v'khol-tz'va'am.

וַיְהִי־עֶרֶב וַיְהִי־בְקֶר, יוֹם הַשִּׁשִּׁי.
וַיְכֻלּוּ הַשָּׁמַיִם וְהָאָרֶץ וְכָל־צְבָאָם.
בראשית א:לא-ב:א

N'vareykh et eyn haḥayim

נְבָרֵךְ אֶת עֵין הַחַיִּים

matzmiḥat p'ri hagéfen

מַצְמִיחַת פְּרִי הַגֶּפֶן

unkadeysh et yom hash'vi'i—

וּנְקַדֵּשׁ אֶת יוֹם הַשְּׁבִיעִי—

yom hashabbat—

יוֹם הַשַּׁבָּת—

zikaron l'ma'aseyh v'reyshit

זִכָּרוֹן לְמַעֲשֵׂה בְרֵאשִׁית

ki hu yom t'ḥilah

כִּי הוּא יוֹם תְּחִלָּה

l'mikra'ey kódesh,

לְמִקְרָאֵי קֹדֶשׁ,

zéykher litzi'at mitzráyim.

זֵכֶר לִיצִיאַת מִצְרָיִם.

V'hayah midey-ḥódesh b'ḥodsho

וְהָיָה מִדֵּי־חֹדֶשׁ בְּחָדְשׁוֹ

umidey shabbat b'shabbato

וּמִדֵּי שַׁבָּת בְּשַׁבַּתּוֹ

v'sas lib'khem

וְשָׂשׂ לִבְּכֶם

v'atzmoteykhem kadéshe tifráḥnah.

וְעַצְמוֹתֵיכֶם כַּדֶּשֶׁא תִפְרַחְנָה.
עַל־פִּי יְשַׁעְיָה סו:כג, יד

Unkadeysh et rosh haḥódesh

וּנְקַדֵּשׁ אֶת רֹאשׁ הַחֹדֶשׁ

ba'arigat p'tiley ḥayéynu

בַּאֲרִיגַת פְּתִילֵי חַיֵּינוּ

l'tokh masékhet hadorot.

לְתוֹךְ מַסֶּכֶת הַדּוֹרוֹת.

Blessing for the New and for Renewal

*L*et us bless the flow of life
that revives us, sustains us,
and brings us to this time.

שֶׁהֶחֱיָנוּ Sheheḥeyánu

N'vareykh et ma'yan ḥayéynu

shchchcyánu v'kiy'mánu v'higi'ánu

laz'man hazeh.

נְבָרֵךְ אֶת מַעְיַן חַיֵּינוּ

שֶׁהֶחֱיָנוּ וְקִיְמָנוּ וְהִגִּיעָנוּ

לַזְמַן הַזֶּה.

Prayer for the New Month

*M*ay the month of _____
(name of the new month)
be a month of blessings:

blessings of goodness,
blessings of joy,

peace and kindness,
friendship and love,

creativity, strength,
serenity,

fulfilling work
and dignity,

satisfaction, success,
and sustenance,

physical health
and radiance.

May truth and justice
guide our acts,

T'filat Haḥódesh תְּפִלַּת הַחֹדֶשׁ

Y'hi ratzon sheyithadeysh aléynu
hódesh _____
(name of the new month)

יְהִי רָצוֹן שֶׁיִּתְחַדֵּשׁ עָלֵינוּ
חֹדֶשׁ _____
(שם החודש)

l'tovah v'livrakhah,
l'sason ulsimḥah,

לְטוֹבָה וְלִבְרָכָה,
לְשָׂשׂוֹן וּלְשִׂמְחָה,

l'shalom v'aḥavah,
rey'ut v'ahavah,

לְשָׁלוֹם וְאַחֲוָה,
רֵעוּת וְאַהֲבָה,

la'avodah vitzirah,
parnasah v'khalkalah,

לַעֲבוֹדָה וִיצִירָה,
פַּרְנָסָה וְכַלְכָּלָה,

l'shalvat hanéfesh
uvri'ut haguf,

לְשַׁלְוַת הַנֶּפֶשׁ
וּבְרִיאוּת הַגּוּף,

l'ḥayim shel dérekh éretz
v'ahavat torah,

לְחַיִּים שֶׁל דֶּרֶךְ אֶרֶץ
וְאַהֲבַת תּוֹרָה,

and compassion
temper our lives

that we may blossom
as we age

and become
our sweetest selves.

May it be so.

לְחַיִּים שֶׁיִּמָּלְאוּ בָם

l'ḥayim sheyimal'u bam

מִשְׁאֲלוֹת לִבֵּנוּ לְטוֹבָה.

mish'alot libéynu l'tovah.

כֵּן יְהִי רָצוֹן.

Keyn y'hi ratzon.

Personal Prayers

May the month of _____
(name of the new month)
be . . .

Group response: May it be so.

Using these opening lines, individuals add their personal prayers to the **Prayer for the New Month.**

תְּפִלּוֹת אִישִׁיּוֹת   T'filot Ishiyot

Y'hi ratzon sheyithadeysh aléynu

ḥódesh _____
(name of the new month)

l' . . .

יְהִי רָצוֹן שֶׁיִּתְחַדֵּשׁ עָלֵינוּ

חֹדֶשׁ _____
(שם החודש)

לְ . . .

Group response: Keyn y'hi ratzon.

הקהל: כֵּן יְהִי רָצוֹן.

Comm.
p. 502

Handwashing Before the Meal

*W*ashing the hands, we call to mind
the holiness of body.

נְטִילַת יָדַיִם לִפְנֵי הָאֲרוּחָה N'tilat Yadáyim Lifney Ha'aruḥah

תִּזְכֹּר נַפְשֵׁנוּ אֶת קְדֻשַּׁת הַגּוּף
בִּנְטִילַת יָדַיִם.

Tizkor nafshéynu et k'dushat haguf
bintilat yadáyim.

Blessing Before the Meal

Let us bless the source of life
that brings forth bread from the earth.

הַמּוֹצִיאָה   Hamotzi'ah

N'vareykh et eyn haḥayim

hamotzi'ah léḥem min ha'áretz.

נְבָרֵךְ אֶת עֵין הַחַיִּים

הַמּוֹצִיאָה לֶחֶם מִן הָאָרֶץ.

Blessing After the Meal

Let us acknowledge the source of life,
source of all nourishment.

May we protect the bountiful earth
that it may continue to sustain us,

and let us seek sustenance
for all who dwell in the world.

בִּרְכַּת הַמָּזוֹן　Birkat Hamazon

Nodeh l'eyn haḥayim
hazanah et hakol.

נוֹדֶה לְעֵין הַחַיִּים
הַזָּנָה אֶת הַכֹּל.

Al ha'áretz hatovah v'har'ḥavah
nishmor na, v'hi t'kay'méynu,

עַל הָאָרֶץ הַטּוֹבָה וְהָרְחָבָה
נִשְׁמֹר נָא, וְהִיא תְּקַיְּמֵנוּ,

unvakeysh mazon l'hasbí'a bo
kol yosh'vey teyveyl.

וּנְבַקֵּשׁ מָזוֹן לְהַשְׂבִּיעַ בּוֹ
כָּל יוֹשְׁבֵי תֵבֵל.

Closing Psalm

Leisure

We had a hidden treasure of leisure

gentle as the morning air,

leisure of stories, kisses, tears,

leisure of holidays,

leisure of mama, grandma, and the aunts

gliding in a boat of light,

slowly floating

in the small boat of peace

with the moon and the heavenly bodies.

ZELDA
(*translation M. F.*)

מִזְמוֹר סִיּוּם

פְּנַאי

הָיָה לָנוּ אוֹצָר סָמוּי שֶׁל פְּנַאי

עָדִין כַּאֲוִיר הַבֹּקֶר,

פְּנַאי שֶׁל סִפּוּרִים, דְּמָעוֹת, נְשִׁיקוֹת

וְחַגִּים.

פְּנַאי שֶׁל אִמָּא, סַבְתָּא, וְהַדּוֹדוֹת

יוֹשְׁבוֹת בְּנַחַת בְּסִירָה

שֶׁל זִיו,

שָׁטוֹת אַט־אַט

בְּדוּגִית הַשָּׁלוֹם

עִם הַיָּרֵחַ וְעִם הַמַּזָּלוֹת.

זלדה

Day of the New Moon Festival

רֹאשׁ חֹדֶשׁ

Blessings for the Morning
of Rosh Hodesh

קִדּוּשׁ וּבְרָכוֹת לִתְפִלַּת שַׁחֲרִית

CELEBRATING ROSH HODESH DAY

For communal celebration of Rosh Hodesh day, the *Shaḥarit:* **Morning Service for the Sabbath** (found on pp. 139–301) may be used, with the following modifications. When Rosh Hodesh falls on a weekday, the fourth section of the ***Amidah:*** **Sevenfold Prayer** (pp. 215–26) is deleted, and the meditation and blessings **Sanctifying Rosh Hodesh** and **May We Be Remembered** (pp. 391–95) are substituted for it. The **Psalm for the Sabbath** (p. 162) is also deleted on weekdays. When Rosh Hodesh falls on the Sabbath, no deletions are made; rather, the meditation and blessings found on pp. 391–95 are inserted into the ***Amidah*** after pp. 215–26 to create an enhanced fourth section. Note that the Rosh Hodesh inclusions for the ***Amidah*** do not contain any poetry but instead provide a supplementary blessing, **May We Be Remembered.**

If the community convenes a *kiddush* after the *Shaḥarit* service, the **Sanctification over Wine for Rosh Hodesh** (pp. 396–97) is recited. When Rosh Hodesh falls on a Sabbath, the **Sanctification over Wine for Rosh Hodesh** is replaced by the **Sanctification over Wine for the Day of Sabbath Rosh Hodesh** (pp. 398–99). The blessings for eating—**Handwashing Before the Meal, Blessing Before the Meal,** and **Blessing After the Meal**—may be found in *Kabbalat P'ney Haḥó- desh:* **Welcoming the New Month** (pp. 376–81).

Sanctifying Rosh Hodesh
קִדֻּשַׁת ראשׁ חֹדֶשׁ

Even in its name, Rosh Hodesh—the festival of the New Moon—symbolizes newness and renewal: ḥódesh, "month," from ḥadash, "new"; Rosh Hodesh, "the head of the month," the very beginning of newness. So, too, the moon, in its eternal turnings, draws us back to beginnings, illumining the paths to self-renewal.

Sanctifying Rosh Hodesh

Renewing the New Moon festival,
hallowing it today,
we weave new threads
into the tapestry of tradition.

———

As we bless the source of life
so we are blessed.

קְדֻשַּׁת רֹאשׁ חֹֽדֶשׁ   K'dushat Rosh Ḥódesh

נְקַדֵּשׁ אֶת רֹאשׁ הַחֹֽדֶשׁ
וּנְחַדֵּשׁ אוֹתוֹ
בַּאֲרִיגַת פְּתִילֵי חַיֵּֽינוּ
לְתוֹךְ מַסֶּֽכֶת הַדּוֹרוֹת.

N'kadeysh et rosh haḥódesh
unḥadeysh oto
ba'arigat p'tiley ḥayéynu
l'tokh masékhet hadorot.

_____

נְבָרֵךְ אֶת עֵין הַחַיִּים
וְכֹה נִתְבָּרֵךְ.

N'vareykh et eyn haḥayim
v'khoh nitbareykh.

May We Be Remembered

May we be remembered
and may those who came before us be remembered
and may all the communities of Israel be remembered

for blessing and for goodness,
for graciousness, kindness, and compassion,
for life and for peace.

On this Rosh Hodesh day
we remember, and we seek to be remembered
in the ongoing history of our people.

After this blessing, return to p. 227 for the continuation of the *Amidah*.

יַעֲלֶה וְיָבֹא   Ya'aleh V'yavo

Ya'aleh v'yavo zikhronéynu

v'zikhron imotéynu va'avotéynu

v'zikhron kol beyt yisra'eyl

יַעֲלֶה וְיָבֹא זִכְרוֹנֵנוּ

וְזִכְרוֹן אִמּוֹתֵינוּ וַאֲבוֹתֵינוּ

וְזִכְרוֹן כָּל בֵּית יִשְׂרָאֵל

l'tovah v'livrakhah,

l'ḥeyn ulḥésed ulraḥamim,

l'ḥayim ulshalom.

לְטוֹבָה וְלִבְרָכָה,

לְחֵן וּלְחֶסֶד וּלְרַחֲמִים,

לְחַיִּים וּלְשָׁלוֹם.

B'yom rosh haḥódesh hazeh

nizkeh l'hizakheyr im kol améynu

b'masóret hadorot.

בְּיוֹם רֹאשׁ הַחֹדֶשׁ הַזֶּה

נִזְכֶּה לְהִזָּכֵר עִם כָּל עַמֵּנוּ

בְּמָסֹרֶת הַדּוֹרוֹת.

Sanctification over Wine for Rosh Hodesh

It shall come to be from one month to the next
that your hearts will rejoice
and your bones will flower like young grass.

AFTER ISAIAH 66:23, 14

Let us bless the source of life
that ripens fruit on the vine,
as we hallow the Rosh Hodesh festival,
weaving new threads
into the tapestry of tradition.

On Sabbath Rosh Hodesh, substitute for this blessing the **Sanctification over Wine for the Day of Sabbath Rosh Hodesh** (pp. 398–99).

Kiddush L'rosh Ḥódesh   קִדּוּשׁ לְרֹאשׁ חֹדֶשׁ

V'hayah midey-ḥódesh b'ḥodsho

v'sas lib'khem

v'atzmoteykhem kadéshe tifráḥnah.

וְהָיָה מִדֵּי־חֹדֶשׁ בְּחָדְשׁוֹ

וְשָׂשׂ לִבְּכֶם

וְעַצְמוֹתֵיכֶם כַּדֶּשֶׁא תִפְרַחְנָה.

עַל־פִּי יְשַׁעְיָה סו:כג, יד

N'vareykh et eyn haḥayim

matzmiḥat p'ri hagéfen

unkadeysh et rosh haḥódesh

ba'arigat p'tiley ḥayéynu

l'tokh masékhet hadorot.

נְבָרֵךְ אֶת עֵין הַחַיִּים

מַצְמִיחַת פְּרִי הַגָּפֶן

וּנְקַדֵּשׁ אֶת רֹאשׁ הַחֹדֶשׁ

בַּאֲרִיגַת פְּתִילֵי חַיֵּינוּ

לְתוֹךְ מַסֶּכֶת הַדּוֹרוֹת.

Sanctification over Wine
for the Day of Sabbath Rosh Hodesh

The people of Israel shall keep the Sabbath,
making it an enduring covenant for generations to come.

AFTER EXODUS 31:16

Let us bless the source of life
that ripens fruit on the vine
as we hallow the seventh day—
the Sabbath day—
in remembrance of creation,
for the Sabbath is first
among holy days,
recalling the exodus
and the covenant.

It shall come to be from one month to the next
and from one Sabbath to the next
that your hearts will rejoice
and your bones will flower like young grass.

AFTER ISAIAH 66:23, 14

And let us hallow the Rosh Hodesh festival,
weaving new threads
into the tapestry of tradition.

Kiddush L'yom

Shabbat Rosh Ḥodesh

קִדּוּשׁ לְיוֹם
שַׁבָּת רֹאשׁ חֹדֶשׁ

V'sham'ru veyt-yisra'eyl et-hashabbat,

la'asot et-hashabbat l'dorotam b'rit olam.

וְשָׁמְרוּ בֵית־יִשְׂרָאֵל אֶת־הַשַּׁבָּת,

לַעֲשׂוֹת אֶת־הַשַּׁבָּת לְדֹרֹתָם בְּרִית עוֹלָם.

עַל־פִּי שְׁמוֹת לא:טז

N'vareykh et eyn haḥayim

matzmiḥat p'ri hagéfen

unkadeysh et yom hash'vi'i—

yom hashabbat—

zikaron l'ma'aseyh v'reyshit

ki hu yom t'ḥilah

l'mikra'ey kódesh,

zéykher litzi'at mitzráyim.

נְבָרֵךְ אֶת עֵין הַחַיִּים

מַצְמִיחַת פְּרִי הַגֶּפֶן

וּנְקַדֵּשׁ אֶת יוֹם הַשְּׁבִיעִי—

—יוֹם הַשַּׁבָּת

זִכָּרוֹן לְמַעֲשֵׂה בְרֵאשִׁית

כִּי הוּא יוֹם תְּחִלָּה

לְמִקְרָאֵי קֹדֶשׁ,

זֵכֶר לִיצִיאַת מִצְרָיִם.

V'hayah midey-ḥódesh b'ḥodsho

umidey shabbat b'shabbato

v'sas lib'khem

v'atzmoteykhem kadéshe tifráḥnah.

וְהָיָה מִדֵּי־חֹדֶשׁ בְּחָדְשׁוֹ

וּמִדֵּי שַׁבָּת בְּשַׁבַּתּוֹ

וְשָׂשׂ לִבְּכֶם

וְעַצְמוֹתֵיכֶם כַּדֶּשֶׁא תִפְרַחְנָה.

עַל־פִּי יְשַׁעְיָה סו:כג, יד

Unkadeysh et rosh haḥódesh

ba'arigat p'tiley ḥayéynu

l'tokh masékhet hadorot.

וּנְקַדֵּשׁ אֶת רֹאשׁ הַחֹדֶשׁ

בַּאֲרִיגַת פְּתִילֵי חַיֵּינוּ

לְתוֹךְ מַסֶּכֶת הַדּוֹרוֹת.

Comm.
p. 506

In the Presence of the Moon

לְאוֹר הַלְּבָנָה

BIRKAT HAL'VANAH

Blessing of the Moon

בִּרְכַּת הַלְּבָנָה

PERFORMING THE *BIRKAT HAL'VANAH* RITUAL

Birkat Hal'vanah takes place outdoors during the moon's waxing phase—that is, between the fourth and fourteenth day of the month—on a clear night when the moon is in view. This ritual may be shared in community or experienced alone. Periods of silence, conducive to reflection or meditation, may be introduced between the readings of the **Opening Psalms** (pp. 409–11) and the concluding blessing, **Renewal of the Moon** (pp. 412–13).

Note that tradition does not assign a specific day for the performance of the *birkat hal'vanah* ritual; however, it is customary to choose a Saturday night, when the community is already gathered to mark the departure of the Sabbath. For the month of Tishrey, the evening after Yom Kippur is chosen, and for Av, the evening after Tish'ah B'av.

Order of the Ritual

Opening Psalms

Renewal of the Moon

סֵדֶר בִּרְכַּת הַלְּבָנָה

מִזְמוֹרֵי פְּתִיחָה

הִתְחַדְּשׁוּת הַלְּבָנָה

Opening Psalms מִזְמוֹרֵי פְּתִיחָה

What Calls You Home

It is neither day nor night.
The sky has no color at all.
The moon has risen, the slimmest
fingernail, or thread.

The thread is white, then silver.
The sky blooms like a rose.
The trees are drained of color,
their green light lifts to the sky.

Above the rose, blue:
light, lightless blue.
The rose turns yelloworange.
A train passes, dogs bark.

The trees are black, are one.
The moon is platinum.
Between the trees and moon
three stars speckle the sky.

A lamp burns in a window,
an airplane crosses the moon.
What house draws you near?
What light calls you home?

Moon in the Rain

Here is the moon shining

on the water at the sides of the roads,

and on the cypresses,

and on the insects

whose lives are a hairsbreadth.

And on the backs of those bent over,

and on the heads of those who stand tall,

and on those fleeing the storm—

its light emerges,

burgeoning.

DALIA RAVIKOVICH
(*translation M. F.*)

הַלְּבָנָה בַּגֶּשֶׁם

זוֹ הַלְּבָנָה עַל מֵי שׁוּחִים

בְּצִדֵּי הַדְּרָכִים הִיא מְאִירָה,

וְעַל הַבְּרוֹשִׁים,

וְעַל רוֹחֲשִׁים,

אֲשֶׁר חַיֵּיהֶם

כְּחוּט הַשַּׂעֲרָה.

וְעַל גַּב שְׁחוֹחִים,

וְעַל רֹאשׁ גְּבוֹהִים

וְעַל הַבּוֹרְחִים

מִן הַסְּעָרָה

נוֹבֵט אוֹרָה

כְּפִטְרִיּוֹת וּכְמֵהִים.

דליה רביקוביץ

Renewal of the Moon

I lift my eyes to the hills:
heaven and earth are my comforts.
By day the sun does not harm me,
by night the moon is my guide.

It renews its light
for those just beginning,
who will one day find
their own renewal.

May the moon
be as praised as the sun
and all be equal
as when we began.

הִתְחַדְּשׁוּת הַלְּבָנָה   Hithad'shut Hal'vanah

Esa eynay el-heharim,

שָׂא עֵינַי אֶל־הֶהָרִים,

ezri yavo

עֶזְרִי יָבֹא

mishamáyim va'áretz.

מִשָּׁמַיִם וָאָרֶץ.

Yomam hashémesh lo yakéni

יוֹמָם הַשֶּׁמֶשׁ לֹא יַכֵּנִי

v'láylah yanhéyni yaréy'ah.

וְלַיְלָה יַנְחֵנִי יָרֵחַ.

Hal'vanah tithadeysh

הַלְּבָנָה תִּתְחַדֵּשׁ

la'amusim mini-véten

לָעֲמוּסִים מִנִּי־בֶטֶן

ulkhol b'riyah

וּלְכָל בְּרִיָּה

bithilat darkah—

בִּתְחִילַת דַּרְכָּה—

v'heym yithad'shu k'motah.

וְהֵם יִתְחַדְּשׁוּ כְּמוֹתָהּ.

Y'hi or hal'vanah

יְהִי אוֹר הַלְּבָנָה

m'vorakh kahamah

מְבֹרָךְ כַּחַמָּה

v'nizkeh kulánu

וְנִזְכֶּה כֻּלָּנוּ

m'heyrah l'orah—

מְהֵרָה לְאוֹרָהּ—

or reyshit b'ri'atéynu.

אוֹר רֵאשִׁית בְּרִיאָתֵנוּ.

Commentary

פֵּרוּשִׁים וְהֶאָרוֹת

Introduction

The following Commentary discusses the individual components of the liturgy in this book; readers should see the Author's Preface and the introductions to the cycles for general background upon which the discussions below are based. All offerings are listed here in the order of their presentation in the liturgy. When an offering appears more than once in the liturgy, it is listed in the Commentary in each of its contexts, although usually it is discussed under its first appearance and thereafter readers are referred to the initial discussion. Sometimes, however, new information is provided under subsequent listings of an item.

The topics treated in the Commentary are of three basic types: history and context of the traditional liturgies on which the particular new offering is based, explanation of linguistic elements of the Hebrew in the traditional prayers and in the new offerings, and theological ramifications. Whenever a Hebrew text is discussed, a literal (word-for-word) translation into English is given (the literal translation of a new offering almost always differs from the English version provided as liturgy in the main section of the book); alternate meanings of a word or phrase are given in parentheses. The titles of the new offerings appear in **bold** type, which distinguishes them from references to components of the traditional liturgy.

Before entering the discussion of the individual liturgical offerings, I want to take a few moments to examine the basic form and content of the traditional Hebrew *b'rakhah*—that genre of prayer we call in English "benediction" or "blessing"—and to explore some of the central theological issues embedded in it. In the process of this exploration, I will attempt to make clear why I have chosen certain kinds of liturgical expression and rejected others.

A rabbinic invention based on a biblical form, the traditional blessing is a statement consisting of two parts: an opening clause declaring God "blessed" and a content-specific phrase or phrases relating this declaration to the occasion being marked. In the latter half of the *b'rakhah*, the rabbis have explored a variety of life experiences. The first half, in contrast, is a formula: *Barukh atah, adonay elohéynu, mélekh ha'olam*, "Blessed are you [masc., sing.], Lord our God, king of the world."

To be precise, one should point out that the term *adonay*, "Lord," is not what actually appears in the text of the blessing formula. What appears there is the Tetragrammaton—the four Hebrew letters *yud-hey-vav-hey* (which I will refer to henceforth in my citations as *y-h-v-h* and in my English translations as "YHVH") used in the Bible to represent the ineffable name of God. (In many of today's standard prayer books, the Tetragrammaton is frequently shortened to two *yud*s—one of its many abbreviated written forms.) However, because only the priests in the Temple were permitted to pronounce God's name, the rabbis designated the word *adonay* to be used as the universal pronunciation of *yud-hey-vav-hey* for purposes of prayer and Bible recitation. While there are many ways to interpret the meaning of the Tetragrammaton's four letters, which would seem to spell a form of the verb "to be," the various nuances of *yud-hey-vav-hey* are not, for the most part, what are conveyed in rabbinic prayer. Rather, it is the word *adonay* that predominates liturgically, because *adonay*—not *yud-hey-vav-hey*—is what is heard each time the traditional prayers are uttered. And, tellingly, it is *adonay*—not *yud-hey-vav-hey*—that is translated when the prayers are rendered into other languages. In fact, *adonay* is so closely associated with God's ineffable name that many religiously observant Jews refuse to pronounce *it* except when praying or reciting from the Bible; instead, they use further substitutions, such as *hasheym*, literally, "the name," and *adosheym* (a combination of *adonay* and *hasheym*). This would seem to demonstrate that, in its traditional liturgical usage, *adonay* itself has come to be identified as *the* name of God.

If *adonay* has, in effect, been consecrated (through use and restraint from use) as the *ultimate* name of God, the statement that opens the basic blessing, *Barukh atah, y-h-v-h [adonay] elohéynu, mélekh ha'olam*, "Blessed are you, YHVH [Lord] our God, king of the world"—which is known as *sheym umalkhut*, "name and sovereignty"—has been similarly consecrated as the ultimate prayer formula. Within Orthodox Judaism this formula has exclusive authority; it opens every blessing, no matter what kind of occasion is being marked, no matter what words form the rest of the speech. This formulaic opening is considered so absolute, so powerful that, once recited, it must not go to waste: it must never be said in vain.

In its brevity and concision, the traditional Hebrew *b'rakhah* has the potential for lyric and spiritual intensity. However, a large part of the reason I first chose to compose new blessings was that I was deeply dissatisfied with the blessing formula—as I would be, in fact, with *any* formula. Indeed, I find the use of *strictly* formulaic language for the divine and *immutable* liturgical forms to be dangerously susceptible to an unwitting form of idolatry, in which reverence for the whole is supplanted by the enshrinement of particular (human-made) images, making the signifier as absolute as what is signified.

Of course, the heavily patriarchal imagery of the rabbinic formula makes it particularly problematic. Yet it is not a satisfying solution merely to replace the direct address of the

Lord-God-king with address of a female image or images (as in *B'rukhah at, sh'khinah*, "Blessed are you [fem.], Shekhinah," one proposal that has circulated widely in alternative liturgies). While it is refreshing to see images other than the single rabbinic icon, the retention of the formulation "Blessed are you" has its own limitations. This passive construction is ultimately disempowering in that it masks the presence of the speaking self (whether personal or communal) that is performing the act of blessing. Perhaps most important, the statement "Blessed are you" leaves the traditional view of God as Other unchallenged—and this theology is clearly problematic for many Jews today.

The question of whether Jewish prayer *needs* to address God as "you" is a highly charged one, perhaps even more provocative than the feminist challenge to the gendered God. Vigorous protests arise when one questions the exclusive authority of the "I-Thou" address of divinity; there is a widely held assumption that this is the only legitimate mode for Jewish prayer. Why this assumption should prevail is not clear. There are certainly people for whom the direct address of God requires a breath-holding suspension of disbelief; while for some this may be an acceptable fiction, for others it feels more like a lie. That one may have an experience of the divine that does *not* assume "otherness" is attested to by many people, Jews clearly among them; this has been true in the past as well as today. The sixteenth-century mystic Moses Cordovero, for example, articulated a nondualistic Jewish theology: "Do not attribute duality to God. . . . Do not say, 'This is a stone and not God.' . . . Rather, all existence is God, and the stone is a thing pervaded by divinity."[20] Speaking personally, I would describe my own experience of the divine as an awareness, or a sensing, of the dynamic, alive, and unifying wholeness within creation—a wholeness that subsumes and contains and embraces me, a wholeness greater than the sum of its parts. Is it reasonable to exclude experiences like this, or formulations like Cordovero's, from the range of conceptualizing that might properly be considered Jewish theology?

Indeed, the movement of Reconstructionism, founded in the mid-twentieth century by Mordecai Kaplan, is explicitly based on a theology that denies that God is either personal or "supernatural."[21] While Kaplan did not seek to abolish the direct address of God in prayer, his eminent disciple Ira Eisenstein, President Emeritus of the Reconstructionist Rabbinical College and an editor of the first Reconstructionist prayer book, has recently called for just that. Eisenstein writes: "Prayer does not necessarily require a 'Thou.' In several cultures, prayer is experienced without reference to a personal being or a Thou. . . . When I pray, I confine myself to the kind of text that enables me to achieve what Walter Kaufmann called 'passionate reflection.' . . . I suggest that traditional Jewish values become the central theme of passionate reflection." Eisenstein goes on to say that prayer today must be "our own, couched in our own idiom, emerging out of our sense of the world." Arguing that "a dialogue with some Other" does not constitute authentic prayer, he urges Reconstruction-ists to try to pray "without the Thou."[22]

Yet the position that God *must* be viewed and addressed as an Other is held today by many Jews, including some liberal theologians and scholars with whom I share dialogue (and with whom I am often in agreement on other issues). Thus feminist theologian Rachel Adler writes: "Eradicating otherness, breaking down all boundaries between self and other, self and God, God and world, simultaneously eradicates relatedness. . . . God's otherness, God's difference from us, is what makes possible relationship and exchange."[23] And liturgy scholar Lawrence A. Hoffman, arguing for the importance of maintaining God's otherness in our prayer, states that "God can be known only in relationship and can never be ade-quately described outside of relationship."[24]

While I would agree that relationship is an important element of theology, I do not see why it is necessary to envision God as a transcendent Other in order to affirm relationship. This view certainly fails to account for the deep sense of connectedness I personally feel when I am in touch with my participation in the greater whole of creation.[25] Moreover, the conception of God as transcendent Other is based on a hierarchical construct of God and world that can be highly problematic for modeling relationships, especially from a feminist perspective, since it provides theological underpinning for the hierarchical dualisms—including the foundational dualistic construct of female and male—that characterize and plague Western culture. It hardly seems coincidental that when the tradition depicts the rela-tionship between God and world in sexual terms, it portrays God as male and the world—often represented by the human community or the people of Israel—as female.[26]

Of course, not all liberal theologians maintain the need to preserve God's otherness; one contemporary scholar who has made a point of challenging the dominant view is Arthur Green. Green writes: "We seek a religious language that goes beyond the separation of 'God,' 'world,' and 'self' that seems so ultimate in most of Western theology. The God of which we speak here is not the 'wholly other,' so widely familiar in our thought and yet so little tested by real understanding. We refer rather to a deity that embraces all of being, a sin-gle One that contains within it all the variety and richness of life, yet is also the Oneness that transcends and surpasses all. . . . But where do we allow room for the truth that all is One if our religious language is that of 'Self' and 'Other'?"[27]

Green makes a stirring case here; and indeed, the importance of speaking honestly of the experience of divine immanence is a central premise of his book. How odd it is, therefore, to find that he declines to abandon the address of God as Other in prayer—in fact, he *insists* upon the use of a personal "you." As he puts it: "For the nondualist, speaking *to* God is as much a betrayal as speaking *of*. Though I insist on using the dualist language in prayer ('blessed are You . . .'), I know that I do not mean it in its simplest sense. This language is a way of addressing the One as though it were possible for me to stand outside that One in such a moment, as though there really were an 'I' who could speak this way to a 'Thou.' But if such prayer is betrayal of our deepest consciousness, it is there to keep faith with our ordinary experience as human beings."[28]

I cannot help but wonder whose "ordinary experience" is being referred to and why we must betray our "deepest consciousness" in order to "keep faith" with it. Why should we be willing to hold one set of beliefs as our truths while we articulate something very different in our worship? If we do not try to touch our deepest faith—our most truthful truths—in prayer, then where?

Striking as it seems, this discrepancy between what one believes and what one is willing to say in prayer is not unique to Green; rather, I would suggest, it reflects an entrenched conservatism on the part of the Jewish community at large in regard to liturgical change. The reasons for this conservatism are open to speculation: the role of nostalgia should perhaps not be underestimated in explaining why people cling to the words they remember (whether accurately or not) from childhood. Still, most people are quite willing to do things differently from their grandparents; this seems to be at least as true in the arena of religion as it is in other areas of life. I would venture to guess that few if any liberal Jews today observe traditional religious customs and laws as their grandparents did. It seems that only when it comes to the actual words of prayer is innovation resisted so fervently. While I cannot adequately explain what causes this phenomenon, I believe I can point to some of its effects. Although liturgical change is often seen as a threat to the continuity of tradition, I would suggest that resistance on the part of the established Jewish community to bringing its prayer in line with its theological, moral, and sociopolitical beliefs has caused many individuals to feel isolated and uncomfortable in synagogue settings, and has dissuaded others from attempting to pray at all. Because communal worship and celebration of the liturgical calendar are central aspects of synagogue experience, many people decline synagogue affiliation and as a consequence have little involvement in Jewish community of any kind. And, as has been documented in recent years, many Jews today pursue spiritual paths in other traditions, such as Buddhism, that seem to speak more authentically to their beliefs. It is my conviction that we *can* articulate our beliefs authentically in a Jewish idiom and a Jewish context, and that it is essential that we try to do so in our prayer if we hope to keep Jewish liturgical tradition alive.

Related to the position that God must be viewed as an Other is the belief that God must be conceptualized and addressed as Person. Thus Lawrence Hoffman states emphatically: "Indeed, it is essential to retain a conception of God as Person, since it is primarily as

Person that we know God in the first place."[29] Feminist theologian Judith Plaskow maintains that we need to use personal imagery for God, at least some of the time, for the following reason: "Because relationships among human beings are unique in containing the potential for the full mutuality and reciprocity that form the foundations of the moral life, it is important that we use anthropomorphic imagery [for God], and that we broaden it as far as possible. But our moral responsibility extends to the entire web of creation, all of which manifests and can symbolize divine presence and activity."[30]

Despite these challenges from thinkers I respect and from whom I have learned a great deal, I have to say that the image of God as Person is not one I find helpful, and I believe that, in this regard, I speak for many others. It is not at all true for me that "it is primarily as Person" that I know God; I experience the divine in many ways, ways that are better represented by nonpersonal images, as well as by other, less direct modes of expression that do not attempt to locate divinity in specific images at all. Moreover, I am seriously troubled by the overwhelming predominance of anthropomorphic imagery in traditional Jewish prayer; it seems to me that this emphasis has led us as a culture into dangerous forms of anthropocentrism (what some call "species-ism"), that is, the belief that the human species is "godlier" than the rest of creation. The detrimental effects of this point of view have been widespread and lasting; one could make the case that this theological perspective buttresses an ideology responsible in large measure for the ecological crisis we face today. With this in mind, I would hold that we ought to explore more fully and more creatively other ways to imagine and conceptualize divinity, and that we should hesitate before adding more anthropomorphisms to our prayer books.

In further response to Plaskow, I would say that I do not believe an anthropomorphic view of the divine is necessary for the foundations of a moral life. The place of morality and values in prayer is a complex and important issue; I confront it specifically in relation to my **Sh'ma: Declaration of Faith** and to my blessings of commandment (see the commentary to the former, pp. 434–35, and to **Sabbath Candlelighting**, pp. 441–43). While I appreciate Plaskow's desire to represent human relationships in our liturgy, I would stress that this needn't take the form of creating images of God as Person (even if that Person is Friend rather than Lord, female rather than male). Instead, I would suggest that we bring human relations *directly* into our liturgy by explicitly affirming in that liturgy our interpersonal values, and by using prayer as an occasion to make commitments to live according to those values. This approach is, I believe, in keeping with the model of "passionate reflection" on traditional Jewish values that Eisenstein is calling for, which he describes thus: "appreciation of the marvels and the mysteries of the universe, dedication to the ideas of human perfectability, individual and social concern for the downtrodden and the stranger, as well as a sense of gratitude for whatever well-being one enjoys. Passionate reflection should revive one's resolution to strive for ethical heights, to resist evil, to engender love and respect for fellow persons—and, finally, to rekindle love of and loyalty to the Jewish people, to Torah in its broadest and deepest sense."[31] I offer examples of moral commitments in various parts of my liturgy, including the **Blessing After the Meal**, the *Sh'ma:* **Declaration of Faith**, and *Aléynu L'shabéyaḥ:* **It Is Ours to Praise**. Other offerings—specifically, the **Blessing of the Children** and the dialogue **Blessing the Beloved**—provide direct address between human beings and attempt, through this form, to model the reciprocity and respect that Plaskow and Eisenstein urge us to seek.

Throughout the rest of this Commentary I will describe the various alternatives I have offered to the direct address of divinity conveyed in the traditional blessing form. The **Blessing Before the Meal** was my initial point of departure from that mode of speech, and I discuss that departure in the commentary to that blessing. But I hope the Commentary as a whole will make clear why I believe there is no single answer to the question of how to speak authentically in prayer.

The Daily Cycle מַחֲזוֹר הַיּוֹם

Morning Blessing בִּרְכַּת הַשַּׁחַר
(pages 10–11; see also 154–55)

The first blessing of the day, the **Morning Blessing**, is one of appreciation. In Hebrew titled ***Birkat Hasháhar***, "blessing of the dawn (or morning)," it is intended to serve in place of the traditional sequence known as *birkhot hasháhar*, "blessings of the dawn (or morning)," discussed in the introduction to THE DAILY CYCLE and in the commentary to **Opening Blessings and Songs** (p. 457). The **Morning Blessing** also appears in THE WEEKLY CYCLE as part of the *Shaharit:* **Morning Service for the Sabbath**, where it serves as a transition from individual to communal prayer.

The opening line of the Hebrew in this new blessing plays upon a phrase in the traditional Sabbath and holiday morning service: *Nishmat kol hay t'vareykh et shim'khah*, "The breath of all that lives will bless your name." Thus the **Morning Blessing** begins *Nishmat hayay t'vareykh*, "The soul of my life will bless." The first word of this line, *nishmat*, is the so-called construct form of *n'shamah*, "breath," or "spirit," or "soul." (The construct in Hebrew grammar is an inflected form of the noun indicating that the word is to be understood as connected by "of" to the noun that follows it. For example, in the phrase *beyt k'néset*, "house of assembly," *k'néset* is "assembly" and *beyt* is the construct form of *báyit*, "house." Possessive forms of the noun are similar to the construct; they consist of the inflected form plus a personal suffix, as in *beyti*, "my house.") A key term in Hebrew liturgy, *n'shamah* derives from the verb meaning "to breathe"; no single English word renders it adequately. In its many appearances throughout biblical, rabbinic, and later literature, it links physical breath with the spiritual life-force, as in this example from the biblical creation story (Gen. 2:7): *Vayítzer y-h-v-h elohim et-ha'adam afar min-ha'adamah, vayipah b'apav nishmat hayim, vayhi ha'adam l'néfesh hayah*, "YHVH God formed the human from the dust of the earth, blowing into its nostrils the breath of life, and the human became a living spirit." *N'shamah* appears in this verse as part of the phrase *nishmat hayim*, "the breath (or spirit, or soul) of life." To say *nishmat hayay*, "the breath (or spirit, or soul) of *my* life," is to personalize an image resounding with myth and history.

The second line of the **Morning Blessing** parallels the first syntactically, elaborating upon and expanding its meaning: *v'kérev libi yashir,* "and the innermost part of my heart will sing." In Hebrew as in English, the word *leyv,* "heart" (which appears here in the possessive form *libi,* "my heart"), refers to both the body and the emotions, although in the context of this line the latter probably comes to mind more readily. Reference to the body is also embedded in the word *kérev,* "innermost part" or "midst," which originally denoted the body's internal organs, specifically the viscera. Because today *kérev* is primarily used as an abstraction, the concrete reference to the body is subtle. I have attempted to draw this association closer to the surface by making *kérev libi,* "the innermost part of my heart," the subject of the statement. A more conventional phrasing of this line would have been *mikérev libi ashir,* the idiomatic English equivalent of which is "from the depths of my heart I will sing." By upsetting the convention, I mean to emphasize the role of the body in the agency of the self, increasing our awareness of body and spirit as one.

The last two lines of this blessing—*Kol od n'shamah b'kirbi / modah* [fem.] (or *modeh* [masc.]) *ani,* "As long as breath is in my innermost being / I give thanks"—are adapted from the traditional *elohay, n'shamah* blessing, which acknowledges and expresses gratitude to God for creating breath or soul. The original line from *elohay, n'shamah* reads: *Kol z'man shehan'shamah v'kirbi modeh ani l'fanékha,* "The whole time my breath is in my innermost being I [masc.] give thanks before you [masc., sing.]." In the new lines, the word *l'fanékha,* "before you," has been omitted, leaving the direction of the prayer open.

In addition, *kol z'man she-,* "the whole time that," has been replaced by *kol od,* "while" or "as long as." In its original biblical contexts, the phrase *kol od* is used much as it is here, to indicate duration of life, as in Job 27:3, *ki-khol-od nishmati vi,* "for while my breath (or spirit, or soul) is within me," and 2 Samuel 1:9, *ki-khol-od nafshi bi,* "for while my spirit (or soul) is within me." I have chosen *kol od* over *kol z'man she-* not only because of its biblical resonance and because it is more concise, but also because it echoes the opening lines of *Hatikvah,* "The Hope," Israel's national anthem (written by Naftali Hertz Imber): *Kol od baleyvav p'nímah / néfesh y'hudi homiyah,* "As long as deep within the heart / the soul of a Jew yearns." Known today by Jews throughout the world, these lines incorporate powerful images of body and spirit to convey an emotional intensity much like what the **Morning Blessing** seeks to express.

Note that in the penultimate line of the **Morning Blessing**, the word *kérev,* "innermost part," reappears, this time as *kirbi,* "my innermost being." Thus the phrase *Kol od n'shamah b'kirbi* intertwines the images *n'shamah* and *kérev* from the blessing's opening lines to portray the body suffused with inspiriting breath. As a whole, this blessing offers an appreciation, expressed by spirit and flesh as one, for the flow of enlivening breath/

spirit/soul throughout the channels and depths of the body—an appreciation, in other words, for human life. In the English version, the two parallel phrases "the breath of my life" and "the cells of my being" are intended to represent the interconnected spirituality and physicality of the self.

Handwashing upon Awakening   נְטִילַת יָדַיִם בְּעֵת הַיְקִיצָה
(pages 12–13)

Handwashing Before the Meal   נְטִילַת יָדַיִם לִפְנֵי הָאֲרוּחָה
(pages 16–17; see also 130–31, 376–77)

Central to rabbinic Judaism's view of the human body are concerns with purity and impurity; an ancient and core part of the liturgy is the purification ritual known as *n'tilat yadáyim*, "lifting (or washing) of the hands." This ritual, which entails the washing and drying of the hands accompanied by the recitation of a blessing, is performed in several contexts: upon awakening, before beginning a meal at which bread is to be eaten, and after contact with a dead body (or upon leaving a cemetery). In the first and last of these contexts, *n'tilat yadáyim* may be seen as symbolizing renewal or rebirth. In the case of its use before a meal, it was originally intended, among other things, to reenact the priestly purification ritual performed when offering a sacrifice at the Temple. One might say that by mandating the washing of hands before eating, the rabbis turned every meal in the daily life of ordinary people into a sacred event.

The general subject of purification in Judaism is too complex to treat meaningfully in the limited context of this discussion. Yet it is important at least to note that it is a problematic area in many regards, especially as it relates to women. For example, the association of impurity with menstruation and childbirth in the context of the rabbinic laws concerning menstruants (the laws of *nidah*, or what later came to be known as *tohorat hamishpahah*, "family purity") has had ramifications far beyond its seemingly limited domain, for centuries affecting a broad spectrum of religious rules and customs, behavioral norms, and attitudes toward women. Yet *nidah* is only one aspect of a still more encompassing problem. To put it simply, we might ask: Why does the body need purification at all? If the body is taken to be inherently sacred, purification is a redundant act.

Some Jewish feminists have suggested that purification rituals might be meaningfully recontextualized today as a way to deal with abuse or violation.[32] Yet even in cases where the body is defiled or violated, we might question whether that body needs to be "purified"— as opposed to cleansed or healed. Indeed, when violation occurs, we might consider which body or bodies—that of the one who is violated or that of the violator—ought to be considered defiled. When sacred boundaries are trespassed, who or what becomes "impure"?

These are but a few of the questions that might be asked about the concept and practice of purification in Jewish life—questions I can but raise here. Yet, to my mind, it is not necessary to resolve these in order to find a meaningful approach to *n'tilat yadáyim*, at least in the contexts of awakening from sleep and beginning a meal. The practice of saying a blessing upon washing the hands has the potential to be spiritually powerful whether or not one chooses to think of it as a purification rite. Its purpose, as I conceive it, is to increase our appreciation for the body while reminding us of our responsibility for that gift.

My new handwashing blessings claim the body's sacrality, affirming the interconnectedness of the traditionally polarized halves of our being: *Tizkor nafshi (nafshéynu) et k'dushat haguf / bintilat yadáyim*, literally, "May my (our) spirit (or soul) recall the holiness of body / in the lifting (or washing) of the hands." The ritual act that accompanies the blessing is at once literal and metaphorical: as we dip our hands in water and raise them to be dried, we elevate them—and, by extension, the whole body—in our awareness.

I have opened these blessings with the word *tizkor*, "recall" or "remember," which is related to the words *zikaron* and *zéykher*, two central liturgical terms meaning "remembrance" found in traditional sanctifications over wine (and in the new ones for the Sabbath and the week provided in this book). These terms connote a deliberate calling to mind that combines memory with signification or symbol, providing connection between important religious concepts (for example, between the Sabbath and the liberation from Egypt, as discussed in the commentary to the **Sanctification over Wine for Sabbath Eve** and the **Sanctification over Wine for Sabbath Day**, pp. 453–54). In the new handwashing blessings, *tizkor* connects *néfesh*, "spirit" or "soul" (given here in the possessive forms *nafshi* and *nafshéynu*), with *guf*, "body," through the concept of *k'dushah*, "holiness." That is, through the act of handwashing, the spirit-self recalls its embodiment and reclaims the sacrality of that embodiment, thus also affirming its own holiness.

I have referred to *néfesh* in this discussion as "spirit," "soul," and "spirit-self"; the Hebrew word—much like the word *n'shamah* in the **Morning Blessing**—is laden with biblical and liturgical associations that make it difficult to render accurately with a single term. Like the English word "soul," *néfesh* is often used to refer to a whole living being. In the English versions of these blessings, I have rendered *néfesh* as "mind," using the phrase "call to mind" to convey the liturgical sense of *tizkor nafshi* (or *nafshéynu*). While for some speakers "mind" may seem more limited than "spirit" or "soul," I want to encourage thinking of the mind as (in the words of Candace Pert quoted previously in the introduction to THE DAILY CYCLE) "enlivening energy . . . throughout the brain and body." In the context of the entire English blessing—"Washing the hands, I (we) call to mind / the holiness of body"—I hope to revivify the common idiom "call to mind," so that it might denote and also stimulate the kind of awareness that the handwashing ritual attempts to call forth.

The traditional handwashing blessing belongs to a category known as "blessings of commandment," which is explained in the commentary to **Sabbath Candlelighting** (pp. 441–43). More information about the use of *néfesh* may also be found in that discussion. Note, too, that *nafshi* and *nafshéynu* are key terms in the *Sh'ma:* **Declaration of Faith**.

Although the traditional handwashing blessing does not vary by context, I have composed the new blessing in two forms, one in the first-person singular and one in the first-person plural. **Handwashing upon Awakening** is given in the singular form, for use by the individual in a private context; thus it is compatible with the preceding **Morning Blessing**, which is also offered in the first-person singular. **Handwashing Before the Meal**, like the **Blessing Before the Meal**, which follows it, is in the first-person plural.

Blessing Before the Meal   הַמּוֹצִיאָה
(pages 18–19; see also 132–33, 378–79)

The twentieth-century German Jewish philosopher Franz Rosenzweig writes: "The sweet, fully ripened fruit of humanity craves community . . . in the very act of renewing the life of the body."[33] If, as Rosenzweig has it, the meal is the foundation of community, bread is often the foundation of the meal. In ancient times, bread itself was considered a meal, and breaking bread was the way people engaged in fellowship. Thus bread was symbolic of both physical and social sustenance. The rabbis, too, saw bread as a double symbol—of God's gift of sustenance to humanity and of humanity's sacrificial offerings to God. For the rabbis, the table was an altar and the meal at which bread was served was a reenactment of the devotional rituals of Temple times.

Throughout Jewish history, from rabbinic times to the present, the blessing over bread, customarily called *hamótzi* (from one of its key words, meaning "which [or who] brings forth"), has been the prayer most commonly recited at the beginning of meals. Based on Psalm 104:14, this blessing praises God as the one "who brings forth bread from the earth," *hamótzi léhem min ha'áretz*. In the original biblical source, God is said to provide grass and plants so that *human beings* may "bring forth bread from the earth." Thus, embedded in the liturgical phrase is the rabbinic idea that divinity and humanity are partners in creation. In this biblical passage, as elsewhere in the Bible, *léhem*, "bread," is a metonymy for food.

Although bread remains a powerful symbol in Judaism, the meal today is often a private experience, and many people find themselves frequently eating alone, without social ceremony. This can be an isolating experience, making the need for a table ritual, with its symbolic connection to history and culture, even more compelling. In my own daily life, saying a blessing over bread has become that ritual.

The **Blessing Before the Meal** was one of the first new blessings I composed, and in doing so I established the fundamentals of my liturgical-poetic process. In creating it, I replaced the phrase *barukh atah*, "blessed are you [masc., sing.]," with an active, first-person plural, gender-inclusive form, *n'vareykh*, "let us bless." With this word, the community exhorts itself to experience oneness with the whole in the very act of blessing. The speech that follows this opening is unrestricted; unlike the word *barukh*, "blessed," which is gender-specific, *n'vareykh* may introduce images in either gender, drawn from any number of contexts.

Thus in this first of my blessings I followed the word *n'vareykh* with the first of my images to replace the rabbinic Lord-God-king. I derived that new image from an ancient text, Deuteronomy 8:7: *éretz náḥaley máyim, ayanot uthomot yotz'im babik'ah uvahar*, "a land of watercourses, wellsprings, and depths emerging from valleys and from hills." In the wellsprings that rise from the land, pouring their waters back into the land, I found what seemed to me the perfect metaphor for my **Blessing Before the Meal**: *áyin*, "wellspring" or "fountain," with the figurative meaning of "source." In the springing up of the fountains, I saw an arc of motion that mirrored the description in the traditional blessing of *hamótzi*, the psalmist's image of bread drawn from the earth. This description from *hamótzi* was one I wished to preserve, rich as it was with associations to the biblical story of our origins—of how we were created from the dust of the earth, drawn from it like the bread we draw forth with our own labors, the bread that at once feeds us and reminds us of our earthliness, of our connection to the ongoing process of creation. It felt right to me to link the bread of the earth with these fountains that rise up from under the earth to suggest a deep ground-of-being, divinity as immanent presence. These connections were what finally led me to form the phrase *eyn haḥayim*, "wellspring (or fountain, or source) of life," and to compose the blessing *N'vareykh et eyn haḥayim / hamotzi'ah léḥem min ha'áretz*, "Let us bless the source of life / that brings forth bread from the earth." (Note that because *eyn haḥayim* is grammatically feminine—although semantically without gender—the word *hamótzi* from the traditional blessing becomes here *hamotzi'ah*.)

Because this blessing was one of the first I wrote, I think of it now as a kind of prototype, but only in a limited sense: in composing it, I had found a way to break through the traditional blessing form and begin my ongoing exploration of new forms and images. But that beginning was *only* a beginning, as should be apparent from the various kinds of blessings in this book, and the line *N'vareykh et eyn haḥayim* remains, to my mind, but one of a multitude of utterances by which one may perform the act of blessing. Should this line ever become formulaic—seen as the ultimate form of expression, to the exclusion of other forms—it would be idolatrous and should be abandoned.

While traditionally *hamótzi* is said only when bread is part of the meal (other blessings are recited for meals without bread), I use this new **Blessing Before the Meal** whenever I eat, understanding *léḥem* as symbolic of all food. In its simplicity, the ritual becomes one I do not fail to do; hence it has the benefit of increasing my awareness of daily gifts.

Blessing After the Meal   בִּרְכַּת הַמָּזוֹן
(pages 20–21; see also 134–35, 380–81)

The traditional grace after the meal, known as *birkat hamazon*, literally, "blessing of the food," is actually a compilation containing three ancient blessings at its core. The themes of these three blessings are gratitude to God for providing food for all creatures; appreciation for *ha'aretz*, "the land" or "the earth," which here means the land of Israel; and hope for the rebuilding of the Temple in Jerusalem. In addition, a fourth blessing, said to be composed later, praises God's goodness to all creation. These four early blessings were gradually embellished over time, resulting in a lengthy chain of prayers intended for daily use, with variations and additions for Sabbaths and holidays.

The new **Blessing After the Meal**, which is considerably shorter than the traditional prayer, is intended for use at any meal on any day of the year. Formed of three statements, each of which is marked by a different verb given in the first-person plural, it encompasses all three of the original core themes, newly interpreted.

The first statement is an acknowledgment of the source of all being and all nourishment. The verb opening this utterance is *nodeh*, "let us acknowledge (or thank)," and the opening line, *Nodeh l'eyn haḥayim*, "Let us acknowledge the source of life," echoes the opening line of the **Blessing Before the Meal**, *N'vareykh et eyn haḥayim*, "Let us bless the source of life." The second line of this statement, *hazanah et hakol*, literally, "which (or who) feeds all," is borrowed directly from the traditional *birkat hamazon* (where, however, it appears in the grammatically masculine form *hazan et hakol*).

The second statement of the blessing refers to *ha'aretz hatovah v'har'ḥavah*, literally, "the good and spacious land," a phrase taken from the traditional prayer, where it denotes the land of Israel. In its new context, this phrase refers both to Israel and to the earth as a whole; the first-person verb here is *nishmor*, "let us protect." The purpose of the second statement is to affirm human partnership with the source of creation in preserving the life of the planet, even as we acknowledge our dependence on the earth for sustenance. At the same time, we acknowledge the role of the land of Israel in sustaining Jewish life, affirming our responsibility to protect it from evil and harm. Thus universalist and particularist concerns, which are present in different parts of the traditional prayer, are here intertwined. Unfortunately, the English version of the blessing fails to preserve the twin meanings of *ha'aretz* as "the earth" and "the land of Israel"—I could find no single word willing to do this double duty. (This is an example of the kind of difficulties that can arise when writing Jewish poetry in a language that has not, historically, been shared by Jews—one reason I believe it imperative to keep the Hebrew liturgical tradition alive.)

The third statement of the **Blessing After the Meal** makes a commitment to work for a world where none will go hungry. This may be seen as a way of striving to make the world in its entirety a sacred space—a symbolic re-creation of the sacred space of the ancient Temple. The verb here is *n'vakeysh*, "let us seek" (appearing here as *unvakeysh*, "and let us seek"), which, like *nishmor*, "let us protect," implies a commitment to ongoing future action beyond the ritual activity of the blessing.

Thus the new **Blessing After the Meal** connects spiritual yearning to social concern and commitment. Taken as a whole, it encompasses the hope of the fourth blessing in the traditional prayer—that goodness may be provided for all living beings.

While rabbinic Judaism mandates the recitation of *birkat hamazon* after any meal at which one has eaten bread, many Jews today recite this prayer primarily at festive meals on the Sabbath and holidays. Having available a short form of the prayer, however, may encourage its use at other times as well; hence the **Blessing After the Meal** appears in THE DAILY CYCLE as well as in subsequent sections of the book.

Sh'ma: Personal Declaration of Faith   קְרִיאַת שְׁמַע עַל הַמִּטָּה
(pages 24–27)

Sh'ma: Communal Declaration of Faith   קְרִיאַת שְׁמַע בַּקְּהִלָּה
(in THE WEEKLY CYCLE)   (במחזור השבוע)
(pages 170–73)

The traditional bedtime prayers center around a biblical passage known as the *sh'ma*, which is an imperative meaning "hear!" Perhaps the most well known piece of liturgy in Jewish life, the *sh'ma* is technically not a prayer at all but a declaration of faith in monotheistic divinity. The full-length *sh'ma* is a compilation of three biblical passages—Deuteronomy 6:4–9; Deuteronomy 11:13–21; and Numbers 15:37–41—but it is the first section alone that is recited upon retiring and that has come to be regarded as the statement of Judaism's central creed. This passage articulates the duty of loving God with all one's being—one's heart, and spirit, and strength—of observing God's commandments, and of teaching these precepts to one's children. It opens with the keynote line *Sh'ma, yisra'eyl, y-h-v-h [adonay] elohéynu, y-h-v-h [adonay] eḥad*, "Hear, O Israel, YHVH [the Lord] is our God, YHVH [the Lord] is One," from which the name *sh'ma* is taken. Later in the passage, the listener (addressed as a male individual) is instructed to speak the commanded words "when you sit in your house and when you walk on the way, when you lie down and when you arise." And indeed, the *sh'ma* has been incorporated into both morning and evening synagogue services and has been used for centuries in the home as part of the bedtime prayers of children and adults. It is among the first prayers that Jewish children have been taught to say and, at least according to popular belief, it is the last prayer that Jewish martyrs have uttered: countless numbers of Jews are said to have gone to their deaths saying the words of this passage. Thus the *sh'ma* and, in particular, its opening line have become emblematic of Jewish identity itself.

How does one dare to rewrite such words?

I have no answer to this question beyond the raison d'être of this book as a whole, which is, simply, that we ought to try to say what we mean when we pray. If we take monotheism seriously—if we take Judaism seriously in our lives—we ought to be able to articulate what a monotheistic belief means to us. To me it means the honoring of diversity within the unity of creation. To my mind and heart, this is the message of faith embodied in the *sh'ma*; this is the message to be heard and conveyed by the people of Israel. I have given more thought to my re-creations of the opening line and first section of the *sh'ma* than to any single blessing in this book—and I present them here not without fear and trembling. *May the words of my mouth and the meditations of my heart be acceptable.*

The following four-line statement, which opens the Hebrew version of the **Sh'ma: Declaration of Faith**, is intended to re-create the opening line of the original *sh'ma*: *Sh'ma, yisra'eyl—/ la'elohut alfey panim, / m'lo olam sh'khinatah, / ribuy panéha eḥad*, literally, "Hear, O Israel—/ divinity has thousands of faces, / the fullness of the world is its presence, / the multiplicity of its faces is One." Three terms in this new declaration may be thought of as replacing the heavily masculine and hierarchical image of *adonay*, "the Lord," which appears twice in the opening line of the original *sh'ma*. (As elsewhere in the traditional liturgy, what actually appears in the text is the unvocalized four-letter name *y-h-v-h*, but the word that is said aloud in prayer is *adonay*; this substitution is explained in the introduction to the Commentary, pp. 417–18.) These three terms are: *elohut*, "divinity"; *sh'khinatah*, "its presence"; and *ribuy panéha*, "the multiplicity of its faces (or facets)." Of these, the first two are grammatically feminine, the third grammatically masculine—although none may be said to have real gender, all being abstract nouns.

The word *sh'khinatah*, "its presence," has double resonance: in Jewish tradition *sh'khinah*, literally, "presence," has itself come to be a name for the divine (sometimes rendered in English as Shekhinah) associated with immanence or indwelling (further explanation of *sh'khinah* appears in the commentary to **Restoring Shekhinah, Reclaiming Home**, p. 474). The phrase *m'lo olam sh'khinatah*, "the fullness of the world is its presence," derives from, and is syntactically parallel to, the traditional liturgical phrase *m'lo khol ha'aretz k'vodo*, "the fullness of the earth is his glory," which can be read as an acknowledgment of divine immanence. Thus the new **Sh'ma: Declaration of Faith** states that the presence of divinity in the world is experienced as indwelling—that is, felt immanently—in all of creation. And the many faces of divinity are revealed in the world as the rich diversity we experience all around us. The world we know—a world we may learn, through awareness, to love more deeply—is a multifaceted manifestation of a unified creation with a unified source: the many are One.

The extended passage that follows this opening and constitutes the rest of the declaration is adapted from the first section of the original *sh'ma*. Its theme is love of life and its ineffable source, a love manifested by adherence to life-preserving and life-enhancing principles that are embraced, enacted, and passed on to the next generation. Unlike the original *sh'ma*, however, which is presented as a direct address to an individual male listener (*V'ahavta . . . b'khol l'vav'kha . . .*, "You shall love . . . with all your heart . . ."), the new **Sh'ma: Declaration of Faith** is a statement of convictions spoken by a first-person voice. This voice is singular in the **Sh'ma: Personal Declaration of Faith**, which is part of the bedtime ritual, and plural in the **Sh'ma: Communal Declaration of Faith**, which is recited in community as part of the new **Shaḥarit: Morning Service for the Sabbath**.

Thus the passage affirms (in ll. 5–8 of the Hebrew, ll. 5–9 of the English): *Ohav (nohav) et-haḥayim / v'eyt eyn haḥayim / b'khol-l'vavi (-l'vavéynu) uvkhol-nafshi (-nafshéynu) / uvkhol-m'odi (-m'odéynu)*, literally, "I (we) shall love life / and the source of life / with all my (our) heart and with all my (our) spirit (or soul) / and with all my (our) might." This parallels the command in the traditional *sh'ma* to "love YHVH [the Lord], your God, with all your heart and with all your spirit (or soul) and with all your might." I have discussed the meanings and resonances of *leyv*, "heart," and *néfesh*, "spirit" (in the commentary to **Morning Blessing**, p. 425, and to **Handwashing upon Awakening** and **Handwashing Before the Meal**, pp. 427–28). The Masoretic cantillation marks (explained on p. 436) in the biblical *sh'ma* passage suggest that these words be read as a unit there, rather than as discrete elements. This supports the interpretation of heart-and-spirit as "whole self," a reading I would encourage in the new prayer as well. Like the terms *néfesh* and *leyv*, the word *m'od*, literally, "might" or "strength," is difficult to translate; primarily because of its meaning in the original biblical context of the *sh'ma*, it has come to be used as a metonymy for the whole human being. Elsewhere in the Bible, as in modern usage, the word *m'od* functions as an adverb meaning "very," as in Genesis 1:31: "God saw all he had done and, behold, it was very good." Here too, *m'od* may be thought of as intensifying what has come before it: we are instructed to love with all our heart and all our spirit—hence, with our very being. I have used two words, "senses" and "strength," to render the concept of *m'od* in my English line. "Strength" follows the traditional understanding of *m'od* in this context, while "senses" emphasizes the role that the body plays in our full appreciation of life.

In the traditional declaration, this command to love God is followed by another, to keep "these words which I command you this day on your heart," a reference that, as found in the original biblical context from which it is taken (Deut. 6:6), calls to mind the Ten Commandments given by God to the people of Israel (in Deut. 5:11–18). The rabbis of the Talmud (b. Berakhot 12a), however, removed the Ten Commandments from the liturgical context of the *sh'ma* to prevent a narrow reading of the phrase "these words which I command you this day," which they preferred to read as a reference to the Torah as a whole. Thus, some readers take this phrase in its liturgical context to include all God's commandments to the people of Israel; others read it as a reference to the opening line of the *sh'ma* or to the commandment to love God with all one's being.

I have followed in the rabbis' footsteps here: just as they departed from the specificity of the biblical context when framing the *sh'ma* in the liturgy, I too (in ll. 9–10 of the Hebrew, ll. 10–12 of the English) have recontextualized the phrase *had'varim ha'éyleh*, "these words" ("these promises" in the English version), omitting the phrase that follows it, "which I command you this day." In moving "these words" out of the specific context of God's speech, I do not mean to give them less authority. On the contrary, I consider them a reference to ultimate values, which define areas in which we might think of ourselves as being "commanded." The idea that as human beings we have moral responsibilities that flow from the unique capacities of our species is, I believe, one sense in which "commandment" may be spoken of meaningfully today by feminists and by Jews. What in fact constitutes proper commandments for human beings today is, of course, the subject of ongoing ethical discourse. In my ***Sh'ma*** (ll. 11–13 of the Hebrew, ll. 13–16 of the English), I have offered three principles that, in my understanding, reflect classical Jewish beliefs as well as feminist ethics: *sh'mirat éretz v'yosh'véha*, "protection of the earth and its inhabitants," *r'difat tzédek v'shalom*, "pursuit of justice and peace," and *ahavat hésed v'rahamim*, "love of kindness and compassion." (The concept of commandment is discussed further in the commentary to **Sabbath Candlelighting**, pp. 441–43.)

The new *Sh'ma: Declaration of Faith* continues (ll. 14–19 of the Hebrew, ll. 17–22 of the English) with an articulation of our commitment to teach "these words" to our children, speaking of them throughout the course of the day; the text of these lines closely parallels that found in the original *sh'ma*. The next section of the new declaration (ll. 20–21 of the Hebrew, ll. 23–24 of the English), however, departs more sharply from the original *sh'ma*. The traditional text prescribes the placing of the words "for a sign upon your hands and for frontlets between your eyes" (in what are called *t'filin*, "phylacteries") as well as "on the doorposts of your house and upon your gates" (in scrolls called *m'zuzot*). These are concrete rituals that serve as reminders to keep the words of the *sh'ma* alive. The new **Sh'ma** replaces the reference to these rituals with the statement "And may my (our) actions / be faithful to my (our) words." I have made this substitution because I believe that, especially as regards communicating ideas to children, there is ultimately no more meaningful exemplification of our values than that of our everyday personal behavior. By omitting the mention of *t'filin* and *m'zuzot* from this passage, I am not at all suggesting that they have no place in Jewish life; on the contrary, I think that they, like many other rituals Jews perform (indeed, like the ritual of prayer itself), can be powerful symbols of identity and of belief.[34] But there is something that must precede any commitment to embody our beliefs in rituals: the promise to enact those beliefs in ordinary, nonritualistic ways. And it is this prior commitment that, I would suggest, belongs in our primary declaration of faith.

The new **Sh'ma** closes with a statement of hope that if we set a wise and loving example for our children, they too will understand and perpetuate the life-affirming values we embrace. The closing four lines of the Hebrew (six lines in the English) are based not on the original *sh'ma* but on two verses from Psalms. The first of these verses, Psalm 78:6, refers to the importance of teaching Torah to our children "so that the next generation will know, the children yet to be born"—*l'má'an yeyd'u dor aḥaron, banim yiваléydu*. For "children," the Hebrew verse specifies *banim*, "sons." As there is no truly gender-inclusive Hebrew word for "offspring," I have substituted for *banim* the phrase *banot uvanim*, "daughters and sons." The second verse I have adopted, Psalm 85:11, adds poignancy to the theme of transcendent, life-embracing love. Envisioning a world in which seeming polarities are reconciled and united, the psalmist declares: *Ḥésed ve'emet nifgáshu, tzédek v'shalom nasháku*, "Kindness and truth have met, justice and peace have kissed." As the concluding lines of the prayer, these two verses link our dedication to future generations with a vision of redemption.

As indicated, this new **Sh'ma** is presented in two forms, for singular and plural speakers. This echoes the two different ways the listener is addressed in the original three passages of the traditional *sh'ma* (in Deut. 6:4–9 a single listener is spoken to, but in Deut. 11:13–21 and Num. 15:37–41 Israel is addressed in the plural—a grammatical distinction that is not discernible in English translation but is explicit in the Hebrew texts). The singular form of the declaration is found in THE DAILY CYCLE, the plural form in THE WEEKLY CYCLE. Readers may experiment with interchanging these forms when a shift of focus is desired.

In the Hebrew version of the **Sh'ma: Declaration of Faith** I have inserted cantillation marks, using the Masoretic system found in traditional Hebrew Bibles. These marks, which appear above and below the words of the text, serve a dual purpose: they are a form of punctuation, telling readers which words and phrases are joined and which are separated, and they are a musical notation, indicating how the lines may be chanted. However, because not all Hebrew readers will be fluent in reading cantillation, I have also retained standard punctuation marks in the Hebrew version of the text. In inserting the cantillation, I have followed traditional patterns, notating words and phrases according to syntax and meaning in accordance with the Masoretic principles. Thus, like the traditional *sh'ma*, the new Hebrew **Sh'ma: Declaration of Faith** may be either recited or chanted. As it has become customary in North American congregations to sing the opening line of the traditional *sh'ma* in a melody distinct from the chant indicated by the cantillation marks, one may choose to use an adaptation of that melody for the opening declaration (four lines) of the new Hebrew **Sh'ma: Declaration of Faith.**

Blessing Before Going to Sleep   בְּרָכָה לִקְרַאת הַשֵּׁנָה
(pages 28–29)

Like the **Morning Blessing**, the **Blessing Before Going to Sleep** is one of gratitude; also like the **Morning Blessing**, it acknowledges the body and spirit as intertwined. The opening lines of the Hebrew—*Ḥevley sheynah al eynay / utnumah al af'apay*, literally, "Cords of sleep upon my eyes / and slumber upon my eyelids"—are taken directly from the traditional blessing said upon retiring, whose source is the Talmud (b. Berakhot 60b, the same context in which the morning blessings are found). To these concrete images of the body, I have added new lines: *mal'ah nafshi hodayah / al mat'not hayom*, "my spirit (or soul) is filled with gratitude / for the gifts of the day," and *mal'ah nafshi hodayah / al matat hayom*, "my spirit (or soul) is filled with gratitude / for the gift of the day." The word *hodayah*, "gratitude," echoes the verb "give thanks" in the **Morning Blessing** (*modah* and *modeh* are verbal forms related to *hodayah*); the reference to *nafshi*, "my spirit (or soul)," recalls **Handwashing upon Awakening** and thus further ties together the beginning and the end of the day. The image *mal'ah nafshi hodayah*, "my spirit is filled with gratitude," mirrors that in the third line of the **Sh'ma: Personal Declaration of Faith**—*m'lo olam sh'khinatah*, "the fullness of the world is its [divinity's] presence." The intention here is to link the personal experience of gratitude with an awareness of larger connections in the world, extending the tradition established by the rabbis (b. Berakhot 60b) of connecting the *sh'ma* declaration with the prayer before going to bed.

After composing this **Blessing Before Going to Sleep**, I was confronted by a friend who takes prayer very seriously: How can I pray these words every night? What do I do at the end of a truly awful day, a day during which everything seems to have gone wrong? Worse, how can I expect this prayer to be uttered by someone whose life is filled with suffering?

I replied that perhaps this blessing could be a stimulus to awareness, a way to help oneself to recognize the unseen gifts one had received during the course of the day. Or perhaps, my friend responded, it might be used to acknowledge the "bitter gifts"—those we might not have wished for but that nonetheless serve us in some way.

The issue my friend raises is complex, touching upon difficult questions such as how prayer might alleviate suffering or transform it into something beneficial, and what to do when prayer has the undesirable effect of increasing our pain. Such questions, which are relevant not just to the particular prayer at hand but to prayer in general, might be seen as variations on even more fundamental concerns, such as how to pray authentically, how and whether to pray with words that do not fit one's feelings, and how to pray at all when one is not inspired to do so.

Throughout the Talmud, the rabbis assume the importance of "fixed" prayer—the Hebrew term for this is *kéva*—which generally refers to specific words recited at set times of day. And indeed, many people who pray on a regular basis report that the practice of fixed prayer can bring about spiritual awakenings that one might otherwise miss. But the rabbis also emphasize the importance of spontaneity and freshness. In the Mishnah, Rabbi Eliezer states definitively that when one makes one's prayer "fixed"—and here he may mean when one says one's prayers by rote—one has not made a (genuine) supplication (Berakhot 4:4). In the Babylonian Talmud, Rabbah and Rav Yosef interpret Rabbi Eliezer as meaning that one should always insert something new into one's prayer (b. Berakhot 29b). In the Jerusalem Talmud, Rabbi Abahu, in the name of Rabbi Elazar, explains Rabbi Eliezer's statement to mean that one should not recite one's prayers as if one were reading an ordinary document (y. Berakhot 4:4). This is taken further, in the same discussion, by Rabbi Aha who says, in the name of Rabbi Yose, that one must add something new each day to one's prayers. The Jerusalem Talmud goes on to report that Ahitofel used to say three new prayers each day,

Rabbi Elazar used to recite a new prayer every day, and Rabbi Abahu used to recite a new blessing every day.

As evidenced in these passages, there is a tension in the rabbinic dialogues between the need for fixed words of prayer and an emphasis on the spontaneous feelings of the individual. The rabbis seem to recognize that the two are not always easily aligned. For myself—and here I part ways with some of the rabbis though not, I think, all of them—to pray *from* the heart and *with* the heart necessarily means not just trying to mean what I say but also trying to say what I mean. And I may not mean—or want to say—the same things every time I pray.[35] (For further discussion of the subject of directing the heart in prayer, see the commentary to **Putting on the Prayer Shawl**, p. 459, and to the *Amidah:* **Sevenfold Prayer for the Sabbath**, p. 469.)

There may well be days that I find I cannot say the **Blessing Before Going to Sleep**. My hope, however, is that there will also be days when the words of this prayer will awaken in me an awareness that was not there before uttering the prayer itself. In an early draft of this blessing, I had written only of *matat hayom*, "the gift of the day," meaning to emphasize the gift of life itself, of having been sustained in life for one more day. It was in a subsequent draft that I added *mat'not hayom*, "the gifts of the day," to increase appreciation of the day's *particular* pleasures and rewards. In attempting to awaken attention to the small, ordinary gifts of daily living, this prayer seeks to make the gift of gratitude—in the end, one of the greatest gifts one can give to oneself—more readily available to the heart.

Daily Psalms   שִׁיר שֶׁל יוֹם
(pages 31–39)

In Jewish liturgical time, the Sabbath is clearly the crown of the week, but the weekdays do not go undistinguished. Each is assigned a biblical psalm to be read at the close of the daily morning service: Sunday, Psalm 24; Monday, Psalm 48; Tuesday, Psalm 82; Wednesday, Psalms 94 and 95:1–3; Thursday, Psalm 81; and Friday, Psalm 93. Known as *shir shel yom*, "song of the day," the daily psalm was an early inclusion in the liturgy: according to the Mishnah (Tamid 7:4), it was once recited by the Levites in the Temple. The themes of the selection are diverse, encompassing God's creation of the universe and sovereignty over it; God's establishment of a holy center in Jerusalem; appeals to the wicked to change their ways; appeals to God to right injustice on earth, punish evil, and redeem the innocent; God's deliverance of Israel from Pharaoh's Egypt and Israel's dereliction; and God's eternal majesty.

I am struck by the beauty of giving each of the weekdays its own distinct piece of liturgy; this assignation at once affirms the diversity and the potential sacredness of everyday life. Indeed, the daily psalm can serve as a metaphor for the uniqueness of all experience. The section in THE DAILY CYCLE entitled **Daily Psalms** is, in part, an attempt to maintain continuity with this ancient part of the liturgy. In creating a new sequence, however, I did not try to parallel the themes of the original biblical selection. Rather, the new psalms are reflections on time, on desire and yearning, and on our deepest connections to the greater whole of life. Intended as an aid to contemplation or meditation, they may be read at any time of the day. No psalm is provided here for Saturday; the **Psalm for the Sabbath** may be found, along with all Sabbath liturgy, in THE WEEKLY CYCLE.

Introductory Recitation for the Daily Psalm   הַקְדָּמָה לְשִׁיר שֶׁל יוֹם
(pages 32–33)

The traditional recitation of the daily psalm is introduced with the line: "Today is the [first, second, etc.] day of the week [literally, "of the Sabbath"], on which the Levites used to say in the Temple." This announcement offers a way to hold one's place in time, specifically focusing on the weekly journey that culminates in the day of rest.

Like the traditional recitation, the new **Introductory Recitation for the Daily Psalm** begins by noting the day, anchoring us in the week. After this, however, it takes a different direction: instead of referring to earlier times, it turns its focus to the present moment.

The Weekly Cycle   מַחֲזוֹר הַשָּׁבוּעַ

Kabbalat Shabbat: Prayer Service Welcoming the Sabbath   קַבָּלַת שַׁבָּת
(pages 53–113)

Though firmly established in Ashkenazic as well as Sephardic traditions, the synagogue service known as *kabbalat shabbat*, literally, "receiving the Sabbath," is in fact not very old; it originated in Safed, Palestine, at the end of the sixteenth century as the creation of a sect of kabbalists (followers of Kabbalah, Jewish mystical tradition).[36] The basis of the service was a passage in the Talmud (b. Shabbat 119a), which reported that certain rabbis welcomed the Sabbath by saying, "Come, let us go out to greet the Sabbath queen" and "Come, bride, come, bride." The kabbalists went out to the fields on Fridays at sunset, reciting these lines along with special prayers and hymns.

The *kabbalat shabbat* service practiced in Ashkenazic synagogues today includes Psalms 95–99 and 29, which praise God as creator and celebrate the wonders of creation, and a song welcoming the Sabbath, which is known by its refrain as *l'khah, dodi*, literally, "go, my beloved." The service also includes Psalm 92, which is known as the psalm for the Sabbath day, Psalm 93, and the *kaddish* prayer, which is said by those in mourning. It is traditionally followed by *ma'ariv* (the evening service). My **Kabbalat Shabbat** takes its basic structure and themes from the traditional *kabbalat shabbat*, adding elements from contemporary synagogue practices.

Opening   פְּתִיחָה
(pages 59–63)

The **Opening** of this new **Kabbalat Shabbat** provides an opportunity to recall one's ancestors, as well as living family and friends, much as women have traditionally done while lighting Sabbath candles in their homes. Thus it begins with a silent meditation, in which the community extends its borders by welcoming into its midst those who are not present. This is followed by the lighting of candles, accompanied by the blessing of **Sabbath Candlelighting** and the **Psalm for Sabbath Candlelighting**.

Sabbath Candlelighting הַדְלָקַת נֵרוֹת שַׁבָּת
(pages 60–61; see also 122–23)

The traditional blessing for Sabbath candlelighting belongs to a category known as *birkhot mitzvah*, "blessings of commandment" (sing. *birkat mitzvah*), which is to say it is a blessing that accompanies an act understood as commanded by God to the people of Israel. This category of blessing contains the formulaic phrase *asher kid'shánu b'mitzvotav v'tzivánu*, "who sanctified us by his commandments and commanded us," following which it specifies the act to be performed. Thus the traditional Sabbath candlelighting blessing reads: *Barukh atah, y-h-v-h elohéynu, mélekh ha'olam, asher kid'shánu b'mitzvotav v'tzivánu l'hadlik neyr shel shabbat*, "Blessed are you, YHVH our God, king of the world, who has sanctified us by his commandments and commanded us to light a Sabbath candle." In traditional practice, the recitation of a blessing of commandment is always followed by the act it specifies, so that it not be "a blessing in vain." Unlike other blessings of commandment, however, the one for candlelighting is said after, rather than before, the act it designates, since its recitation marks the onset of the Sabbath and the lighting of candles is prohibited once the Sabbath has begun.

The category of *mitzvah*, "[divine] commandment," which is central to traditional Jewish life, presents dilemmas for feminist Jews. How does one honor commandment, or feel oneself commanded, without conceptualizing the divine as commander and, hence, reinforcing hierarchical structures of power and authority in the world? For those who understand divinity as immanent in all creation, where is the source of divine commandment found? These questions, which are central to a theology of Judaism, deserve much more extensive treatment than I can engage in here. The following reflections point toward some directions for further discusssion.

Commandment is a concept inextricably linked to human consciousness, specifically, to our capacity for moral understanding. While I believe that the divine inheres in all of creation, I see commandment as applicable to the human species alone. I understand the experience of being commanded as a perception of overarching moral values accompanied by a recognition that these values make demands upon us. Without engaging here in debate about the nature of values—whether their source is external or internal and whether they are properly understood as absolute or as relatively determined—one may allow that the embracing of specific moral values is an act of human will. We acknowledge the authority of certain values and accept the responsibility to act in accordance with them; in this sense, we may say we hear or receive commandment. In its concept of covenant, Judaism emphasizes a reciprocal relationship between God and Israel. It is not enough to be commanded;

one must take the obligation of commandment upon oneself. Thus even from a traditional perspective, the concept of commandment always contains a component of human will, of choice and agency. As a feminist and a Jew, I personally experience being commanded as a sense of clarity about what helps to create a more just and more harmonious world.

In Jewish religious life, however, far more blessings of commandment are provided for ritual acts, such as lighting the Sabbath candles, than for commandments in the domain of *g'milut ḥasadim*, "deeds of lovingkindness," such as visiting the sick or donating to the poor. Although this fact may at first seem surprising, on reflection it is understandable: while ritual acts require a focused awareness in order to have meaning, deeds of lovingkindness—actions performed by one person on behalf of another—do not seem to need a formal blessing in the same way, since *in themselves* they bring blessing into the world.[37] How might one understand commandment then, as I have interpreted it, in the ritual domain?

I suggest that while particular ritual acts may not seem to be commanded in the sense I have just described, they may *stand for* our commitments to live in consonance with our transcendent values. So, for example, as we light the Sabbath candles, we pause to feel our gratitude for the gifts of creation, renewing our commitment to care for those gifts. As we perform the handwashing ritual, we recall the sacrality of our embodiment and renew our promise to treat the body with respect. It may seem like it is asking a lot of our rituals that transcendent meaning be found in each of them—discovered and recovered, from generation to generation—but without this ongoing process of renewal, ritual grows stagnant and empty.

My re-creations of the commandment blessings focus on our experience—and on our awareness of that experience—at the moment when we perform a ritual act that has meaning for us. The imagery of these blessings derives in particular from two biblical passages addressing how we are to approach divine commandment, Deuteronomy 6:4–9 and 11:13–21, which constitute the first two paragraphs of the keynote prayer *sh'ma*, "Hear, O Israel" (see the commentary to the *Sh'ma:* **Declaration of Faith**, pp. 431–36). These passages explicate the command to love God with all one's "heart," *leyv*, and all one's "spirit," *néfesh*; *leyv* and *néfesh* emphasize here the importance of intentionality, of engaging the *whole self*, in performing acts of *mitzvah* (*leyv* is discussed further in the commentary to the **Morning Blessing**, p. 425; discussion of *néfesh* may be found in the commentary to **Handwashing upon Awakening** and **Handwashing Before the Meal**, pp. 427–28). I have adopted these words (in the possessive forms *libéynu*, "our heart," and *nafshéynu*, "our spirit") as the central images of my new commandment blessings.

Thus, the emphasis of the new blessings of commandment is on the human community—on our experience of the sacred *within* the personal or communal self, represented by the terms *libéynu* and *nafshéynu*. Hence the opening verbs in these blessings direct the act of blessing back onto the speaker or speakers. So **Sabbath Candlelighting** reads: *Yitromeym libéynu, / t'shovav nafshéynu, / b'hadlakat neyr shel shabbat*, literally, "May our heart be lifted (or lift itself), / may our spirit be refreshed, / in the lighting of the Sabbath candle." In other blessings of this category, I preserve similar syntax along with one or both of the key terms *leyv* and *néfesh*, but I vary verbs and add images as suggested by context. When appropriate, the blessing is given in a singular rather than communal voice (using the forms *libi*, "my heart," and *nafshi*, "my spirit"). Other re-creations of blessings of commandment in this volume are **Handwashing upon Awakening, Handwashing Before the Meal, Putting on the Prayer Shawl,** and the **Torah Blessings.**

The commandment to light Sabbath candles was assigned to women in the Mishnah (Shabbat 2:6), and it has been generally thought of as a "women's *mitzvah*" since mishnaic times. According to Jewish law, however, candlelighting is incumbent on every household, whether or not women are present. And while historically women lit the candles for the home, in many places today the members of the household perform the ritual together. Although traditionally a part of home observance, in modern times Sabbath candlelighting has been incorporated into communal services as well, particularly among Reform and *ḥavurah*-style communities. Therefore I have included the new blessing in both *Kabbalat Shabbat* and *Kabbalat P'ney Shabbat:* **Home Ritual for Sabbath Eve.**

Psalm for Sabbath Candlelighting מִזְמוֹר לְהַדְלָקַת נֵרוֹת שַׁבָּת
(pages 62–63)

Like the glass that is shattered at the conclusion of a Jewish wedding, reminding us of sorrow at a time of great joy, this poem by the modern Hebrew poet Zelda Mishkovsky (known to her readers simply as Zelda) emphasizes loss and longing at the uplifting moment of the Sabbath's entrance. There is a simple but deep truth in Zelda's poem: the more we feel connected, the more we are open to bereavement. Lighting the Sabbath candles is, for many Jewish women, a special moment of connection to their mothers and grandmothers; for some, it is a link added to a long historical chain. Traditionally, women have offered their own personal prayers for family and loved ones at this time. Thus, at a moment laden with connection to the past, Zelda's poem gives voice to our awareness of life's passing—and to its continuity.

Psalms of Creation מִזְמוֹרֵי הַבְּרִיאָה
(pages 65–97)

In this, the heart of the service, poems of twentieth-century women writing in Hebrew and Yiddish (authors' names appear beneath their poems), along with some of my own English poems (which are unattributed), take the place of the biblical psalms found in the traditional *kabbalat shabbat* (Pss. 95–99; 29), which celebrate the creator and the creation. What the new poems have in common with each other—and what also links them to the biblical psalms—is their focus on the natural world. Unlike the traditional selection of psalms, however, the new poems are primarily concerned with human connections to the rest of nature rather than with the exaltation of a creative force beyond nature.

In introducing poems by Jewish women into the traditional liturgical place of the biblical psalms, I mean to establish a multivocal conversation that affirms continuity with ancient sources even as it shifts the focus away from traditional God-world relationships and toward connections between the species. My aim was also to make a place in the tradition for the voices of Jewish women psalmists, which have not been included in the liturgical canon. To my regret, I was unable to include women's voices from the more distant past because hardly any have been preserved; those few texts that have come down to us are not, for the most part, literary in genre. Similar obstacles stood in the way of including poems by women from Sephardic and other Eastern Jewish cultures. I made an effort to choose poems by women with distinct sensibilities, yet in the end, a thread of sorrow winds through them all. Perhaps this is a truism of nature poetry, perhaps it's just a paradox of our existence: when we are most aware of the beauty surrounding us, we are simultaneously reminded of its—and our—transience.

Greeting the Sabbath לְקְרַאת שַׁבָּת
(pages 99–102)

With song and dance, the Sabbath is welcomed in joy: as the song *l'khah, dodi* is the high point of the traditional *kabbalat shabbat* service, so ***L'khu, Rey'ot V'rey'im: Greeting the Sabbath Bride*** is the climax of this new ***Kabbalat Shabbat***. The moment following ***L'khu, Rey'ot V'rey'im*** is one of silent, attentive listening, signaled in the **Psalm for the Sabbath**. Together, ***L'khu, Rey'ot V'rey'im*** and the **Psalm for the Sabbath** represent complementary aspects of Sabbath experience: exuberant, communal celebration and personal, reflective quietude.

L'khu, Rey'ot V'rey'im: Greeting the Sabbath Bride   לְכוּ, רֵעוֹת וְרֵעִים
(pages 100–101)

Unlike other elements of the **Kabbalat Shabbat** service, **L'khu, Rey'ot V'rey'im: Greeting the Sabbath Bride**, a song welcoming the Sabbath in the figure of a bride, is neither a new creation nor a re-creation of an ancient text. Rather, it is a close adaptation—a shortened and modified version—of the kabbalistic song known as *l'khah, dodi*, written by Rabbi Solomon Alkabetz Halevi (who memorialized his name through an acrostic within the poem) in the mid-sixteenth century. A mystical poem heavily laden with biblical allusions, *l'khah, dodi* has been extremely popular for four centuries and remains so among diverse Jewish communities today, including progressive and feminist communities. In Orthodox synagogues in Israel, where singing is a negligible part of prayer services, *l'khah, dodi* is unique in being the only part of the service that is always sung aloud by the congregation.

Indeed, the singability of *l'khah, dodi* would seem to account in large measure for its appeal, since the meaning of the text is extremely difficult to decipher: one can barely tell who is speaking and to whom. While the refrain is specifically addressed to a male beloved (*dodi*) who is exhorted to greet the "bride," many of the stanzas are addressed to a female, usually assumed to be the Sabbath bride herself. If one tries to read the poem as a unified whole, one finds that the traditional allegory of God as groom and Israel as bride doesn't fit, nor does that of Israel as groom and the Sabbath as bride. In accordance with the kabbalistic symbolism upon which the poem is based, both the male and female figures in the refrain should probably be understood as personifications of the divine: God the male lover and God the bride and queen.[38] Whether or not the text of *l'khah, dodi* is comprehensible to most readers, however, there is no doubt that it has captured Jewish imagination. Today, in particular, many people seem to enjoy the celebration of the feminine implicit in this piece of the liturgy.

A major change in my adaptation, **L'khu, Rey'ot V'rey'im**, occurs in the refrain, which addresses not an individual male beloved but the community as a whole—female friends (*rey'ot*) as well as male friends (*rey'im*). In addition, five of the nine stanzas have been dropped, and the remaining four have been modified so as to replace male images with references to the Shekhinah, divine presence (for explanation of the term "Shekhinah," see the commentary to **Restoring Shekhinah, Reclaiming Home**, on p. 474, and to the **Sh'ma: Declaration of Faith**, on p. 433). Beyond these alterations, however, I have made no attempt to update or rework the poem; I have even retained the standard form of the original vocalization, despite its inconsistencies. The markedly artificial style and archaic diction of **L'khu, Rey'ot V'rey'im** distinguish it significantly from the other Hebrew prayers and blessings in this book; these characteristics also make the poem difficult to render into a new English version suitable for singing. For purposes of explication, a near-literal English translation is provided opposite the Hebrew.

Psalm for the Sabbath מִזְמוֹר שִׁיר לְיוֹם הַשַּׁבָּת
(page 102; see also 162)

In the traditional liturgy, Psalm 92 is known as the psalm for the Sabbath day and is recited during both *kabbalat shabbat* and the Sabbath morning service. Originally sung by the Levites in the Temple during the Sabbath sacrificial offering, its main subject is the greatness of God's creations, and its metaphors are drawn from the natural world. "The righteous," proclaims the psalmist, "will flourish like the date palm, like the cedar in Lebanon" (v. 13).

In both **Kabbalat Shabbat** and the **Shaḥarit: Morning Service for the Sabbath** found in this book, a contemplative poem replaces Psalm 92. Focusing on a state of inner quiet and attentiveness, it is intended to awaken our senses to creation within us and around us.

Closing Prayers סִיּוּם
(pages 103–113)

All traditional synagogue services conclude with a recitation of the *kaddish*; most services today also have closing songs. The **Closing Prayers** of this new **Kabbalat Shabbat** include the **Kaddish: Mourners' Prayer** and the **Closing Blessing**. These offerings are also found (along with certain additions) in the **Closing Prayers** of the **Shaḥarit: Morning Service for the Sabbath.**

Kaddish: Mourners' Prayer קַדִּישׁ
(pages 105–9; see also 291–95)

The traditional mourners' prayer, known as the *kaddish*, is an Aramaic hymn praising God's name; it begins with the words *Yitgadal v'yitkadash sh'meyh raba*, "May his great name be magnified and sanctified." Not a dirge but a chant of affirmation, the *kaddish* provides a celebration of continuity in the face of rupture and loss. Traditionally, Jews recite the *kaddish* on a daily basis for eleven months after the death of a parent, child, or spouse; thereafter, it is recited on the anniversary of the death. The *kaddish* is included in every traditional synagogue service, with mourners reciting it while the congregation listens and says "amen"; in many Reform congregations today, it is said in unison by all.

Because one aim of this book is to encourage a community of worshipers that is diverse and inclusive, and a related goal is to increase the names by which we evoke and invoke divinity, I have chosen a poem of naming as the basis of my new *Kaddish:* **Mourners' Prayer.** *L'khol B'riyah Yeysh Sheym*, literally, "each creature has a name," rendered in the English version as *Each of Us Has a Name*, is adapted from the poem by Zelda *L'khol Ish Yeysh Sheym*, literally, "each man (or person) has a name."

Zelda's poem, which takes the form of a list of different aspects of our lives that give us our names, appears to be an elaboration on a rabbinic theme. In the midrash (Ecclesiastes Rabbah 7:1), the rabbis teach that "a person is called by three names: one that his father and his mother call him by, one that others call him by, and one that he is called in the book telling the story of his creation." The Midrash Tanḥuma (Parashat Vayak'heyl) reads, "One finds three names by which a person is called: one that his father and his mother call him by, one that people call him by, and one that he acquires for himself. The best of all is that which he acquires for himself."

In Hebrew (as in English), the word *sheym* means not just "name" but "identity" or "reputation"; the Bible proclaims "a good name is better than fine oil" (Eccl. 7:1). Names represent the variety of ways in which we are known to ourselves and to each other. Zelda's poem pays tribute to the multifaceted nature of the individual life and to the ways in which a life accrues meaning over time through its connections to others. Hence this poem can serve as an effective memorial to one whose life has ended; and indeed, it is widely used as a supplementary reading in memorial services in Israel.

I have made one significant change in my adaptation of Zelda's poem. Wherever the word *ish*, "man," appears (in the title and in the opening line of each stanza), I have substituted the word *b'riyah*, "creature." Although *ish* is used by some Hebrew speakers to mean "person" or "individual," it is in fact heavily weighted with gender; distinct from the word *ishah*, which means "woman," it is not only grammatically masculine but masculine in meaning. (Despite this, it seems reasonable to assume that Zelda intended *ish* to be read in her poem more inclusively, to mean "individual.") Other Hebrew words meaning "person" (such as *adam*, the word found in the two passages of midrash quoted above) are perhaps somewhat less heavily masculine in meaning; they are all, nonetheless, gender-marked. Therefore I have replaced *ish* with *b'riyah*, a grammatically feminine noun that is semantically gender-neutral (making the necessary grammatical adjustments throughout the rest of the poem). While this substitution clearly alters the poem's meaning, it does so in a way that expands rather than constricts. The shift from "person" to "creature" is, I would suggest, particularly relevant to this new liturgical context: we are perhaps never more aware of our "creatureliness"—the transience and mortality that we share with all of creation—than at times of death.

Note that *Each of Us Has a Name* also appears in the third section of the **Amidah: Sevenfold Prayer for the Sabbath**. See the commentary to **Hallowing Our Namings** (p. 473).

Closing Blessing   בִּרְכַּת סִיּוּם
(pages 111–13; see also 297–99)

The **Closing Blessing** for **Kabbalat Shabbat** and for the **Shaḥarit: Morning Service for the Sabbath** is based on the final blessing of the traditional Sabbath morning *amidah* prayer, which petitions: *Sim shalom, tovah uvrakhah, ḥeyn vaḥésed v'raḥamim aléynu v'al kol yisra'eyl amékha*, "Bestow peace, goodness and blessing, graciousness and lovingkindness and compassion upon us and upon all Israel, your people." The new prayer expresses the wish that these blessings will flow *among* us and all communities of Israel, and *among* all peoples of the world. The shift from "upon" to "among" emphasizes the need for our own active participation in the process of generating peace, and turns the prayer from a petition into a statement of hope and commitment.

Kabbalat P'ney Shabbat: Home Ritual Welcoming the Sabbath
קַבָּלַת פְּנֵי שַׁבָּת
(pages 115–35)

Judaism has traditionally attached names to its synagogue services but not to the sequences of blessings and songs that make up home ritual. In the process of compiling the liturgy for this book, it occurred to me that giving a name to home ritual for Sabbath eve would be a step in the direction of honoring the home as ritual domain—a domain that historically has been associated with women. The name **Kabbalat P'ney Shabbat**—like the name **Kabbalat Shabbat**, borrowed from the traditional term for one of the synagogue services—means "welcoming the Sabbath." Both names are based on an idiom of rabbinic origin, *l'kabeyl panim*, literally, "to receive [the] face [of]," which means "to greet" or "to welcome." Although I have not seen the phrase *kabbalat p'ney shabbat* (literally, "receiving the face of the Sabbath") used this way before, it is not an entirely original invention; it echoes a well-known phrase from the refrain of the kabbalistic hymn *l'khah, dodi*: *L'khah, dodi, likrat* kalah; p'ney shabbat n'kab'lah, literally, "Let us go, beloved, to greet the bride; we shall receive the face of the Sabbath." (See **L'khu, Rey'ot V'rey'im** on pp. 100–101 and the commentary to it on p. 445.)

Like the traditional series of blessings and songs that usher the Sabbath into the home, my **Kabbalat P'ney Shabbat** centers around the meal. In accordance with a talmudic provision (b. Shabbat 117b), the Sabbath is traditionally celebrated with three meals, referred to as s'udot, "feasts" (sing. s'udah). The first is dinner on Sabbath eve; the second is the main meal of the Sabbath day, which takes place after the morning prayers; the third occurs toward the end of the Sabbath day, in the twilight time between the afternoon and evening prayers. At these meals, two ḥalot (Sabbath breads) are customarily served, in commemoration of the léḥem mishneh, the double portion of manna gathered on the sixth day of the week by the children of Israel when they were in the desert (Exod. 16:22); the double provision made it possible for the Israelites to rest rather than gather food on the Sabbath. It is also customary to sing Sabbath songs, called z'mirot, during the meals; these songs vary widely from community to community and new ones are continually being introduced. The liturgy provided in **Kabbalat P'ney Shabbat** includes the three blessings for meals (also found in the other cycles of this book) along with blessings and other offerings that are special for the Sabbath.

Opening Psalm   מִזְמוֹר פְּתִיחָה
(page 121)

Modern Jews who do not consider themselves bound by the proscriptions of Jewish law face the challenge of choosing for themselves those practices, and perhaps those restraints, that will make the Sabbath day unique. (In some sense, everyone does this: even the most strict Sabbath observers are choosing, at some level, which authorities and which customs to follow.) The poem *Will*, to be read before Sabbath candlelighting, focuses on acts of self-imposed disengagement from routine, acts at once real and symbolic that locate us in a historical continuum.

Sabbath Candlelighting   הַדְלָקַת נֵרוֹת שַׁבָּת
(pages 122–23)

See pp. 441–43.

Blessing of the Children   בִּרְכַּת יַלְדָּה וָיֶלֶד
(pages 124–25; see also 360–61)

The custom of blessing one's children on the eve of the Sabbath and holidays is an especially poignant Jewish ritual, but the content of the traditional blessing is rather puzzling. Based on words said by Jacob to his grandsons in Genesis 48:20, it asks God to make the male child like Ephraim and Menasheh; an adaptation for girls asks that they be like the foremothers Sarah, Rebecca, Rachel, and Leah. Why Ephraim and Menasheh, one cannot help but wonder—indeed, why any *particular* ancestors at all? In its specificity, this blessing seems restrictive rather than expansive: it doesn't open out to the range of possibility and promise that ought to characterize youth.

I am reminded, in this context, of the famous Hassidic story about the righteous Rabbi Zusya. One day his disciples found him weeping and they asked him why. Rabbi Zusya explained that he trembled at the thought of being asked at the end of his life, as he approached the gates of heaven, not the question "Zusya, why were you not Moses?" but "Zusya, why were you not Zusya?" It doesn't seem from this story that Zusya would have been at peace having lived the life of Ephraim or Menasheh—and why should we expect that he would?

Indeed, why should we wish for a child to be anything other than her or his best self? Not living one's own life—not being true to the unique configuration of gifts and potential that nourish the self from within—is a tragedy. Yet letting a child be herself, himself—letting go of expectations that do not emerge from the reality of who the child is—is one of the hardest lessons parents have to learn. So once a week, at the onset of the Sabbath just after lighting the Sabbath candles, I remind myself gently, as I kiss my son's hair, what it is I really want for him. "Abraham Gilead," I say, "be who you are, *heyeyh asher tihyeh*." The Hebrew words deliberately echo the biblical voice of divinity announcing (in Exod. 3:14) *ehyeh asher ehyeh*, "I am that I am," which I understand as the ultimate expression—the very model—of authentic being.

The traditional ritual closes with a recitation of the priestly blessing (Num. 6:24–26): "May God bless you and keep you; may God shine his face on you and be gracious to you; may God turn his face to you and give you peace." The new ritual closes by blessing the child directly with these words: *vahayi b'rukhah / ba'asher tihyi* [for a girl] or *veheyeyh barukh / ba'asher tihyeh* [for a boy], literally, "and may you be blessed / in what you are."

The purpose of this new blessing is twofold: to provide affirmation for the child and to foster awareness in the giver of the blessing. It was not my intention to encapsulate in this blessing the complex totality of being a parent. Rather, I saw it as a spur to a particular kind of knowledge at a particular moment in time, that pause that occurs at the onset of the Sabbath during which we let go of strivings and take note of the world's abiding gifts. In this framework of appreciation on Sabbath eve, as we celebrate the whole of creation, we pay special attention to the children in our midst, thankful for their being, accepting of who they are, hopeful that they will blossom into their best selves.

A personal postscript: Honesty prods me to confess that sometimes it is a challenge to capture this ideal state of acceptance, even in the conducive setting of Sabbath eve. I recall in particular a time when my son, not quite three, was still very much in the throes of naysaying characteristic of his age. As I bent over his head and whispered the words that were by then familiar to him, "Abraham Gilead, be who you are," he bellowed back at me, "I don't want to!" "All right, then," I said, with as much patience as I could muster, "be who you want to be."

Blessing the Beloved   בִּרְכַּת אֲהוּבוֹת וַאֲהוּבִים
(pages 126–27)

Following the blessing of the children on Sabbath eve, it has become customary to recite Proverbs 31:10–31, a hymn known as *éyshet-ḥáyil*, "a woman of valor," which sings the praises of the ideal mother and wife. Originally introduced on Sabbath eve by the kabbalists, who recited it as a wedding song to the Shekhinah, *éyshet-ḥáyil* has come to be recited in traditional homes as a tribute to the wife and mother of the family.

While the intent behind this recitation may be loving, many Jewish women today find it patronizing. Not only does *éyshet-ḥáyil* present an idealized portrait of womanhood that no real woman could possibly live up to, it suggests that a woman's worth lies essentially in her value to others—specifically, her husband and children. And yet the underlying idea of honoring one's partner seems worth preserving: just as we bless our children on the eve of the Sabbath, it seems fitting that we should pause to appreciate others with whom we share our lives, in particular, life partners and intimate friends. For this purpose I offer three Hebrew dialogues, for same-sex and opposite-sex couples, adapted from the Song of Songs 1:15–16 and 7:7. The only collection of love poetry in the Bible, the Song of Songs has long been associated with the Sabbath, particularly among Sephardic communities, many of whom chant it in its entirety on Sabbath eve. This unique biblical book, with its lyric celebration of eros, is a fitting expression of the sensual pleasure that tradition especially encourages on the Sabbath. It is also an inspiring portrayal of mutuality in relationships. The lovers in the Song of Songs declare affection, invite each other to lovemaking, and share compliments and praise using language that is entirely free of sexual stereotyping. Women and men both take initiative, and no matter who initiates a particular encounter (in the dialogue on which **Blessing the Beloved** is based, it happens to be the male who speaks first), the relationship grows from a to-and-fro exchange and is never based on domination and subordination. For people in couples, the Song of Songs offers a model of intimacy and reciprocity that is particularly fitting for the Sabbath—a day set aside for appreciation, rather than utilization, of the world's gifts.[39]

Of course, not everyone is part of a couple, and even members of a couple are not always in each other's company. By choice or by chance, many of us find ourselves without partners, at least some of the time, on Sabbath eves. For those who are celebrating the Sabbath alone, the Sabbath itself may be embraced as a faithful friend who accompanies one in self-restoration. This concept is not a purely modern one: it has roots in the early midrash proposing that the people of Israel is the Sabbath's rightful partner, compensating the Sabbath for not having been given a mate in creation (Genesis Rabbah 11:9). Over the centuries, poets have written many paeans to the Sabbath day, some of which portray it as a beloved or a longed-for friend (the tenth-century Hebrew poet Yehudah Halevi has written magnificently on this subject). The figure of the Sabbath bride depicted in the kabbalistic poem *l'khah, dodi*—and re-created in my **Kabbalat Shabbat** ceremony as **L'khu, Rey'ot V'rey'im: Greeting the Sabbath Bride**—is another embodiment of this idea. Thus **L'khu, Rey'ot V'rey'im** is another possible reading for this moment in the **Kabbalat P'ney Shabbat** ritual.

Sanctification over Wine for Sabbath Eve   קִדּוּשׁ לְלֵיל שַׁבָּת
(pages 128–29)

Sanctification over Wine for Sabbath Day   קִדּוּשׁ לְיוֹם שַׁבָּת
(pages 300–301)

The *kiddush*, literally, "sanctification," is a category of blessings that mark holy days, including the Sabbath and the major festivals, as well as special occasions such as weddings and baby namings. Traditionally recited over wine, which is referred to in the blessings as "the fruit of the vine," the *kiddush* gives embodiment to the psalmist's claim, "Wine gladdens the human heart" (Ps. 104:15).

The *kiddush* for the Sabbath was originally one of two main liturgical events that took place in the home, the other being the *havdalah* ritual that ends the Sabbath. Sabbath *kiddush* and *havdalah* are both ancient, ascribed by the rabbis in the Talmud (b. Berakhot 33a) to the Men of the Great Assembly (a legendary body once assumed to be in existence from the end of the era of the prophets in the fifth century B.C.E. until the beginning of the rabbinic period in the second century B.C.E.).[40] The wording of these prayers was not fixed, however, until talmudic times, and it was during this period that both the *kiddush* and the *havdalah* were transferred to the synagogue. Today, the *kiddush* for Sabbath eve is recited in the home as part of the Sabbath meal; in Ashkenazic communities outside of Israel, it is also recited in the synagogue at the conclusion of the evening service. The *kiddush* for Sabbath day is recited in the home at the start of the midday meal and sometimes in the synagogue after morning services.

The texts of the different sanctifications vary according to the occasion being marked. The traditional text of the *kiddush* for Sabbath eve begins with a biblical quotation describing the completion of the creation of the world (Gen. 1:31b–2:3). This is followed by the standard blessing over wine and then by another longer blessing that praises God for sanctifying Israel with commandments, for giving the Sabbath to Israel with love, for choosing the people of Israel from all nations, and for sanctifying the Sabbath.

On Sabbath day, the text of the *kiddush* opens with a different biblical passage (Exod. 31:16–17), which emphasizes the Sabbath as the covenant between God and Israel. This citation is followed by the line "Therefore God blessed the Sabbath day and sanctified it" (Exod. 20:11), after which the blessing over wine is said. (In some traditions, this second citation is longer, consisting of Exod. 20:8–11, which contains the commandment to "remember the Sabbath day to hallow it.") In comparison with the *kiddush* for Sabbath eve, the *kiddush* for Sabbath day is noticeably brief, despite its Aramaic name, *kiddusha raba*, literally, "the great sanctification."

The biblical passages recited at the beginning of each *kiddush*, on Sabbath eve and on Sabbath day, emphasize the major themes associated with those parts of the Sabbath: creation on Sabbath eve, revelation (the giving of the covenant) on Sabbath day. However, in the *kiddush* for Sabbath eve, the themes of creation and revelation are both referred to in a pair of key phrases: *zikaron l'ma'aseyh v'reyshit*, "in remembrance of the creation," which is to say, the creation story told at the beginning of the book of Genesis, and *zéykher litzi'at mitzráyim*, "in commemoration of the exodus from Egypt," a reference to the central event of Israel's history, the liberation from slavery, which precedes the revelation of Torah on Mount Sinai. The words *zikaron* and *zéykher* are essentially synonyms, deriving from the root *z-kh-r*, meaning "recall" or "remember," and they are best understood here as "calling to mind" (these terms are also related to the verb *tizkor*, found in my **Handwashing upon Awakening** and **Handwashing Before the Meal** and discussed in the commentary to those blessings, on p. 427). This double commemoration reflects the two variant texts of the commandment to observe the Sabbath, found in Exodus 20:8–11 and Deuteronomy 5:12–15. In the former, Israel is told to "remember" the Sabbath day because "six days God made the heavens and the earth and the sea and all that is in them, and he rested on the seventh day";

in the latter, the Israelite is enjoined to "keep" the Sabbath and to "remember that you were a slave in the land of Egypt and God brought you out of there with a strong hand and an outstretched arm." Thus the traditional sanctification for Sabbath eve is not only longer than that for Sabbath day, it is also thematically richer, calling to mind key events of myth and history as it juxtaposes the story of the universe with the story of Israel.

In my re-creations, I have reproduced this juxtaposition in both sanctifications, for Sabbath eve and Sabbath day, distinguishing between the two occasions only in the introductory biblical citations, which are excerpted from the citations in the traditional sanctifications. In the **Sanctification over Wine for Sabbath Day**, I have made a small adaptation to the excerpt from the biblical citation, changing *V'sham'ru v'ney-yisra'eyl et-hashabbat*, literally, "The sons of Israel shall keep the Sabbath," to *V'sham'ru veyt-yisra'eyl et-hashabbat*, literally, "The house of Israel shall keep the Sabbath" ("house of Israel" is a common biblical term meaning "people of Israel"). The text of the blessing *per se* is identical in both contexts, signaling the equal importance of each part of the Sabbath experience.

This text begins with a re-creation of the traditional blessing over wine, which reads: *Barukh atah, y-h-v-h elohéynu, mélekh ha'olam, borey p'ri hagáfen*, literally, "Blessed are you, YHVH our God, king of the world, who creates the fruit of the vine." Because this moment is intended to acknowledge the divine as provider or nurturer, I have reprised here the theological metaphor *eyn haḥayim*, "wellspring (or fountain, or source) of life," found in my **Blessing Before the Meal** and **Blessing After the Meal**. This metaphor is discussed in the commentary to the **Blessing Before the Meal** (p. 429), as well as in the Author's Preface (pp. xvi–xviii).

I have re-created the second half of the traditional blessing over wine by altering its key verb. In place of *borey*, "create," which refers specifically to divine creation—a concept explained by the rabbis as the making of *yeysh mey'áyin*, "something from nothing"—I have substituted the word *matzmiḥat*. *Matzmiḥat* is the construct participle, grammatically feminine form, of the verb *hitzmí'aḥ*, which means "brings plants from the earth" and which is used metaphorically to mean "causes (or enables) to grow (or to flourish)." In biblical and liturgical contexts the verb *hitzmí'aḥ* is also used metaphorically in various other ways (to mean "bring about," "reveal," "renew," etc.). The following passage provides examples of both literal and figurative usages of this word: *Ki kha'aretz totzi tzimḥah, ukhganah zeyru'ehah tatzmí'aḥ, keyn adonay y-h-v-h yatzmí'aḥ tz'dakah uthilah néged kolhagoyim*, literally, "For as the earth brings forth its growth, and as the garden causes the things that are sown in it to grow, so the Lord YHVH will cause righteousness and praise to flourish before the nations" (Isa. 61:11).[41] Another example of metaphorical usage may be found in the first section of the traditional *amidah* prayer, which contains the phrase *matzmí'aḥ y'shu'ah*, "who causes salvation to flourish," as an attribution of God. In my blessing, I return to the word's original association with growth from the earth to acknowledge the source of all creation as that which nurtures the vine into fruition: *N'vareykh et eyn haḥayim / matzmiḥat p'ri hagéfen*, literally, "Let us bless the source of life / that causes (or enables) the fruit of the vine to grow (or to flourish)."

Just as the word *matzmiḥat* has symbolic resonance, the phrase *p'ri hagéfen*, "fruit of the vine," may be thought of as extending beyond its literal denoting of the grape to suggest fruition in other realms of our lives. The metaphor of the vine as community is made explicit in the **Meditation for the Sanctification over Wine for Rosh Hodesh** (found on p. 363, commentary on p. 499).

This first part of the blessing is followed by the lines *unkadeysh et yom hash'vi'i— / yom hashabbat— / zikaron l'ma'aseyh v'reyshit / ki hu yom t'ḥilah / l'mikra'ey kódesh / zéykher litzi'at mitzráyim*, literally, "and let us sanctify the seventh day— / the Sabbath day— / in remembrance of the creation / for it is the first / among holy days / that commemorate the exodus from Egypt." As in the traditional sanctification for Sabbath eve, the phrases *zikaron l'ma'aseyh v'reyshit* and *zéykher litzi'at mitzráyim* are joined by the words *ki hu yom t'ḥilah l'mikra'ey kódesh*, "for it is the first among holy days," a reference to Leviticus 23, in which the Sabbath is named first in a list of holy days.

Perhaps the most noticeable theological shift in these new sanctification blessings is their appropriation of the activity of sanctification from the realm of the divine into human hands. Like the other sanctifications in this book (the **Sanctification over Wine for the Week** and the three variations of the **Sanctification over Wine for Rosh Hodesh**), these blessings all make a statement beginning with the word *unkadeysh*, literally, "and let us sanctify (or hallow)." Here the phrase is *unkadeysh et yom hashabbat*, literally, "and let us sanctify the Sabbath day." In contrast, the traditional sanctification for Sabbath eve praises God for sanctifying the Sabbath. Though the declaration in the new blessing may at first seem daring, it is, I believe, merely honest. If sanctification means finding what is holy in a context or a situation, is this not fundamentally a human act? While we are not the only species that participates in divinity, we are, I believe, the only species capable of appreciating and giving meaning to the category of sanctification. If one believes that divinity inheres in all creation, then hallowing is the act of recognizing divinity wherever it resides, the act of acknowledging the sacred and making a place for it in our lives. This is the charge of humanity; it is we who may choose to sanctify time, we who are capable, through our actions, of hallowing and profaning. To sanctify the Sabbath is to set it apart for ourselves as a time in which creation is treated reverentially rather than instrumentally. The symbolic words of the **Sanctification over Wine for Sabbath Eve** and the **Sanctification over Wine for Sabbath Day** remind us of our acceptance of this charge—our *choice* to remember and keep the Sabbath—and of our broader commitment to the continuation of Jewish civilization.

If we look at the tradition carefully, we may decide that this view is not such a radical departure from rabbinic teaching after all. In the fourth blessing of the traditional *amidah* prayer, the blessing of *k'dushat hayom*, "sanctification of the day," we find the words *am m'kad'shey sh'vi'i*, "a people that sanctifies the Sabbath." And in the midrash (Exodus Rabbah 15:24), the rabbis discuss how Rosh Hodesh gets its sanctity, and they answer that it gets it from the people of Israel: "If Israel does not sanctify it [Rosh Hodesh], it has no sanctity at all. And do not be surprised by this: for The-Holy-One-Blessed-Be-He sanctified Israel, as it is said, 'You shall be holy to me, for I, God, am holy' (Lev. 20:26). And since they are sanctified to God, therefore whatever they sanctify is sanctified." Of course, the rabbis make explicit that the original source of holiness is "The-Holy-One-Blessed-Be-He," who sets Israel apart from other nations; thus holiness is transferred by a chain of command, as it were. But I, too, believe that the source of sanctity is the divine and that sanctification takes place in a kind of chain—a lateral chain of interconnections. By virtue of our participation in the wholeness and holiness of creation, by dint of our unique capacities as human beings within that whole, and by virtue of our choice to exercise those capabilities in transmitting and creating the culture of Israel, we come to sanctify the Sabbath, the holidays, and other aspects of Jewish liturgical time as well as moments in our daily lives.

Handwashing Before the Meal   נְטִילַת יָדַיִם לִפְנֵי הָאֲרוּחָה
(pages 130–31)

See pp. 426–28.

Blessing Before the Meal   הַמּוֹצִיאָה
(pages 132–33)

See pp. 428–30.

Blessing After the Meal   בִּרְכַּת הַמָּזוֹן
(pages 134–35)

See pp. 430–31.

Shaḥarit: Morning Service for the Sabbath שַׁחֲרִית לְשַׁבָּת
(pages 139–299)

The traditional morning service, which is called *shaḥarit* (from the word meaning "dawn"), contains the following sections: *birkhot hashaḥar*, "blessings of the dawn"; *p'sukey d'zimrah*, "verses of song"; *k'ri'at sh'ma uvirkhotéha*, "recitation of the *sh'ma* and its blessings"; *amidah*, "[the prayer said while] standing"; and prayers following the *amidah*. On the Sabbath and holidays, various expansions and changes occur. After the *amidah*, the Torah is read and special blessings are recited. Supplicatory prayers that form part of the last section of the daily service are not said, but the prayer known as *aléynu* (literally, "it is upon us") and various closing psalms and songs are included. In Orthodox and most Conservative congregations, a *musaf* (literally, "addition," referring to a supplementary service based on the ancient sacrifices at the Temple) is recited before *aléynu*. The *kaddish* (in Aramaic, "sanctification," referring to a prayer sanctifying God's name) is recited at several points in the service, at least once in a version specifically for mourners. The Reform and Reconstructionist movements have made many adaptations to this basic structure, as have *havurah*-style and Jewish renewal communities. But one should recognize that even the Orthodox version of the service has not always had the form it takes today. The original *shaḥarit* service was much shorter than today's version, and many of the customs regarding participation and leadership have also changed over time. Today's alterations and innovations of text and practice may rightly be viewed as part of a larger historical continuum. My **Shaḥarit**, while innovative in content, parallels quite closely the structure and themes of the traditional *shaḥarit*.

Opening Blessings and Songs בִּרְכוֹת הַשַּׁחַר וּפְסוּקֵי זִמְרָה
(pages 151–62)

This opening section of the new **Shaḥarit** service is based on the first two sections of the traditional *shaḥarit*: *birkhot hashaḥar*, "blessings of the dawn," and *p'sukey d'zimrah*, "verses of song." Both of these sections were relatively late inclusions in the service. *Birkhot hashaḥar* was originally said not in the synagogue but at home as a preparation for public prayer; the whole of it did not find a place in the synagogue until the ninth century. A compilation of various blessings along with texts for study, *birkhot hashaḥar* contains within it a sequence of blessings, itself referred to by the term *birkhot hashaḥar*, that mirrors the activities of rising in the morning. This sequence, which is also discussed in the introduction to THE DAILY CYCLE (p. 5), has its source in the Talmud (b. Berakhot 60b), where the intention is only to encourage an attitude of daily thankfulness, not to prescribe fixed prayers.

P'sukey d'zimrah is a compilation of prayers and songs, the core of which is a sequence of six biblical poems, Psalms 145–150 (Ps. 145 is prefaced by Pss. 84:5 and 114:15; Ps. 145 concludes with an additional verse, Ps. 115:18). Focusing on the works of the creator, with praise as the dominant theme, all of these psalms begin with a form of the word *haleyl*, which means "praise." On the Sabbath, supplemental psalms and prayers are added to this section of the service. Among the additions are Psalm 92 (psalm for the Sabbath day) and the prayer known as *nishmat kol ḥay*, "the breath of all that lives."

I have distilled the themes of the original *birkhot hashaḥar* sequence into a single blessing, the **Morning Blessing**, which is included in THE DAILY CYCLE as well as in the *Shaḥarit:* **Morning Service for the Sabbath**. In the *Shaḥarit*, it is preceded by **Putting on the Prayer Shawl** and followed by **How Good the Dwellings**. These three offerings correspond to the first part of the traditional *shaḥarit* service, *birkhot hashaḥar*. They are followed, in this new *Shaḥarit*, by *Hal'lu:* **Praise, The Breath of All Life**, and the **Psalm for the Sabbath**, which correspond to the second part of the traditional service, *p'sukey d'zimrah*.

Note that instead of the Aramaic phrase *p'sukey d'zimrah*, I have used the Hebrew equivalent, *p'sukey zimrah*, in my Hebrew title for this section of the service.

Putting on the Prayer Shawl   עֲטִיפַת טַלִּית
(pages 152–53)

It is customary to wear a *tallit* (prayer shawl) for morning prayer, and tradition mandates a blessing of commandment to be recited when one puts it on. **Putting on the Prayer Shawl** is based on the traditional ritual for donning the *tallit*, which usually includes the recitation of preparatory and concluding lines before and after the recitation of the actual blessing. In one tradition, the opening lines include the following statement of intention: *Hin'ni mit'ateyf b'tallit shel tzitzit k'dey l'kayeym mitzvat bor'i*, "Here I envelop myself in a prayer shawl of fringes in order to fulfill the commandment of my creator"; this is followed by a citation of the biblical source of this commandment (Num. 15:38).

My new ritual, too, opens with a statement of intention: *Hin'ni mit'atéfet* [fem.] (or *mit'ateyf* [masc.]) / *b'tallit shel tzitzit* / *k'dey lizkor v'lishmor* / *et masóret hadorot* / *ukhdey l'khaveyn et libi*, literally, "Here I envelop myself / in a fringed garment / in order to recall and to preserve / the tradition of the generations / and in order to direct my heart." In the English version, this statement is compressed: "Recalling the generations, / I wrap myself / in the *tallit*." In place of a reference to the biblical source of the commandment, the new ritual refers to the historical transmission of the ritual and to the role it may play in one's personal prayer.

L'khaveyn et libi, "to direct my heart," is the first-person form of an expression that appears repeatedly in talmudic literature (for example, throughout b. Berakhot chaps. 2, 4, 5). By "directing the heart" in prayer, the rabbis seem to mean focusing one's attention on the words one is saying and also directing those words to God. The related concept of *kavanah*, "intention" or "attention" (in prayer), is central in talmudic thought; it is also the basis of later discussion, especially in kabbalistic and Hassidic writing, where it accrues further meaning.[42] In general, "directing the heart" may be thought of as an orientation or stance toward worship, and I think it is one that has not outlived either its usefulness or its potential for new meaning.

For me, "directing the heart" is less about the willed or deliberate focusing of awareness than about the alignment of thought and feeling. It has to do with authenticity, by which I mean both honesty and sincerity. I cannot pray with my heart if the words I am saying do not ring with truth for me; at the same time, sometimes all words are wrong, and one must allow the heart to speak with silence. In one sense, the whole of this book is my attempt to provide words that will help the head to align with the heart (to borrow the dualistic language of our culture, in which we are sometimes trapped). It is, in other words, an attempt to let the *whole self* speak and to help the many selves of the community to speak together. I have chosen to bring this posture, this intentionality, to the foreground here by putting the words *l'khaveyn et libi* into the context of a blessing, **Putting on the Prayer Shawl**—the first blessing uttered in the **Shaḥarit** service, the one that begins the individual's preparation for the communal service that is to come. (I have also adopted the term for one of my new liturgical genres, the meditation, or *kavanat haleyv*, "intention [or attention, or direction] of the heart," which is discussed in the commentary to the **Amidah: Sevenfold Prayer for the Sabbath**, p. 469.)

The Hebrew phrase *masóret hadorot*, "the tradition of the generations," and the English phrase "recalling the generations" appear also in **Recalling Our Ancestors, Remembering Our Lives** (the first section of the new **Amidah** prayer, found on pp. 179–91), as does a form of the word *lizkor*, "to recall" (the form given there is *nizkor*, "let us recall"). Thus **Putting on the Prayer Shawl** is deliberately linked to the portion of the service that honors ancestry and history. Another form of the verb *lizkor* (*tizkor*, "may it recall") appears in **Handwashing upon Awakening** and in **Handwashing Before the Meal**, and its meaning is discussed in the commentary to those blessings (p. 427).

Putting on the Prayer Shawl continues with the following blessing: *Yipataḥ libi, / tizdakeykh nafshi, / b'hit'at'fi batallit*, literally, "May my heart be opened, / may my spirit become clear, / as I envelop myself in the *tallit*." The Hebrew lines follow the syntactic pattern of my other re-creations of commandment blessings, such as **Sabbath Candlelighting** (*Yitromeym libéynu, / t'shovav nafshéynu, / b'hadlakat neyr shel shabbat*, literally, "May our heart be lifted, / may our spirit be refreshed, / in the lighting of the Sabbath candle"). In **Putting on the Prayer Shawl**, as in **Sabbath Candlelighting**, sacrality is embedded in human action; in the case of **Putting on the Prayer Shawl**, the act is individual and private, and therefore the blessing is in the first-person singular. The form of the blessing and the key terms *leyv*, "heart," and *néfesh*, "spirit," are discussed in the commentary to **Sabbath Candlelighting** (pp. 442–43).

Morning Blessing   בִּרְכַּת הַשַּׁחַר
(pages 154–55)

This blessing, which appears also in THE DAILY CYCLE where its context is a private one, becomes part of the transition leading from individual to communal prayer in the *Shaharit* service. Its placement in both THE DAILY CYCLE and THE WEEKLY CYCLE parallels the placement of the *birkhot hasháhar* sequence in both the daily and Sabbath services of the traditional liturgy. However, its intended use here as a *private* prayer on the weekdays and as part of the *public* service on the Sabbath is different from current usage of the traditional *birkhot hasháhar*, representing instead the historical stages of the *birkhot hasháhar* sequence, which began as private devotions and ultimately became part of the synagogue service. Commentary to the **Morning Blessing** may be found on pp. 424–26.

How Good the Dwellings   מַה־טֹּבוּ מִשְׁכְּנוֹתֶינוּ
(pages 156–57)

The traditional morning service begins with a passage referred to as *mah-tóvu*, which is uttered upon entering the synagogue. A compilation of biblical citations (Num. 24:5; Pss. 5:8; 26:8; 95:6; 69:14), the passage as a whole is not strongly coherent, although the word *va'ani*, "I," which opens three of the five biblical verses, seems to act as a linking term. The opening line (Num. 24:5)—*mah-tóvu ohalékha, ya'akov, mishk'notékha, yisra'eyl*, "how good are your tents, Jacob, your dwelling places, Israel"—is interpreted in the Talmud (b. Sanhedrin 105b) as a reference to Israel's synagogues and houses of study; this interpretation makes the passage meaningful as an introduction to synagogue prayer. The image of the tents also mirrors the ritual of the *tallit*, in which the prayer shawl is raised like a tent or canopy above the head as it is donned.

How Good the Dwellings, which opens the communally recited portion of the new *Shaḥarit* service, begins with the following adaptation of Numbers 24:5: *Mah-tóvu oha-léynu, / mishk'notéynu, yisra'eyl*, literally, "How good are our tents, / our dwelling places, Israel." It continues with an adaptation of Numbers 24:6, the original text of which reads: *kinḥalim nitáyu, k'ganot aley nahar, ka'ahalim nata y-h-v-h, ka'arazim aley-máyim*, literally, "like winding streams, like gardens at the sides of the rivers, like aloes that God has planted, like cedars beside the waters." The adaptation replaces *ahalim nata y-h-v-h*, "aloes that YHVH has planted," with *ahalim n'tu'im*, literally, "planted aloes." Thus the opening of **How Good the Dwellings**, like the original passage in the Bible, compares the gathering places of the community to a scene in the natural world. This image is followed by an adaptation of another biblical image of communal harmony, Psalm 133:1, the original text of which reads: *Hineyh mah-tov umah-na'im shévet aḥim gam-yáḥad*, literally, "How good and how pleasant [it is] for brothers to sit (or to dwell) together." In the adaptation, *aḥim*, "brothers," becomes *kulánu*, "all of us."

Thus **How Good the Dwellings** celebrates the vibrancy of an inclusive community gathered together for a common purpose. Although the *mah-tóvu* passage is the first prayer in the traditional morning service, I have placed **How Good the Dwellings** after **Putting on the Prayer Shawl** and the **Morning Blessing** so that it will be said after individuals have had a chance to focus their personal awareness.

Hal'lu: Praise   הַלְלוּ
(pages 158–59)

This offering is an adaptation of Psalm 150, the quintessential psalm of praise and a popular part of the traditional morning service. As with other biblical adaptations in this book, the Hebrew is not modernized but retains its original biblical style. Many details of the original, with its catalogue of creative suggestions for how to praise, are preserved here intact, but references to the power of the (male) creator have been eliminated and, in some lines, replaced by references to the beauty of creation. The English version of this psalm is not even an approximate translation of the Hebrew; rather, it is a poem inspired by the original psalm and intended to complement the Hebrew adaptation.

For reference, below is a literal translation of the new Hebrew text:

> Praise the world,
> praise its fullness,

praise with the blast of the horn,
with harp and lyre.

Praise with drum and dance,
with strings and flute,

praise with resounding cymbals,
with cymbals ringing out.

Every living being [literally, breath, or spirit, or soul] will praise
the world,

every living being will praise
its beauty.

The Breath of All Life   נִשְׁמַת כָּל חַי
(pages 160–61)

The traditional hymn known, by its opening words, as *nishmat kol ḥay*, literally, "breath (or spirit, or soul) of all that lives (or of every living thing)," and sometimes referred to simply as *nishmat*, "breath of," is one of the most moving prayers in the Sabbath morning service. Rabbinic in origin, it is, like the biblical psalms in the morning prayer sequence, a hymn of praise. Containing vivid imagery of the natural world and concrete description of the human body, it builds its poetic momentum through the accretion of detail.

My adaptation of this prayer, **The Breath of All Life**, quotes extensively from the original. The opening couplet in the Hebrew is an abbreviation of the original opening, which reads: *Nishmat kol ḥay t'vareykh et shim'kha, y-h-v-h elohéynu, v'rú'aḥ kol basar t'fa'eyr utromeym zikhr'kha, malkéynu, tamid*, literally, "The breath of all that lives will bless your name, YHVH our God, and the spirit of all flesh will praise and exalt the knowledge of you, our king, forever." As in other blessings, I have left open the direction of this prayer, specifying no recipient for its praise; hence, the adaptation reads *Nishmat kol ḥay t'vareykh / v'rú'aḥ kol basar t'fa'eyr*, literally, "The breath of all that lives will bless / and the spirit of all flesh will praise." The middle three couplets of the new prayer are borrowed intact from the original prayer; they consist of a catalogue of metaphors describing the body proclaiming praise. In quoting these lines, I have preserved the traditional language exactly, retaining the vocalization of the original (which more or less follows biblical convention) as found in standard prayer books. The concluding two couplets of the new Hebrew prayer (one couplet in the English) are an adaptation of the original, which states that we cannot sufficiently express our gratitude to God for even one of the many favors performed for Israel. This may be understood broadly: although the liturgical text goes on to specify interventions in human history, such as the redemption from slavery, the Talmud quotes some of this passage in connection with the prayer thanking God for rain (b. Berakhot 59b; b. Ta'anit 6b). I have adopted the hyperbolic style of the original here: *gam az, lo naspik l'hodot / v'lu al p'li'ah aḥat / mini-élef alfey alafim / v'ribey r'vavot*, literally, "even then, we would not be able to acknowledge sufficiently / even one wonder / from among thousands of thousands of thousands / and a multitude of many more." The English version of these lines replaces hyperbole with compression: "it would not be enough to tell / the wonder."

Psalm for the Sabbath   מִזְמוֹר שִׁיר לְיוֹם הַשַּׁבָּת
(page 162)

See p. 446.

Sh'ma and the Surrounding Blessings   קְרִיאַת שְׁמַע וּבִרְכוֹתֶיהָ
(pages 163–75)

The traditional *k'ri'at sh'ma uvirkhotéha*, "recitation of the *sh'ma* and its [three] blessings," is one of the two oldest sections of the service, the other being the *amidah*; today, these are still considered, along with the Torah reading, its most important components. In the traditional morning service, *k'ri'at sh'ma uvirkhotéha* begins with a call to blessing and continues with the blessing known as *yotzeyr or*, "creator of light," which praises God for creating light and darkness. The second blessing of this section, referred to as *ahavah rabah*, "abounding love," praises God for giving the Torah to Israel with love. After this comes the *sh'ma*, a declaration of faith beginning with the words "Hear, O Israel." Following the *sh'ma* is the third blessing, called *emet v'yatziv*, "true and firm," also known as the blessing of *g'ulah*, "redemption." Thus as a whole, *k'ri'at sh'ma uvirkhotéha* articulates the three major themes of the Sabbath: creation, revelation, and redemption. My re-creation of this section of the service follows the five-part structure of the traditional section, with the **Bar'khu: Call to Blessing** as the opening, the ***Sh'ma*: Communal Declaration of Faith** as the focal point, and the ***Sh'ma***'s surrounding blessings highlighting the three central themes of the Sabbath.

Bar'khu: Call to Blessing בָּרְכוּ
(pages 164–65)

The traditional call to blessing begins with the words *Bar'khu et y-h-v-h hamvorakh*, "Bless YHVH, the blessed one," to which the congregation replies *Barukh y-h-v-h hamvorakh l'olam va'ed*, "Blessed is YHVH, the blessed one, forever." The new *Bar'khu:* **Call to Blessing** is, like the traditional call, in the form of a dialogue. But in the new call, another kind of reciprocity between part and whole parallels that between prayer leader and congregation: this is embedded in the meaning of the words, which express belief in a reciprocal relationship of blessing between the human community and the divine. The leader calls out, *Bar'khu et eyn haḥayim*, literally, "Bless the source of life" (the English version of this line reads, "Let us bless the source of life"), and the congregation responds, *N'vareykh et eyn haḥayim / v'khoh nitbareykh*, literally, "Let us bless the source of life / and thus (or in so doing) we will (or may we) be blessed." (The English version of these lines reads: "As we bless the source of life / so we are blessed.") This response is then repeated by the leader, following the custom of the traditional liturgy. (This time the English version is given in a variation, "As we bless the source of life / so may we be blessed.") The rabbis spoke of a partnership between humanity and divinity, and it is this idea that is at the heart of this invitation-and-response, which also serves as the first part of the **Torah Blessings**. The lines *N'vareykh et eyn haḥayim / v'khoh nitbareykh* are reprised again as a refrain to close each section of the **Amidah: Sevenfold Prayer for the Sabbath** and to embellish the **Closing Blessing** of the *Shaḥarit* service.

Blessing of Creation בִּרְכַּת יְצִירָה
(pages 166–67)

The **Blessing of Creation** is a re-creation of the first of the traditional blessings in the *k'ri'at sh'ma* section of the Sabbath morning service. Like its traditional counterpart, the new blessing is based on Isaiah 45:7, which reads: *Yotzeyr or uvorey ḥoshekh, oseh shalom uvorey ra*, "[I] form light and create darkness, make peace and create evil." In Isaiah, these words are spoken by the prophet in the name of God. The traditional *yotzeyr or* blessing praises God for the same acts mentioned here—with one difference. In place of the word *ra*, "evil," the *yotzeyr or* blessing offers *hakol*, "everything." The rabbis of the Talmud (b. Berakhot 11b) acknowledge that this is a euphemism (the term they use is *lishana ma'alya*, "elevated [or preferred] language"). Many commentators on the prayer book have also noted this emendation, but they have not debated its efficacy; rather, they tend to treat it as a stylistic modification that renders the biblical text more suitable for prayer.[43] This seems disingenuous. An important theological shift occurs with the removal of the word *ra* from this text. One might argue that the word *hakol* is inclusive; thus the rabbis have not excluded evil from their statement about God. But this is begging the point: if God indeed created *everything*, why erase evil from the attribution?

It seems almost tautological to note that the concept of "good" has no meaning without the concept of "bad"; yet it may be worth stating the obvious here. The refusal to name that with which we are uncomfortable does not make it disappear. It would seem that, in a truly inclusive monotheistic vision, the divine domain includes what is "bad"; and, at times, the "bad" needs to be named. Of course, we might debate for a long time what we mean by good and evil; Jewish teaching certainly does so, although not usually in the context of prayer. While prayer is probably not the best place to engage in theological argument, it *is* the right place, I believe, to name our truths and, insofar as possible, to do so inclusively— which is to say, not to name half-truths, which are, effectively, lies.

I have returned to the biblical source for the new blessing, which reads: *N'vareykh et eyn haḥayim, / m'kor haḥóshekh v'ha'or, / m'kor hash'leymut v'hatóhu, / m'kor hatov v'hara, / m'kor kol y'tzirah*, literally, "Let us bless the source of life, / source of darkness and light, / source of wholeness and chaos, / source of goodness and evil, / source of all creation." I have deliberately reversed the order of *or* and *ḥóshekh*, "light" and "darkness," from the way they appear in the original blessing, lest one infer that *or* is to be identified with *hash'leymut*, "wholeness," and *hatov*, "goodness," while *ḥóshekh* is equated with *hatóhu*, "chaos," and *hara*, "evil." The dualism of light and darkness is widely regarded as a value-laden opposition in Western thought, and this hierarchy has been applied in especially problematic ways to racial differences among people. If, in grappling with the images embedded in our culture, we choose to talk about light and darkness as polarities (as opposed, for example, to viewing them as points on a spectrum), I believe it important that we try to subvert the hierarchy normally associated with them.

Blessing of Revelation   בִּרְכַּת תּוֹרָה
(pages 168–69)

The second of the three blessings surrounding the reading of the *sh'ma* in the morning service is referred to in the Babylonian Talmud (Berakhot 11b) and subsequent Ashkenazic tradition by its opening words, *ahavah rabah*, "abounding love," and in the Jerusalem Talmud (Berakhot 1:5) as *birkat hatorah*, "blessing of the Torah"; it is from the latter that I take the Hebrew name of my new **Blessing of Revelation**. In the traditional blessing, God is praised for having loved and chosen Israel from among all nations and is beseeched to teach the people of Israel his Torah. Within the blessing is this plea: *Raḥeym aléynu v'teyn b'libéynu l'havin ulhaskil, lishmó'a, lilmod ul'lameyd, lishmor v'la'asot ulkayeym et kol divrey talmud toratékha b'ahavah*, literally, "Have mercy on us, and place within our heart [the ability, or the willingness] to understand and to be wise, to listen, to learn, and to teach, to observe and to do and to fulfill all the words of the teachings of your Torah with love." I have adapted these lines for the heart of my **Blessing of Revelation**, which opens, echoing the **Blessing of Creation**, thus: *N'vareykh et eyn haḥayim, / m'kor havanah v'havḥanah*, literally, "Let us bless the source of life, / source of understanding and discernment." The blessing then continues: *Nizkeh na l'havin ulhaskil, / lishmó'a, lilmod ul'lameyd, / lishmor v'la'asot ulkayeym / divrey torah b'ahavah*, literally, "May we merit to understand and to be wise, / to listen, to learn, and to teach, / to observe and to do and to fulfill / the words of Torah with love." The English version unfolds the meaning of the Hebrew lines with a slightly different emphasis: "Let us bless the source of life, / source of the fullness of our knowing. / May we learn with humility and pleasure, / may we teach what we know with love, / and may we honor wisdom / in all its embodiments." The last couplet of the English is a reference to the diversity of forms that wisdom takes in life, which include the wisdom of the body itself. Thus Torah is understood here in the broadest possible way, as sacred teaching and learning.

Sh'ma: Communal Declaration of Faith   קְרִיאַת שְׁמַע בַּקְּהִלָּה
(pages 170–73)

In the traditional service, the full text of the *sh'ma*, consisting of three passages, is read: Deuteronomy 6:4–9; 11:13–21; and Numbers 15:37–41. This new service contains a re-creation of the first passage. The **Sh'ma: Communal Declaration of Faith** is discussed together with the **Sh'ma: Personal Declaration of Faith**, pp. 431–36.

Blessing of Redemption   בִּרְכַּת גְּאֻלָּה
(pages 174–75)

Following the recitation of the *sh'ma* in the traditional morning service is a long blessing referred to by its opening words, *emet v'yatziv*, "true and firm." It ends by praising God for redeeming Israel, which is why it has also come to be known as the blessing of *g'ulah*, "redemption." In it, the third theme of the Sabbath day is articulated, for the Sabbath celebrates not only creation and the giving of Torah but hope for future redemption. While redemption is specifically associated here with God's leading the Israelites out of slavery in Egypt, it cannot help but also allude to the future, traditionally understood as the messianic era.

Like creation and revelation, the theme of redemption has been the subject of a wide spectrum of interpretations; I shall offer but one. I understand redemption as the saving of the world through positive actions that correct and undo human wrongs. Specifically, the world needs to be redeemed from the forces of narrow self-interest that have led to widespread injustice, social and economic inequities, violence, waste of resources, and destruction of the environment. We might think of this as the work of "salvation" incumbent on all humanity. To be sure, the future is not wholly in our control. Yet it is clear that the human species plays a uniquely powerful role in the interconnected systems of life on the planet, and with this role come responsibilities. Both biblical and rabbinic theology encourage human mastery over the rest of creation—what is often called "nature" or "the earth." Today, however, it seems clear that many of our attempts to control "nature" have led to dangerous imbalances in the whole of the natural world, of which we are an inextricable part. Yet it is not enough for us now to stand back and, as the saying goes, let nature take its course. Recognizing ourselves as part of the web, we must work consciously and conscientiously to make the whole web healthy and viable.

The kind of commitment I am seeking on the part of humanity might be expressed by the term *tikun olam*, "repair of the world"—a phrase first used by the rabbis of the Talmud to refer to the establishment of the social good. And I believe that dedication to *tikun olam* begins with hope, with the faith that we can, with our actions, affect the world for good. Therefore the **Blessing of Redemption** (which opens like the **Blessing of Creation** and the **Blessing of Revelation**) reads: *N'vareykh et eyn haḥayim, / m'kor emunah v'tikvah, / ma'yan shirah ḥadashah, / m'kor tikun olam*, literally, "Let us bless the source of life, / source of faith and hope, / fountain of new song, / source of repair of the world." (Further discussion of *tikun olam* may be found in the commentary to *Aléynu L'shabéy'aḥ:* **It Is Ours to Praise**, pp. 485–86.)

The term *shirah ḥadashah*, "new song," is borrowed from the traditional blessing, which proclaims that the "redeemed praise [with] a new song," but the motif actually originates in the Bible (where it appears in the variant form *shir ḥadash*; see Pss. 33:3; 40:4; 96:1; 98:1; 144:9; 149:1; and Isa. 42:10). In its biblical contexts, this motif is associated not only with praise and joy but with hope and the desire for salvation, themes that are all embedded in the phrase *shirah ḥadashah*.

Amidah: Sevenfold Prayer for the Sabbath
עֲמִידָה: תְּפִלַּת שֶׁבַע לְיוֹם הַשַּׁבָּת
(pages 177–259)

The prayer known as the *amidah*, which means, literally, "standing," was also called by the rabbis *hat'filah*, "the prayer" (because, in their eyes, it was the prayer par excellence), and *sh'moneh esreyh*, "eighteen" (because the version for daily services originally contained eighteen blessings). It is one of the two most ancient and important parts of the synagogue service; its origins and structure are discussed in the Talmud (see, for example, b. Megillah 17b; y. Berakhot 2:4). Its structural integrity is generally attributed to Rabbi Gamliel II, circa 90 C.E., although wide variation in wording remained the norm for centuries after him. The *amidah* exists today in a variety of versions, reflecting the traditions of different Jewish communities around the world.

The *amidah* in the daily prayer service may be thought of as having three parts: three blessings of praise, which are considered the introduction; thirteen blessings of petition; and three blessings of conclusion, one of which is a thanksgiving. However, the Sabbath *amidah* (like the holiday *amidah* and the *amidah* recited at *musaf* services on the intermediary days of the festivals and on Rosh Hodesh) contains seven rather than nineteen blessings; the middle thirteen blessings are absent, and a blessing sanctifying the day appears in their place. The traditional explanation for the shorter *amidah* on Sabbaths and holidays is that the petitionary blessings are inappropriate for holy days, which present us with a state of perfection. Because of its seven-blessing form, the Sabbath *amidah* is sometimes called *t'filat shéva*, "prayer of seven"; from this I derived my title **Amidah: Sevenfold Prayer for the Sabbath**.

The seven blessings of the traditional Sabbath *amidah* are referred to as follows: *avot*, "fathers [i.e., the forefathers, or Patriarchs]"; *g'vurot*, "[divine] power"; *k'dushat hasheym*, "sanctification of the [divine] name," often referred to today simply as the *k'dushah*, "sanctification"; *k'dushat hayom*, "sanctification of the day"; *avodah*, "service" or "worship"; *hodayah*, "thanksgiving"; and *birkat kohanim*, "blessing of the priests," also known today as *birkat shalom*, "blessing of peace." Each blessing begins by praising, petitioning, or thanking God for particular deeds or attributes related to its theme. The conclusion of each blessing is a formulaic summation opening with the words *Barukh atah, y-h-v-h [adonay]*, "Blessed are you, YHVH [Lord]"; this summation is referred to as the eulogy.

The prayer offered in this book is a re-creation of the Sabbath *amidah*; hence it comprises seven sections that are thematically based on those of the traditional prayer. Each section contains blessings, meditations, and poetry; the blessings, which are the core of the prayer, are each discussed below in the commentaries to the individual sections.

Each section begins with a meditation, which I refer to as a *kavanat haleyv*, "intention (or direction) of the heart" (pl. *kavanot haleyv*). This term is related to the talmudic phrase *l'khaveyn et haleyv*, "to direct the heart," which is discussed in the commentary to **Putting on the Prayer Shawl** (p. 459). However, the actual idea for my genre of *kavanot haleyv* comes from later traditions of reading introductory passages before saying prayers. The medieval poets wrote special supplications called *r'shuyot*, literally, "permissions," which the cantor recited before praying on behalf of the congregation; the kabbalists composed other kinds of introductory recitations to be used by all worshipers, passages that they called *kavanot*, literally, "intentions" (sing. *kavanah*), which focused on the underlying mystical meaning of the prayer about to be uttered. In modern Hebrew, the word *kavanah* does not usually denote this kabbalistic usage; rather, it means "intention" in a more general sense. I am adopting here the more specialized meaning of *kavanah* as a liturgical genre, adding to the term the talmudic connection with the heart; hence *kavanat haleyv*, "intention of the heart." It is the purpose of my *kavanot haleyv* to help the heart open to the words of the individual blessings.

The poetry in this new *Amidah* further elaborates on the themes articulated in the blessings. Composed by a variety of Jewish women poets writing in Hebrew, Yiddish, and English (authors' names appear beneath the poems; unattributed poems are mine), it has a multivocality similar to that of the **Psalms of Creation** in *Kabbalat Shabbat*. This multivocality corresponds to what is found in the traditional *k'rovot*, special poems that were individually composed and added to the traditional *amidah* prayer on Sabbaths, holidays, and special weekdays. *K'rovot* came from various periods and locales and offered poetic expansion of the themes of the prayer; I think of them as my historical precedent for incorporating poems into the new *Amidah*.

At the end of each section of this new prayer, the blessing for that section is repeated, followed by a two-line refrain that reads: *N'vareykh et eyn haḥayim / v'khoh nitbareykh*, "As we bless the source of life / so we are blessed." These lines are also found in the **Bar'khu: Call to Blessing** and in the **Torah Blessings**; thus they serve as a motif linking the three major elements of the **Shaḥarit: Morning Service for the Sabbath**—**Sh'ma and the Surrounding Blessings**, **Amidah: Sevenfold Prayer for the Sabbath**, and **Honoring Torah**. They are reprised for a final time at the end of the *Shaḥarit* service, following the **Closing Blessing**. (Note that in some places, the English version of the refrain is rendered with slight stylistic variations.)

Rabbi Gamliel II is credited with demanding the public recitation of the *amidah* by all worshipers. Not all could recite it successfully, however, as no written prayer books existed in talmudic times; therefore an official representative of the congregation was charged with the responsibility of reciting it aloud on behalf of those unable to say it. To this day, the *amidah* is generally recited privately but then repeated aloud by the one leading the prayer; thus it combines private and communal liturgical expression. The new prayer, too, is meant for use by both the individual and the community (with suggestions for different forms of implementation found in the guidelines for conducting the *Shaḥarit* service, on p. 141).

Recalling Our Ancestors, Remembering Our Lives   מָסֹרֶת הַדּוֹרוֹת
(pages 179–91)

The first blessing of the traditional *amidah*, called *avot*, "fathers," praises God as the protector of Israel's forefathers Abraham, Isaac, and Jacob; in many congregations today, the names of the foremothers Sarah, Rebecca, Rachel, and Leah are inserted here as well. Although the insertion has been sanctioned by all the major non-Orthodox branches of Judaism, and although it appears in several modern prayer books, a good many congregations still resist this first step toward recording the presence of Jewish women in history.[44] This resistance is a telling sign of the tenacity with which patriarchal attitudes can pervade communal consciousness, such that the invisibility of women is taken to be normative and even minimal attempts to address absences in the liturgy are seen as intolerable. Indeed, this resistance tells us that we need to do much more than make token gestures such as including the names of the foremothers in our prayers. We need to bring women's lives *fully into the foreground* of our awareness in order to begin to create correctives that will ultimately lead to a genuinely inclusive community.

The first section of my new **Amidah** emphasizes our relationship to our ancestors, both distant and close, and to historical tradition. One of the poems in the section, the Yiddish poet Malka Heifetz Tussman's *I Am Woman*, is a sweeping account of the history of Jewish women told in a personal voice. The inclusion of this poem in the **Amidah** is an attempt to begin to compensate for some of the imbalance in Jewish liturgy by making women's names and stories visible.

The blessing for the section reads: *Nizkor et masóret hadorot / v'nishzor bah et sarigey ḥayéynu*, literally, "Let us recall the tradition of the generations / and let us weave into it the branches (or tendrils) of our lives." Adapting the metaphor somewhat, the English version reads: "Recalling the generations, / we weave our lives / into the tradition." The word *nizkor*, "let us recall," is also found in **Handwashing upon Awakening** and **Handwashing Before the Meal** (where it takes the third-person form *tizkor*) and in **Putting on the Prayer Shawl** (where it is in the infinitive form, *lizkor*). It is also related to the words *zéykher* and *zikaron*, both meaning "remembrance," found in the traditional sanctification blessings over wine for the Sabbath as well as in the new sanctifications in THE WEEKLY CYCLE of this book. All these contexts emphasize a calling to mind that effects a significant connection. Here, the emphasized relationship is that between our lives and the lives of those in our past as a people.

The image of weaving and the reference to the historical generations are motifs found also in other parts of the new liturgy, including the **Sanctification over Wine for Rosh Hodesh** (pp. 364–65 and 396–97), **Sanctifying Rosh Hodesh** (pp. 392–93), and **May We Be Remembered** (pp. 394–95). See pp. 500–501 for discussion.

Sustaining Life, Embracing Death   מַעְגַּל הַחַיִּים
(pages 193–203)

The second blessing of the traditional *amidah*, known as *g'vurot*, "might," praises divine power in the world; some versions of the *amidah* particularly note that power as it is manifested in nature. Thus during the winter season, between the festivals of Sukkot and Passover, the words *mashiv harú'ah umorid hagáshem*, "who causes the wind to blow and the rain to fall," are inserted into this section; in the summer, some prayer books insert *morid hatal*, "who causes the dew to fall." An important aspect of divine power mentioned three times in this blessing—once in the opening, once in the middle, and once in the eulogy—is that of "reviving the dead," *m'hayeyh meytim*—an attribution that has been eliminated in recent times from a number of standard prayer books. In place of the words *m'hayeyh meytim*, the Reform movement's prayer book offers the more general phrase *m'hayeyh hakol*, literally, "who revives all"; the Reconstructionist movement replaces *m'hayeyh meytim* with *m'hayeyh kol hay*, literally, "who revives all that lives."[45] (Interestingly, both denominations retain the phrase *mélekh meymit umhayeh*, "king who kills and revives," in a middle paragraph of the blessing.)

Although understandable, the substitution of *hakol*, "all," or *kol hay*, "all that lives," for *meytim*, "the dead," seems to me misguided. Presumably, Reform and Reconstructionist objections to the phrase *m'hayeyh meytim* have to do with the literal interpretation of it as referring to the resurrection of the dead in messianic times. While that may once have been its primary meaning, there are a number of other ways to read it and to reconstruct the idea behind it. The selective elimination of this phrase—among only a handful of phrases seen as absolutely unacceptable by these two modern movements in Judaism—lends a tacit approval to other words in the liturgy that would surely seem equally preposterous today if understood in a fundamentalist way. Indeed, of all theological concepts, that of *t'hiyat hameytim*, "revival of the dead," seems to me one that is worth saving and grappling with.

To avoid addressing it is to evade one of the monumental concerns of human life—our relationship to mortality.

My restoration of the concept of *t'ḥiyat hameytim* to the new **Amidah** is based on the conviction that it can be meaningfully read as an acknowledgment and even affirmation of the presence of death in our lives. For what is life without death? And what life is not part of the circle of dying, and what death is not part of the circle of living? The second section of the new **Amidah** focuses on the relationship of death and dying to all life. The new blessing reads: *N'vareykh et hama'yan / adey-ad m'fakeh—/ ma'gal haḥayim / hameymit umḥayeh*, literally, "Let us bless the spring (or fountain, or well) / that eternally flows—/ the circle of life / that kills and revives." The phrase *hameymit umḥayeh* is taken directly from the traditional *amidah*, where God is called *mélekh meymit umḥayeh umatzmí'aḥ y'shu'ah*, "king who kills and revives and causes salvation to flourish." In the traditional prayer, "killing" and "reviving" are acts of an agent (God) upon something else (the world). The new blessing, in contrast, speaks of the circle of life as that which kills and revives; no separate object is implied here. At first, this idea may seem puzzling. What this new blessing seeks to convey is a sense of life in continuous regenerative movement, continually dying and renewing itself. In the English version, this idea is rendered as "the circle of life / ever-dying, ever-living"—which is, in effect, another way of understanding the Hebrew.

One of the poems in this section, Malka Heifetz Tussman's triolet *Leaves*, perhaps captures the theme of the section best. Tussman uses the triolet's circular form—in which lines are repeated, rhymed, and repeated again, so that the closing returns us to the beginning—to connect the idea of revival with the unending cycles of nature.

Hallowing Our Namings   נִשְׁמַת כָּל שֵׁם
(pages 205–13)

The words of the third traditional blessing, *k'dushat hasheym*, "sanctification of the name," are few and emphatic: "You are holy and your name is holy and holy ones every day praise you. Blessed are you, Lord, the holy God." A longer passage containing several biblical citations and elaborating on the theme of God's holiness appears alongside these words in the text of the *amidah* but is not meant to be recited by the individual during the silent prayer; rather, it is recited only during the prayer leader's repetition.

The key words here—"holiness" and "name"—are integrally connected to each other, for the way in which we name something is the way we set it apart, and holiness, according to rabbinic teaching, is the quality of being set apart. The new blessing created around these words honors and celebrates the sanctity of all life; at the same time, it honors our *naming* of life, that is, our specifically human connection to the whole of creation. It reads: *Nashir l'nishmat kol sheym / ulsheym kol n'shamah, / nashir l'nishmat kol sheym / v'likdushat kol n'shamah*, literally, "Let us sing to the soul (or breath, or spirit) of every name / and to the name of (or for the sake of) every soul, / let us sing to the soul of every name / and to the holiness of every soul." A discussion of the meaning of *n'shamah*, "soul," or "breath," or "spirit," and of its construct form, *nishmat*, may be found in the commentary to the **Morning Blessing**, p. 424.

Note that *Each of Us Has a Name*, the adaptation of a poem by Zelda that is included in this section of the **Amidah**, also serves as the new **Kaddish: Mourners' Prayer**, found in the **Shaḥarit** and in **Kabbalat Shabbat** (and discussed in the commentary to the **Kaddish**, pp. 447–48). The link between these parts of the liturgy follows tradition, in that the traditional *kaddish* prayer is another sanctification of God's name (its opening words are "May his great name be magnified and sanctified").

Sanctifying the Sabbath Day   קְדֻשַׁת יוֹם הַשַּׁבָּת
(pages 215–25)

The fourth blessing of the traditional *amidah*, *k'dushat hayom*, "sanctification of the day," is fundamentally related to the Sabbath *kiddush* ("sanctification" over wine): both praise God for sanctifying the Sabbath. The *kiddush* for Sabbath day is usually preceded by Exodus 31:16–17, which is also found in the *k'dushat hayom* section of the *amidah*.

Similarly, the fourth blessing of my **Amidah** is related to the **Sanctification over Wine for Sabbath Eve** and the **Sanctification over Wine for Sabbath Day**; it reads: *N'kadeysh et yom hashabbat / v'nishmor oto— / zikaron l'ma'aseyh v'reyshit, / zéykher litzi'at mitzráyim*, literally, "Let us hallow the Sabbath day / and let us keep it— / in remembrance of the creation, / in commemoration of the exodus from Egypt." Both creation and revelation are recalled in the phrases *zikaron l'ma'aseyh v'reyshit* and *zéykher litzi'at mitzráyim*. The theme of revelation, which is especially associated with the daytime part of the Sabbath, is evoked a second time in the phrase *v'nishmor oto*, "and let us keep it." This commitment to preserve the Sabbath as hallowed time echoes the wording of the commandment (given as part of the Ten Commandments at Sinai) *shamor et-yom hashabbat*, "you shall keep the Sabbath day" (Deut. 5:12). To make the association with revelation more accessible in the English version of the blessing, I have rendered "the exodus from Egypt" as "the covenant," because it was the exodus that led to the giving of Torah at Sinai.

Restoring Shekhinah, Reclaiming Home   הַחֲזָרַת הַשְּׁכִינָה
(pages 227–39)

The fifth blessing, *avodah*, "service," is probably the most ancient part of the *amidah* and has undergone the most change over the course of time. Originally a petition recited at the time of the Temple sacrifices, in one of its oldest extant versions it asks that God "dwell in Zion." The current version asks that God restore the Temple service (i.e., the sacrifices) and concludes by praising God who "restores his presence to Zion," *hamaḥazir sh'khinato l'tziyon.*

Despite its seemingly archaic nature, I believe this blessing contains promising potential for re-creation. *Sh'khinato*, "his [God's] presence," is a possessive form of the word *sh'khinah*, "presence" or "indwelling," which over the course of Jewish history has been used as a name for the divine and, specifically, for divine immanence. The Shekhinah (now also a term in the English language) was explicitly portrayed as a female figure in Kabbalah, although one would be hard pressed to make the claim that the kabbalistic images were liberating for women, in that they were always defined in subordinate relationship to the male God.[46] The word *sh'khinah* itself is grammatically feminine, and today the term has gained new life in some Jewish feminist circles, where it is used as a way to name divinity.

The mention of Zion in this blessing is also resonant and might be retained meaningfully in the liturgy as a reference to the Jewish homeland (rather than as a reference to the ancient Temple). Asking that the Shekhinah be restored to the Jewish homeland can be a way of seeking at least two distinct but related aims: that Israel be a place in which we live with reverence for all life; and that the sense of the divine as immanent, and the valuing of women's experience as part of the divine immanence, be honored in Israel and wherever else we make our homes. I have tried to weave these ideas together in my new blessing: *Naḥazir et hash'khinah limkomah / b'tziyon uvateyveyl kulah*, literally, "Let us restore the Shekhinah (or divine presence) to its place / in Zion and in all the world." The English version separates out the interwoven meanings of the Hebrew: "Let us restore Shekhinah to her place / in Israel and throughout the world, / and let us infuse all places / with her presence."

This section of the **Amidah** includes a famous poem by the early-twentieth-century Hebrew poet and Zionist pioneer Rachel Bluwstein, known best to the Israeli population simply as Rachel. *To My Land* is the humblest of nationalistic hymns, eschewing battle cries and celebrating instead the planting of a tree. Following Rachel's poem I have placed Malka Heifetz Tussman's *Holy Quiet*, a reverent and loving recollection of an orchard in Russia—a country she was forced to leave (in 1912, at the age of sixteen) because of anti-Semitism. Tussman, like so many Jews of her generation, made the United States her new home. I have juxtaposed her poem with Emma Lazarus's paean to the United States, *The New Colossus*, which is inscribed on the Statue of Liberty. Each time I read Lazarus's poem, I am struck by how much the United States has meant to its immigrants—and how far we still have to go in fulfilling the commitment to make this land, too, a haven, a holy place where "the homeless, tempest-tost" will find refuge. Finally, the poem *Recovery*, which is mine, speaks of home as the experience of feeling oneself in place, fully belonging, in the natural world.

The Gift of Gratitude בְּפֶה מָלֵא שִׁירָה
(pages 241–47)

The traditional blessing of *hodayah*, "gratitude," which occupies the sixth section of the *amidah* prayer, is re-created in the **Amidah: Sevenfold Prayer for the Sabbath** primarily through silence. The briefest of meditations introduces six Hebrew words (ten in English) that constitute not a whole blessing but the beginning of one. What follows may come spontaneously in the form of words or as silent feeling. No poetry is provided in this section.

The six Hebrew words are: *B'feh maley shirah / uvlashon shofá'at rinah*—, literally, "With mouth full of song / and tongue overflowing with joy (or singing)—." These words are based on lines from the traditional prayer *nishmat kol ḥay*, "the breath of all that lives"— lines that also appear in the Hebrew version of my prayer **The Breath of All Life** (in the **Opening Blessings and Songs** of the **Shaḥarit** service): *Ílu fínu maley shirah kayam / ulshonéynu rinah kahamon galav*, literally, "If our mouth were as full of song as the sea [is with water] / and our tongue [as full of] joy (or singing) as the sound (or multitude) of its waves." In their original context and in the new context given them in **The Breath of All Life**, these lines are the beginning of a statement of appreciation for the wonders of creation—a statement that concludes by acknowledging that no amount of praise can suffice to encompass all there is to be grateful for. Having said these lines earlier in the service, one now returns to reflect upon the state of appreciation and to enter into it more personally, contributing, if one desires, one's own words. If the *amidah* was, for the rabbis, the ultimate prayer, then in this new **Amidah** the section of silent gratitude might be viewed as the prayer within the prayer—the prayer of the heart, which may not require words at all.

Blessing of Peace בְּרְכַּת שָׁלוֹם
(pages 249–59)

The seventh blessing of the traditional *amidah* is called *birkat kohanim*, "blessing of the priests," originally because of its inclusion of the priestly blessing; today it is also referred to as *birkat shalom*, "blessing of peace." Beginning with a petition whose opening words are

Sim shalom, "Grant peace," it concludes by praising God for blessing Israel with peace. In the **Closing Blessing** found in both the *Kabbalat Shabbat* and *Shaḥarit* services, I have re-created the *sim shalom* passage, retaining much of its original language (see the commentary to the **Closing Blessing**, p. 448). For the final blessing of the new *Amidah*, I have composed a new petition for peace based on biblical passages.

The new blessing reads: *Nish'al mey'eyn hashalom: / Yizal katal, / ya'arof kamatar hashalom, / v'timla ha'áretz shalom / kamáyim layam m'khasim*, literally, "Let us ask of the wellspring (or source) of peace: / May [it] flow like the dew, / may peace drop like the rain, / until the earth is filled with peace / as the waters cover the sea." The lines *Yizal katal, / ya'arof kamatar hashalom* are adapted from a verse in the biblical poem known as *ha'azínu*, "give ear," in which Moses calls upon the people of Israel to be faithful to God, who has redeemed them. The speaker introduces his speech with a metaphor: *Ya'arof kamatar likḥi, yizal katal imrati*, "My portion shall flow like the dew, my speech shall drop like the rain" (Deut. 32:2). The concluding lines of my blessing, *v'timla ha'áretz shalom / kamáyim layam m'khasim*, are based on a passage in Isaiah that depicts with vivid imagery a vision of the world at peace. The particular verse from which the lines of the blessing are adapted (Isa. 11:9) reads: *ki-mal'ah ha'áretz dey'ah et-y-h-v-h kamáyim layam m'khasim*, literally, "for the earth shall be full of knowing YHVH (or the knowledge of YHVH) as the waters cover the sea."

In the biblical texts on which the new blessing is based, water is a metaphor for redemptive knowledge and speech. In the new blessing itself, water—in its various manifestations as wellspring, dew, rain, and sea—is a metaphor for the redemptive gift of peace. The use of water as an image of peace is also informed by other biblical passages: "Had you only listened to my commandments, your peace would have been like the river and your righteousness like the waves of the sea" (Isa. 48:18) and "I will extend peace to her like a river and the honor of nations like a flowing stream" (Isa. 66:12). Because all the biblical sources for this blessing are prophetic in tone or context (exhorting the audience to act or implicitly seeking to bring about human action as a response), the Hebrew version of the blessing implies a connection between our own efforts and the bringing of peace to the world. In the English version, I have made the human role explicit. The image of water as a metaphor for peace is continued in the poems by Zelda, *Pause* and *First Rain*, which embellish the theme of the section.

Honoring Torah   לְכְבוֹד תּוֹרָה
(pages 261–81)

It is impossible to overstate the importance of Torah, sacred teaching, in Jewish life. "On three things the world stands," comment the rabbis in Pirkey Avot, "on Torah, on worship, and on deeds of lovingkindness" (3:7). It is clear from many sources, and from the structure of the liturgy as well, that for the rabbis Torah was itself a form of worship and that it was also inseparable from the righteous acts to which it was supposed to lead.

The word "Torah" has several meanings in Judaism, the primary one being the Five Books of Moses, or Pentateuch, which constitutes the first part of the Bible. The Hebrew Bible as a whole, comprising the Pentateuch along with the Prophets and the Writings, is a second meaning of Torah, for the entire Bible is considered divinely given. Moreover, the term *torah sheb'al peh*, "oral Torah," is used to refer to postbiblical rabbinic teachings; and although a distinction is made between *torah sheb'al peh* and *torah shebikhtav*, "written Torah," both are seen as authoritative and foundational to Judaism.

But the meaning of Torah in Jewish thought goes beyond even rabbinic teaching to encompass an ongoing process throughout Jewish history. While the term *torah misinay*, "Torah from Sinai"—a reference to the biblical story of the revelation—designates the highest form of sacred text, every Jew living in every period of history is to feel personally present at the historical moment when Israel was given Torah by God.

Martin Buber puts it this way: "Creation is the origin, redemption the goal. But revelation is not a fixed, dated point poised between the two. The revelation at Sinai is not this midpoint itself, but the perceiving of it, and such perception is possible at any time. That is why a psalm or a prophecy is no less 'Torah,' i.e., instruction, than the story of the exodus from Egypt."[47] And, we might add, that is why a psalm or a prophecy written today may be no less Torah than one composed two or three thousand years ago.

The recitation of biblical passages was an integral part of Jewish worship in ancient times when the transition was being made from sacrificial offerings at the Temple to verbal communal prayer. Indeed, it is likely that the reading of passages from the Bible was the reason for the earliest communal prayer assemblies. And so today, two millennia later, a portion of the Pentateuch is read in traditional Jewish communities at least four times a week—on Monday and Thursday mornings, and on Sabbath mornings and afternoons—as well as on festivals and fast days. On Sabbaths and holidays, an additional portion is read from the Prophets. On certain festivals and fast days (Passover, Shavu'ot, Tish'ah B'av, Sukkot, and Purim), whole books from the Writings are read (these books, collectively referred to as the Five Scrolls, are the Song of Songs, Ruth, Lamentations, Ecclesiastes, and Esther). Like certain other components of the service, the Torah reading on Sabbath morning must take place in the presence of a *minyan* (a quorum of ten), indicating its sacrality and significance as a communal event. The Torah scroll itself is removed from its ark, unwound, and chanted aloud with a care that aims for exactitude. The whole ritual is accompanied by blessings and recitations. This is what is usually called "the Torah reading" or "the Torah service."

Yet this is not the only way to conceive of a Torah reading.

If it is true that each of us is to feel as though she or he stood at Sinai, if it is true that Torah is an ongoing process, not a static thing, then the body of knowledge we call our sacred teachings or texts, and the community we refer to as our rabbis or teachers, should be constantly evolving, responsive to life and to change. In Hebrew, the word *torah* also means, simply, "teaching"—as in the teaching of grammar or the teaching of a particular individual. I have used the Hebrew word *torah* in this section of the service, **Honoring Torah**, both with and without the definite article, to allow it to be interpreted as broadly and flexibly as possible. A Torah reading, for the purposes of this service, could be either a recitation of, or a study session on, a sacred Jewish text—which is to say, any text of Jewish origin or context that leads in a path toward deeds of righteousness and lovingkindness. By "text" I mean to include written objects as well as other forms of teaching. I do not mean that we ought to discard traditional teachings—what Jews in the past might have called Torah. A community that obliterates its history cannot understand itself, cannot meaningfully shape where it is heading. I mean, rather, that we must continue to add to our understanding of these texts—and to our broader understanding of truth and justice—so that both the idea and the practice of Torah as sacred teaching continue to thrive in our communities today.

Gates of Righteousness שַׁעֲרֵי־צֶדֶק
(pages 264–65)

The removal of the Torah scroll from its ark and the replacement of the scroll after the reading are traditionally accompanied by the recitation or singing of biblical verses, the selection of which varies among Jewish cultures. The traditional Ashkenazic text consists of Numbers 10:35 and Isaiah 2:3. Numbers 10:35 speaks of the journey of the holy ark in the desert, where it accompanies Israel in battle, and it includes a line about the scattering of Israel's enemies; Isaiah 2:3 heralds Torah emerging from Zion. Today, new selections for this purpose have been suggested by both the Reform and Reconstructionist movements. To accompany the opening of the ark and the removal of the Torah scroll, the Reconstructionist movement inserts Psalm 118:19–20 in its new prayer book.[48] This passage reads: *Pithu-li sha'arey-tzédek; avo vam, odeh yah. Zeh hashá'ar la-y-h-v-h; tzadikim yavó'u vo*, literally, "Open for me the gates of righteousness (or Open for me, O gates of righteousness); I will

enter them, I will thank YH. This is the gate to (or of) YHVH; the righteous will enter it."
Although two distinct readings of the Hebrew opening line, as shown here in the literal
translation, are theoretically possible, I think the one shown second is less plausible. While
reading "gates of righteousness" as an appositive accounts specifically for the plural form of
the imperative verb *pithu*, "open," it is just as likely that the plural form here refers to a non-
specific "you" (the so-called *s'tami* form). Moreover, the verb *pithu* is transitive; if the gates
are the addressee, the phrase would have to be read as elliptical ("open [yourselves] for me"),
which seems awkward. The use of the third person ("them") to refer to the gates in the
immediately ensuing clause makes this reading even less likely.

I have adapted these lines for my new service as follows: *Pithu-li sha'arey-tzédek, / avo
vam v'odeh. / Zeh hashá'ar latorah, / navo vo unvareykh*, literally, "Open for me the gates of
righteousness (or Open for me, O gates of righteousness), / I will enter them and give
thanks. / This is the gate to (or of) Torah, / let us enter it and bless." As I have not altered the
original Hebrew of the opening line, no ambiguity has been lost. In the English version of the
offering, this line is left similarly open to interpretation: "May the gates of righteousness
open."

Torah Blessings בִּרְכוֹת הַתּוֹרָה
(pages 266–69)

The traditional liturgy includes recitations before and after the reading of Torah. The recitation before the reading begins with a call to blessing and a congregational response identical to what are found in the beginning of *k'ri'at sh'ma uvirkhotéha*, "*sh'ma* and its
blessings." So too, the new recitation provided here begins with the dialogue found in the
Bar'khu: Call to Blessing (discussion of this dialogue may be found in the commentary to
the **Bar'khu: Call to Blessing**, p. 464).

The second part of the traditional recitation before reading Torah is a blessing praising
God for choosing Israel from among all peoples and for giving Israel his Torah; its source is
the Talmud (b. Berakhot 11b). The blessing recited after the Torah reading is similar, praising God for giving Israel a Torah of truth and for planting everlasting life in Israel's midst;
unlike the blessing before the reading, however, it does not explicitly mention Israel's chosenness.

The idea of Israel as God's chosen people—the people to whom God gave Torah—is
a key concept in rabbinic Judaism. Yet it is particularly problematic for many Jews today, in
that it seems to fly in the face of the monotheistic belief that all humanity is created in the

divine image—and, hence, all humanity is equally loved and valued by God. Israel's chosenness has been the subject of much discussion (including hard analysis as well as apologia) in modern Jewish theology, and it is clearly a subject requiring more attention than I can devote to it here.[49] It will have to suffice to say that the Reconstructionist movement has abandoned all reference to chosenness in its liturgy, and I find it difficult to conceive of a feminist Judaism that would incorporate it in its teaching: the valuing of one people *over and above* others is all too analogous to the privileging of one sex over another. Moreover, in honoring the sacred teachings of one's people, it is neither necessary nor helpful to state or imply that the teachings of other peoples cannot be sacred as well.

My new **Torah Blessings** honor Torah, in the sense of Israel's teaching, without making any statement about chosenness. They are based not on the Torah blessings found at this point in the traditional morning service but on other traditional blessings for Torah that share the same talmudic source. The first of these is the blessing of commandment that reads: *Barukh atah, y-h-v-h elohéynu, mélekh ha'olam, asher kid'shánu b'mitzvotav v'tzivánu la'asok b'divrey torah*, "Blessed are you, YHVH our God, king of the world, who has sanctified us with his commandments and commanded us to be occupied with words of Torah." This blessing has been incorporated in the traditional liturgy into the sequence of *birkhot hasháhar*, "blessings of the dawn," which is recited daily. Because for many Jews today the Sabbath is the primary occasion on which Torah is studied, heard, or read on a regular basis, I have carried over the language of this blessing into the first of the **Torah Blessings** of the *Shaharit:* **Morning Service for the Sabbath.**[50]

To do so, I have taken the phrase *la'asok b'divrey torah*, "to be occupied with words of Torah," and rephrased it to fit the form of my new blessings of commandment, a form established with **Sabbath Candlelighting** (see the commentary on pp. 442–43). To the lines *Yitromeym libéynu, / t'shovav nafshéynu*, "May our heart be lifted, / may our spirit be refreshed," which open **Sabbath Candlelighting**, I have added here *ta'amik havanatéynu / b'oskéynu b'divrey torah*, literally, "may our understanding deepen / through the occupation with words of Torah."

For the blessing after the Torah reading, I have repeated these lines and followed them with three more lines based on yet another blessing proposed in the same discussion in the Talmud (b. Berakhot 11b), which reads (in a literal translation): "Make pleasant the words of Torah in our mouths, and in the mouths of your people, the house of Israel, and we and our offspring and the offspring of your people, the house of Israel, all of us, will know your name and study your Torah. Blessed are you, Lord, who teaches Torah to his people Israel." In its talmudic context, this is proposed as a conclusion to the blessing for studying Torah; in the traditional liturgy, it follows the blessing for studying Torah in the daily morning service. I have re-created it to serve as the conclusion to the **Torah Blessings**, which reads: *V'ye'ervu divrey torah b'finu / uvfi tze'etza'éynu / uvfi kol tze'etza'ey yisra'eyl*, literally, "And may the words of Torah be pleasant in our mouths / and in the mouths of our offspring / and in the mouths of all the offspring of Israel." After this is recited, the congregation once again responds *N'vareykh et eyn haḥayim / v'khoh nitbareykh*, "As we bless the source of life / so we are blessed."

As Those Who Came Before Us Were Blessed	כְּמוֹ שֶׁנִּתְבָּרְכוּ
For one who has honored Torah	לעולה לתורה
(pages 270–71)	

As Those Who Came Before Us Were Blessed	כְּמוֹ שֶׁנִּתְבָּרְכוּ
For one in need of healing	למען חולה
(pages 272–75)	

As Those Who Came Before Us Were Blessed	כְּמוֹ שֶׁנִּתְבָּרְכוּ
For one gravely ill	למען חולה אנוש/ה
(pages 276–79)	

As part of the Torah section of the traditional Sabbath morning service, a blessing known by its opening words as *mi shebeyrakh*, "[the One] who blessed," is said on behalf of the entire congregation, with special variations of the blessing also recited on behalf of individuals. While originally designated for individuals called to the Torah, the *mi shebeyrakh* blessing was also used traditionally to honor those who performed good deeds and those who made donations to the community. Today it is often said on behalf of those who are ill, and a special version of it is recited for mothers on the occasion of a birth. The *mi shebeyrakh* rubric has become extremely popular in recent times, especially as a prayer for the ill; in many congregations, variations are also recited for other kinds of personal circumstances. The Reconstructionist movement suggests in its latest prayer book that *mi shebeyrakh* blessings be recited for those who are ill and for their caretakers, for those celebrating a birthday, for those reaching bar mitzvah or bat mitzvah, for those celebrating an anniversary, for those traveling to Israel, and more.[51] Women's prayer groups have used this rubric to celebrate all kinds of occasions, from getting a new job to completing a university degree.[52] The broad use of *mi shebeyrakh* blessings is indicative of a need, one that is perhaps growing today, to have the experiences of the individual recognized by the community.

The traditional prayer is a simple petition to God, asking that the person mentioned in the prayer be protected and blessed and, in the case of illness, speedily and completely healed. The prayer begins with the following words: *Mi shebeyrakh avotéynu avraham, yitzhak v'ya'akov, hu y'vareykh et* . . . , literally, "He who blessed our fathers Abraham, Isaac, and Jacob, may he bless [the name of the individual is said]"; the new prayer books of the Reconstructionist and Conservative movements include mention of the foremothers here as well.[53] My new blessing, entitled in Hebrew **K'mo Shenitbar'khu**, literally, "as [they] were blessed," opens: *K'mo shenitbar'khu imotéynu va'avotéynu / keyn titbareykh* [fem.] (or *yitbareykh* [masc.]) . . . , literally, "As our mothers and fathers were blessed, / so may [the individual's name is inserted here] be blessed." The opening lines of the English version, "As those who came before us were blessed / in the presence of the communities that sustained them," make explicit what I believe may have been the impetus behind the original prayer: to connect the individual to the greater whole of community, both historical and present. The evocation of such a connection is a powerful effect of the traditional *mi shebeyrakh* blessings, as I hope it will be for these new blessings as well.

In the traditional blessings (and in the new ones), this effect is highlighted by the insertion of the individual's name into the body of the prayer. In Orthodox use of the *mi shebeyrakh* prayer for those who are ill, a person is called by her or his first name followed by that of her or his mother; in Orthodox use of all other forms of the prayer, it is the father's name that is mentioned. (So too, in Orthodox synagogues, when a man is called upon to recite a Torah blessing, he is referred to by his first name and the first name of his father; in Orthodox practice, women are not called to the Torah at all.) However, in much non-Orthodox practice today, both parents' names are used for all *mi shebeyrakh* blessings (and all Torah blessings as well). To have one's name said aloud in a congregation can be quite moving in itself; when one includes, as part of one's name, the names of both one's parents, the sense of connection is intensified.

Indeed, the uttering of names is powerful, and it doesn't even need to be done publicly to have an impact. Not long ago, I was visiting a very sick friend who asked me to say a blessing for her. We were in her hospital room, with only a few close family members present. When I asked what names she would like to have included in the blessing, she began by giving me her Hebrew name and her mother's Hebrew name; then she paused and asked if she might add her grandmother's name as well. Within a few moments, she was adding others to the list—father, brothers, spouse, aunt—and it wasn't long before both she and I realized what was happening. She was making a chain of names to connect herself to others, and this connection was an important part of the blessing that she needed and sought.

I have included several variations of **As Those Who Came Before Us Were Blessed** in this *Shaharit* service: for an individual who has honored Torah, which may be interpreted broadly to include anyone who has taught or read sacred texts, recited Torah blessings, or helped to spread Torah in the congregation; for one in need of healing; and for one gravely ill.[54] I have distinguished between those in need of healing and those gravely ill because it seems to me that it is not always helpful to ask, as the traditional prayer does, for *r'fu'ah sh'leymah, r'fu'at hanéfesh urfu'at haguf*, literally, "complete healing, healing of the spirit and healing of the body." How does one say such a prayer in the name of someone who, in her own mind, has no hope for such recovery? Unfortunately, with diseases such as AIDS and breast cancer claiming the lives of relatively young members of many communities, this situation is not rare. Recovery from even "incurable" illness does occur, of course; yet it seems insensitive to impose the hope for it on those who are trying to make peace with their reality in a different way, trying to accept whatever is to come.

It has been suggested to me that all of us—no matter what our circumstances—would do well to accept what is to come without denial, for mortality is our common condition. I agree, yet I cannot help but feel that it is also human to hope for recovery when recovery seems possible, and that it is helpful to hear others wishing it for you as well. So I have written two different blessings for those who are ill, one of which asks, much like the traditional blessing, *lirfu'at hanéfesh v'lirfu'at haguf, / r'fu'ah sh'leymah*, literally, "for healing of the spirit and for healing of the body, / complete healing." The other blessing asks for a different kind of wholeness—one that comes from a deep acceptance of one's place in the greater whole of being. I leave it to individuals to choose which variation serves their needs.

The closing lines of the blessing for those gravely ill reprise an image from the second blessing of the **Amidah: Sevenfold Prayer for the Sabbath (Sustaining Life, Embracing Death)**: *hama'yan / adey-ad m'fakeh*, "the spring (or fountain, or well) / that eternally flows." Thus the blessing for those who may be facing imminent death echoes the affirmation of death as a part of life (for further discussion of this theme, see the commentary to **Sustaining Life, Embracing Death**, pp. 471–72).

Tree of Life   עֵץ־חַיִּים הִיא
(pages 280–81)

In the traditional service, after the reading of the Torah and again at the very end of the Torah ritual, selections of biblical verses are recited. One popular excerpt that is sung in many congregations today is made up of two verses, Proverbs 3:17–18, presented in reverse order. Known by its opening words, *eytz-ḥayim hi*, "it is a tree of life," this passage has become so familiar a part of the liturgy—and so beloved to congregants—that it seems to have taken on a completely new life outside its biblical context, leading one to forget that the liturgical order of the verses is an inversion of its original form. So too, one may easily fail to notice that the original subject of this passage in the Bible—the referent of the Hebrew pronoun "it"—is not *torah* but *ḥokhmah*, "wisdom," and *t'vunah*, "understanding." Calling to mind the original context of these verses when one sings or recites them in the Torah ritual can underscore a broad view of Torah as not just a fixed set of books and oral teachings but the ongoing pursuit and transmittal of wisdom and understanding.

The image of Torah as a "tree of life" is indeed one of the most satisfying metaphors in liturgical tradition, combining an appreciation of the vitality of the natural world with the life-enhancing gift of human understanding—at once an image of divine immanence and of transcendent revelation. I have presented the biblical verses here without emendation (preserving the inverted order canonized by centuries of liturgical use), accompanied by a new English translation.

Birkat Haḥódesh: Heralding the New Month　בִּרְכַּת הַחֹדֶשׁ
(page 283)

On the Sabbath before Rosh Hodesh, at the conclusion of the Torah section of the morning service, the ritual of *Birkat Haḥódesh*: **Heralding the New Month** is performed. This ritual is found in THE MONTHLY CYCLE, on pp. 335–47, and commentary is found on p. 494.

Closing Prayers　סִיּוּם
(pages 285–99)

The traditional Sabbath morning service concludes with the *aléynu* prayer and the *kaddish*, followed by one or more closing songs. The **Closing Prayers** to the new *Shaḥarit* contain *Aléynu L'shabéy'aḥ:* **It Is Ours to Praise** (a re-creation of *aléynu*) along with the *Kaddish:* **Mourners' Prayer** and the **Closing Blessing**. The *Kaddish* and the **Closing Blessing** are also found in the **Closing Prayers** of *Kabbalat Shabbat:* **Prayer Service Welcoming the Sabbath**. However, in the *Shaḥarit*, the **Closing Blessing** is embellished with an additional two lines at the end: *N'vareykh et eyn haḥayim / v'khoh nitbareykh*, "As we bless the source of life / so we are blessed." This is the same refrain that is found in the *Bar'khu:* **Call to Blessing**, in each section of the *Amidah*, and in the **Torah Blessings**; thus the *Shaḥarit* service ends on the motif that unites it throughout.

Aléynu L'shabéy'aḥ: It Is Ours to Praise עָלֵינוּ לְשַׁבֵּחַ
(pages 287–89)

Toward the end of traditional synagogue services for morning, afternoon, and evening, the prayer known as *aléynu*, literally, "it is [incumbent] upon us," is recited. Taken originally from the Rosh Hashanah service, where it introduces the *malkhuyot*, "kingship verses," the *aléynu* prayer expresses belief in God-as-king and relates this belief to the future unity of humanity in the world to come. At the end of the second paragraph of the prayer, known as *al keyn n'kaveh*, "therefore we hope," Zechariah 14:9 is quoted: *V'hayah y-h-v-h l'mélekh al-kol-ha'aretz; hayom hahu yihyeh y-h-v-h eḥad ushmo eḥad*, literally, "YHVH will be king over all the earth; on that day YHVH will be one and his name one."

I do not believe that I am alone in finding this prayer as a whole to be one of the more problematic pieces of the traditional liturgy. The body of the prayer contains blunt disparagement of other cultures and communities, in lines praising God for not making the people of Israel like the other peoples of the world. Moreover, the *aléynu* prayer seems self-contradictory: in singling out the Jews as the only ones who serve the proper God, it does not seem to bespeak the spirit of unity toward which it purports to aim. Rather than wishing for a world in which all worship as Jews, we might instead strive toward harmony within diversity, toward unity achieved through mutual respect.

And yet *aléynu* is so deeply ingrained in the texture of the synagogue service that to excise it entirely would leave a disturbing gap. Structurally and thematically, the service calls out for a concluding prayer, one in which the redemptive theme is reiterated. In **Aléynu L'shabéy'aḥ: It Is Ours to Praise**, I re-create the *aléynu* prayer as a conclusion to the Sabbath morning service, bringing back the major themes of the Sabbath and concluding with the vision of redemption.

The opening of the new prayer echoes that of the traditional one: *Aléynu l'shabéy'aḥ*, literally, "It is upon us to praise," or, as I translate it here, "It is ours to praise." However, the new prayer continues not as the traditional prayer does, exalting "the master of all," but instead reprises the motif *yif'at teyveyl*, literally, "the beauty of the world," from **Hal'lu: Praise** in the **Opening Blessings and Songs**. It continues by stating what is incumbent on us: *lif'ol v'la'amol l'tikun olam, / ki b'khoḥéynu livnot ultakeyn, / uvyadéynu l'hatzmí'aḥ g'ulah*, literally, "to act and to work for repair of the world, / for [it is] within our power to build and to mend, / and [it is] in our hands to help bring about redemption."

These lines, and specifically the phrase *lif'ol v'la'amol l'tikun olam*, are based on a line in the traditional prayer that reads, *l'takeyn olam b'malkhut shaday*, "to repair the world under the reign of God." The *aléynu*'s vision of a perfected cosmos is one of the earliest contexts of the idea of *tikun olam*, "repair of the world"—a concept that has been revived today in Jewish discussions of social justice issues. In the new *Aléynu L'shabéy'aḥ, tikun olam* refers to human efforts to bring about a better world, which is how I understand the idea of redemption. (This idea is discussed in the commentary to the **Blessing of Redemption**, on pp. 466–67.)

The final couplet of the new *Aléynu L'shabéy'aḥ* opens with a phrase from the last line of the traditional prayer, *bayom hahu*, "on that day," leading, like its traditional counterpart, into the climactic vision. The couplet reads: *Bayom hahu yishk'nu lavétaḥ / kol ba'ey olam*, literally, "On that day [they] will dwell in security / all the creatures of the world." Thus *Aléynu L'shabéy'aḥ:* **It Is Ours to Praise** begins with an appreciation of the realm of creation, moves into revelation of human responsibilities, and concludes with the vision of a redeemed world, a world of peace, brought about, at least in part, by our own actions.

Kaddish: Mourners' Prayer   קַדִּישׁ
(pages 291–95)

See pp. 446–48.

Closing Blessing   בִּרְכַּת סִיּוּם
(pages 297–99)

See p. 448.

Sanctification over Wine for Sabbath Day   קִדּוּשׁ לְיוֹם שַׁבָּת
(pages 300–301)

Following services on Sabbath morning, the sanctification over wine (*kiddush*) and the second feast of the Sabbath take place (discussion of the Sabbath feasts may be found in the commentary to **Kabbalat P'ney Shabbat**, p. 449). Although the *kiddush* is technically a part of home ritual, many synagogues today convene a *kiddush* after the Sabbath morning service. I have therefore appended the **Sanctification over Wine for Sabbath Day** to the end of the *Shaḥarit* service, for use in either the communal or home setting. For commentary to this blessing, see pp. 452–56.

Havdalah: Parting Ritual for the Sabbath   הַבְדָּלָה לְמוֹצָאֵי שַׁבָּת
(pages 305–23)

Like the Sabbath *kiddush,* the *havdalah* ritual, which ends the Sabbath and separates it from the week, is ancient. (See the commentary to the **Sanctification over Wine for Sabbath Eve,** pp. 452–53.) Also like the *kiddush,* the *havdalah* has origins attributed by some to communal meals. At nightfall during these meals, light was brought in, and at the close of the meal incense was burned, with blessings recited for both the incense and the light. In the grace after the meal, a blessing called *havdalah,* "separation," was inserted for the conclusion of the Sabbath; on Saturday nights, this blessing was also added to the *amidah* prayer recited by individuals (inserted in the fourth section, which petitions God for knowledge and wisdom). Later, when the communal meals fell out of custom, the whole ritual— including blessings over wine, spices, light, and distinctions—was transferred to the evening service in the synagogue. In certain communities, however, the *havdalah* was also performed in the home, where individuals added their personal choices of biblical verses containing petitions for blessing in the coming week. Today the *havdalah* takes place in synagogues as well as homes. Much like the sequence of blessings that ushers the Sabbath into the home, the ritual for the Sabbath's departure is performed with candles, wine, sweet fragrance, and songs, in a vivid appeal to the senses of sight, taste, smell, and hearing.

As Sabbath eve is associated with the theme of creation and Sabbath day with revelation, the close of the Sabbath is thematically linked to redemption; it is therefore traditional to add to the *havdalah* ceremony special poems and songs containing messianic images. The **Havdalah: Parting Ritual for the Sabbath** re-creates the traditional ritual, preserving the main elements of wine, spices, light, and distinctions. It also contains two new offerings for its opening and its conclusion. The theological meanings of the traditional ritual and of this new one are discussed in the introduction to THE WEEKLY CYCLE (pp. 45–47).

Opening Psalm   מִזְמוֹר פְּתִיחָה
(page 311)

The poem entitled *Open Gate,* which opens the new **Havdalah,** sets the context for transition into the week, much as *Will* (the **Opening Psalm** of *Kabbalat P'ney Shabbat*) sets the context for transition into the Sabbath. In *Open Gate,* "the corridor / where night / bares its maze" mirrors the "passages" with which night fills the house in *Will.* The reference to the open gate itself echoes a traditional liturgical metaphor for access to *t'shuvah,* "returning" (often translated "repentance," but intended here to be understood as a return to new beginnings). The reference to "three stars" alludes to the talmudic ruling that, for religious purposes, a day ends (and the next day commences) when three stars may be seen in the evening sky (b. Shabbat 35b).

Sanctification over Wine for the Week   קִדּוּשׁ לַשָּׁבוּעַ

(pages 312–13)

The traditional blessing over wine recited at the *havdalah* ceremony is a simple blessing over the fruit of the vine. In the introduction to THE WEEKLY CYCLE (pp. 45–47), I discuss why I chose to elaborate on the *havdalah*'s blessing over wine, re-creating it as a full sanctification (*kiddush*). In the commentary to the **Sanctification over Wine for Sabbath Eve** and the **Sanctification over Wine for Sabbath Day** (pp. 452–56), the elements of the sanctification blessings are explained. The **Sanctification over Wine for the Week** is parallel in every regard to these other new sanctifications: it is introduced by a biblical citation, proceeds to a two-line blessing over the wine (identical to that used in the other sanctifications), and concludes with the statement of sanctification particular to the occasion.

The introductory citation here is excerpted from the introductory passage to the traditional home ritual of *havdalah*. It includes Esther 8:16, *Lay'hudim hay'tah orah v'simḥah v'sason vikar*, literally, "The Jews had light and joy and gladness and honor," followed by a phrase of emphasis that was added by the rabbis, *keyn tihyeh lánu*, "so may they be ours." The image of light found in these lines at once recalls the candlelighting performed on Sabbath eve and points ahead to the *Havdalah*'s blessing of **Lights of Fire**. Thus it underscores the parallel between the ritual opening the Sabbath and the one opening the new week, which this new *Havdalah* seeks to call to mind. I have excerpted these lines in the Hebrew exactly as they appear in the traditional *havdalah*, although I have rendered them anew in English.

The introductory lines contain another element that is central to the thematic focus of the new *Havdalah* ritual—the connection of the past to the present, which provides a sense of ongoing history. This theme is articulated in the second half of the **Sanctification over Wine for the Week**, which reads: *unkadeysh et shéyshet y'mey hama'aseh / zéykher l'toldotéynu*, literally, "and let us sanctify the six days of work / in commemoration of our generations (or of our history)."

The sanctification of the week, or what tradition calls *shéyshet y'mey hama'aseh*, "the six days of work," is a hallowing of an aspect of time as well as a sanctification of work. In the Ten Commandments, not only is Israel enjoined to remember or keep the Sabbath by not working on that day, it is also positively enjoined to work on the other six days of the week:

shéyshet yamim ta'avod v'asíta kol-m'lakhtékha, "six days you shall work and do all your labor" (Exod. 20:9; Deut. 5:13); this commandment is also repeated in Leviticus 23:3: *shéyshet yamim tey'aseh m'lakhah*, "six days shall work be done." If to honor the Sabbath is to honor *being* itself—the being of all creation—to honor the weekday and its work is to honor our *doing* in the world. It is during the week that we work to effect change, and thus, we might say, it is during the week that we strive to bring about redemption. There is a traditional acronym for the *havdalah* ritual made up of the four letters beginning the words *yáyin, b'samim, neyr,* and *havdalot* ("wine," "spices," "candle," and "distinctions"); this acronym spells the word meaning "build." We might think of the week as a time of building, a time to create and renew, to mend and repair. To hallow the work week is to acknowledge its potential for redemption and to commit to seeking opportunities to do fulfilling work in the course of our daily lives.

The phrase *zéykher l'toldotéynu*, literally, "in commemoration of our generations," parallels the two phrases in the Sabbath sanctifications, *zikaron l'ma'aseyh v'reyshit*, "in remembrance of the creation," and *zéykher litzi'at mitzráyim*, "in commemoration of the exodus from Egypt." If the Sabbath commemorates our origins in creation and our release from slavery, the central event of our people's history, then the week represents our ongoing journey through time, through history, as a people, as a civilization. This is one meaning of *toldotéynu*, represented in the English version of the blessing as follows: "Let us bless the source of life / that ripens fruit on the vine / as we hallow the week, / calling to mind our history."

But *toldotéynu* has another association, another connection to its context. Just as the phrase *ma'aseyh v'reyshit* refers to our beginnings—*v'reyshit* contains within it the root that means "head" (hence, "start")—the word *toldotéynu* also implies beginnings, for its root means "birth." To recall past generations is to remember that life is ever regenerating. Aware of the transformations occurring all around us and within us, we remind ourselves to let go, clearing the way for something new. As the Sabbath leaves, the work week enters: we escort one out as we welcome the other in.

Spices בְּשָׂמִים
(pages 314–15)

It is speculated that the origin of the blessing over spices had to do with the use of incense over coals at the end of meals, but there are also more poetic interpretations of this blessing. The twelfth-century scholar Maimonides explained that the fragrance of spices was cheering to the soul, saddened by the Sabbath's departure (Hilkhot Shabbat 29:29). (Note that when a holiday follows immediately after the Sabbath ends, the spices are omitted from the *havdalah* ritual, and one explanation for this is that the spices are unnecessary because the incoming holiday is enough to cheer the soul.) Others say that a bit of the Sabbath itself wafts with the fragrance, helping us to keep its spirit with us as we enter the week.

If fragrance is cheering, it is also more than merely ornamental; indeed, smell is often intimately associated with identity. The English word "essence," which derives from the Latin *esse*, "to be," and which means both "identity" and "scent," demonstrates this association.[55] In the traditional blessing, God is praised not just for creating aromatic spices but for creating the (many) *kinds* of such spices: *Barukh atah, y-h-v-h elohéynu, mélekh ha'olam, borey miney v'samim*, literally, "Blessed are you, YHVH our God, king of the world, who creates the kinds (or varieties) of spices (or fragrances)." If fragrances are taken metaphorically to mean identities, this blessing might be said to celebrate the diversity of individual identities within creation.

This idea brings to mind once again the image *nishmat kol ḥay*, "breath (or soul, or spirit) of all that lives (or of every living thing)," which is found in the traditional liturgy (see the commentary to **The Breath of All Life**, p. 462). It is neither coincidental nor irrelevant that the word for "soul," *n'shamah*, is related to the word for "breathing," *n'shimah*, an activity directly connected to the sense of smell. While the traditional liturgy offers the line *nishmat kol ḥay t'vareykh et shim'kha*, "the breath of all that lives will bless your name," it struck me, in re-creating the blessing for fragrances, that we might meaningfully invert this statement so that we, as a community, would praise the breath of all that lives. *Nishmat kol ḥay*—the breath that unites us in creation even as it distinguishes us from each other in our individuated beings. *Nishmat kol ḥay*—the spirit that breathes in each of us, uniting us with the breath and flow of life. Blessing the image of *nishmat kol ḥay* means honoring the uniqueness of each creature within the infinite diversity of creation. Thus my blessing reads: *N'haleyl et nishmat kol ḥay / unvareykh al miney b'samim*, literally, "Let us praise the breath (or spirit, or soul) of all that lives / and bless (or say a blessing over) the varieties of fragrances."

Often things get lost in translation, but sometimes there are unexpected gains. The dual resonance of the English word "essence" perhaps compensates for the loss of the subliminal association between *n'shamah* and *n'shimah*. Thus the English version of my blessing reads: "Let us celebrate the breath / of all living things / and praise all essences."

Lights of Fire   מְאוֹרֵי הָאֵשׁ
(pages 316–17)

The traditional blessing over the light in the *havdalah* ritual praises God for creating *m'orey ha'eysh*, literally, "lights of fire"—an image resonant with metaphoric possibility. Where there is a blaze, there is first a kindling, and so to me the lights of fire call to mind the image of the hidden sparks, familiar from mystical tradition where "uplifting" them is said to bring about *tikun*, "repair [of the cosmos]."[56] If we extend this metaphor to the psychological domain, the sparks may represent inner potential that is revealed through self-awareness. In the social realm, the sparks may signify external sources of inspiration and encouragement, such as people who provide caretaking and support, enabling others to act. This kind of "kindling," too, is often hidden from view. On both personal and interpersonal levels, the imagery of "lights of fire" seems to call for a searching out of that which is concealed or unrecognized, a foregrounding of the background, an illumination of the depths.

In re-creating this blessing, I chose the verb *n'vakeysh*, "let us search (or seek)," and I linked it with the kabbalistic image of the sparks: *N'vakeysh et nitzotzot hanéfesh / matzitey m'orey ha'eysh*, literally, "Let us seek the sparks of the spirit / that kindle the lights of fire." In the English version, the element of concealment is explicit: "Let us seek the unseen sparks / that kindle the greater lights." The word *matzitey*, "kindle," is used metaphorically here, echoing its use in a famous poem by the Hungarian Jewish poet Hannah Szenes, who died in 1944 at the age of twenty-three trying to rescue Jews from the Nazis. In *Ashrey Hagafrur*, "Blessed Is the Match," Szenes writes: *Ashrey hagafrur shenisraf v'hitzit lehavot*, "Blessed is the match that has been consumed and that has kindled flames." The "match" in Szenes's poem is the person whose death "kindles" inspiration in others; in the new blessing, unseen sparks kindle the lights of insight and enlightened action in the world.

Distinctions   הַבְדָּלוֹת
(pages 318–19)

Distinctions   הַבְדָּלוֹת
For the onset of a holiday   ללֵיל חג
(pages 320–21)

The traditional *havdalah* blessing for distinctions is discussed in the introduction to THE WEEKLY CYCLE (pp. 45–47), where I analyze what I find problematic in the formulation. The key phrases of this blessing describe God as *hamavdil beyn kódesh l'ḥol, beyn or l'ḥóshekh, beyn yisra'eyl la'amim, beyn yom hash'vi'i l'shéyshet y'mey hama'aseh*, literally, "[the one] who distinguishes between the holy and the profane (or ordinary), between light and darkness, between Israel and the [other] nations, between the seventh day and the six days of work." In the new blessing, I preserve the act of making distinctions but formulate them differently: *Navhin beyn ḥelkey hashaleym / v'al hahevdeylim n'vareykh. / Navdil beyn yom hash'vi'i / l'shéyshet y'mey hama'aseh, / ukdushah b'khol yom n'vakeysh*, literally, "Let us distinguish among the parts of the whole / and say a blessing over the differences. / Let us separate the seventh day / from the six days of work, / and in each day let us seek holiness." The word *havdalah* is echoed twice here: once in the word *hahevdeylim*, "the differences," and once in the word *navdil*, "let us separate." Rather than make hierarchical distinctions, this blessing asks that we affirm difference as a positive value and celebrate the particular differences that make things distinguishable from each other. The English version of the blessing makes explicit the analogies that are embedded in the Hebrew.

Above all, what this blessing seeks to do is to humanize the act of making distinctions and to subvert the hierarchical assumptions embedded in oppositional thinking. If we recognize that *we* are the ones making discriminations, we are more likely to take responsibility for making honorable and compassionate ones, which will support truth and justice in our lives.

This idea is not without basis in the tradition. Although they attributed the ultimate power of discrimination to God, the rabbis, too, implicitly connected distinctions with human intelligence. In a talmudic discussion concerning the placement of the *havdalah* blessing within the fourth section of the daily *amidah*, which asks God to grant us knowledge, one of the rabbis remarks: "I am surprised that the blessing for granting knowledge is eliminated [from the *amidah*] on the Sabbath. For without knowledge, where does prayer come from? Likewise, without knowledge, where would *havdalah* [the ability to make distinctions] come from?" (y. Berakhot 5:2).

Note that traditionally, when the Sabbath ends at the onset of a holiday, a different version of the *havdalah* blessing is recited. I, too, have provided a special version of the blessing, which acknowledges the distinction between Sabbath and festival. In this blessing (as well as in the rest of the **Havdalah** ritual as adapted for the onset of holidays), the entrance of the holiday overrides the onset of the week, since the ordinary work week does not begin until the holiday is over. (Instructions for adapting the whole of the ritual to the eve of holidays are found on p. 307.)

Blessing for the New Week   בִּרְכַּת הַשָּׁבוּעַ
(pages 322–23)

On Saturday night, immediately preceding and during the evening service, it is customary to read a selection of psalms and other biblical passages to escort the Sabbath in its departure. In Ashkenazic tradition, this collection of verses includes nearly all the blessing formulas in the Pentateuch. One segment of this reading is made up of verses selected from Deuteronomy 28:1–14, in which Israel is promised a blessing if it will keep God's commandments. The verses are quoted out of order—3, 6, 5, 4, 8, 12—and are followed by Deuteronomy 15:6 and 33:29; yet they work together as a whole, as an affirmation of daily working life.

The **Blessing for the New Week** is based on the traditional excerpts from Deuteronomy 28. It is included at the end of the *Havdalah:* **Parting Ritual for the Sabbath** to take the place of the additional blessings for the new week that were once appended to the *havdalah* service when it was performed in the home.

The Monthly Cycle   מַחֲזוֹר הַחֹדֶשׁ

Birkat Hahódesh: Heralding the New Month   בִּרְכַּת הַחֹדֶשׁ
(pages 335–47)

The traditional ritual known as *birkat hahódesh*, "blessing of the month," is a composite of prayers surrounding an announcement of the upcoming festival of the New Moon. It is recited in synagogue on the Sabbath preceding Rosh Hodesh, called *shabbat m'var'khim*, "the Sabbath [during which] we bless." The most poignant part of *birkat hahódesh* is a passage usually referred to by its opening words, *y'hi ratzon*, "may it be [your] will." Essentially a catalogue of requested blessings, *y'hi ratzon* is an adaptation of a private prayer recited by Rav, a rabbi of the third century, and recorded in the Talmud (b. Berakhot 16b); it was not incorporated into the public *birkat hahódesh* ritual until the eighteenth century. The ritual also includes a prayer for the gathering of the Jewish people from exile and closing petitions for well-being and salvation. Despite its name, *birkat hahódesh* does not contain a single blessing formula.

Like the traditional ritual, **Birkat Hahódesh: Heralding the New Month** is a composite of prayers surrounding an announcement. Unlike the traditional ritual, the new ritual opens with an expression of gratitude for the month that is drawing to a close before proceeding to the announcement of the upcoming Rosh Hodesh festival. It closes with a prayer for blessings in the month about to begin.

Gifts of the Month: A Thanksgiving   מַתְּנוֹת הַחֹדֶשׁ: הוֹדָיָה
(pages 340–41)

In anticipation of the new month, we pause to recall what we have received during the month that now draws to an end. This prayer of gratitude, which has no counterpart in the traditional liturgy, echoes some of the language of the **Blessing Before Going to Sleep**, found in THE DAILY CYCLE.

Announcing the New Month הַכְרָזַת הַחֹדֶשׁ
(pages 342–43)

The Hebrew version of this announcement is identical to that found in the traditional *birkat haḥódesh* ritual. The English version contains the expanded wish that the upcoming holiday will be "a day of blessings, / goodness, and joy."

Prayer for the New Month תְּפִלַּת הַחֹדֶשׁ
(pages 344–47; see also 370–73)

The Hebrew version of this prayer is based on the *y'hi ratzon* portion of the traditional *birkat haḥódesh* ritual. It contains phrases taken from *y'hi ratzon* as well as from other sources, in particular, the blessing of sanctification for Rosh Hodesh, found in the fourth section of the *amidah* of the *musaf* (supplementary service) for Rosh Hodesh day; it also contains several original phrases. Much of the phrasing, traditional and new, takes the form of conventional word pairs. Thus the Hebrew version employs the standard poetic convention of listing attributes in pairs to create the effect of abundance through accretion, a convention emphasized by the use of couplets. The English version of the blessing is also in couplets, but it does not rely as heavily as the Hebrew on the convention of word pairing; also, unlike the Hebrew, it is composed entirely in a contemporary diction.

The following is a literal translation of the Hebrew blessing:

> May the month of [name of the new month]
> be renewed for us
>
> for goodness and for blessing,
> for happiness and for joy,
>
> for peace and brother/sister-hood,
> friendship and love,
>
> for work and creativity,
> livelihood and income,
>
> for peace of spirit
> and bodily health,
>
> for a life of *dérekh éretz* [explained below]
> and love of Torah,

for a life in which the wishes of our heart
will be fulfilled for goodness.

So may it be.

The opening and closing words of the prayer, *Y'hi ratzon*, "May it be," and *Keyn y'hi ratzon*, "So may it be," are traditional liturgical phrases of petition. The **Prayer for the New Month** is distinct from most of the offerings in this book in that it uses a petitionary form to express wishes and desires.

The last couplet of the Hebrew, *l'ḥayim sheyimal'u bam* / *mish'alot libéynu l'tovah*, "for a life in which the wishes of our heart / will be fulfilled for goodness" (lines that are closely adapted from the traditional Hebrew prayer), broadens the scope of the rest of the prayer by seeking fulfillment over the course of a lifetime. It asks, in an elliptical way, that only our worthwhile wishes be fulfilled—that is, only those desires whose fulfillment will be for the good—implying that we do not always know what is ultimately best for ourselves or for others. No matter how well we plan our lives, we can be sure that at least some of the time we will be surprised; we can only hope we learn well from these surprises. These ideas are recast in the English blessing as the wish "that we may blossom / as we age / and become / our sweetest selves."

The term *dérekh éretz* in line 11 is especially difficult to translate; literally, it is "the way of the land," but it refers to appropriate behavior in a sense that pertains more to ethics and decency than to manners or etiquette. It is traditionally linked with the idea of Torah, as in Pirkey Avot: "The study of Torah with *dérekh éretz* is beautiful" (2:2). As a pair, the terms *dérekh éretz* and *ahavat torah*, "love of Torah," represent a central value of Jewish life. In the English version of the blessing, this value is articulated in these lines: "May truth and justice / guide our acts, / and compassion / temper our lives."

The **Prayer for the New Month** is recited in both *Birkat Haḥódesh:* **Heralding the New Month** and *Kabbalat P'ney Haḥódesh:* **Welcoming the New Month**, which takes place on Rosh Hodesh eve. This dual appearance echoes a pattern in the traditional liturgy, which requests blessings for the new month on two occasions—in the *y'hi ratzon* portion of *birkat haḥódesh*, which takes place during the Sabbath preceding Rosh Hodesh; and on Rosh Hodesh day itself, in the fourth section of the *amidah* of the *musaf* service. Note that in the context of *Kabbalat P'ney Haḥódesh*, which is the spiritual high point of the cycle, the **Prayer for the New Month** is embellished with **Personal Prayers**, in which individual members of the community contribute their own words.

Kabbalat P'ney Haḥódesh: Welcoming the New Month
קַבָּלַת פְּנֵי הַחֹֽדֶשׁ
(pages 351–83)

Special mealtime ritual for the eve or day of Rosh Hodesh has not been a part of traditional Jewish practice for many centuries, although it was observed in earlier periods. Indeed, the feast of Rosh Hodesh has ancient origins, first recorded in 1 Samuel 20, where David tells Jonathan of his custom of sitting with the king for a meal on the day of the New Moon. Tractate Soferim, an eighth-century Palestinian document normally delineated as one of the "minor tractates" of the Talmud (that is, not actually part of the Talmud but appended to it in the standard printed versions), describes postbiblical practice of the feast in the land of Israel. Soferim outlines the liturgy and customs associated with the feast, which commenced with the afternoon prayers on the day preceding the New Moon and continued until the moon appeared in the evening sky (19:7, ed. Higger). The liturgy specifically included a blessing over wine, which noted the sanctity of the day with the words *hamkadeysh yisra'eyl v'rashey ḥodashim*, "who sanctifies Israel and the beginnings of months." Soferim also makes reference to passing the winecup to one's wife "to cause a blessing to rest on your house" (19:8). From this we may deduce that women as well as men participated in this aspect of Rosh Hodesh observance. Although the blessing recorded in Soferim is no longer recited, I view it as a historical basis for including a sanctification over wine in today's new Rosh Hodesh celebrations.

 Kabbalat P'ney Haḥódesh: **Welcoming the New Month** is intended for use by the family or the community on Rosh Hodesh eve (or a date shortly thereafter); it takes its structure from that of mealtime ritual for the eve of festivals, adding to it some enhancements. Its name is based on *Kabbalat P'ney Shabbat:* **Home Ritual Welcoming the Sabbath** (that name is explained on pp. 448–49).

Opening Psalm   מִזְמוֹר פְּתִיחָה
(page 357)

The poem *Witnessing* depicts the ancient ritual of witnessing the appearance of the crescent moon prior to announcing the New Moon holiday. It sets the context for Rosh Hodesh candlelighting, which may be seen as a way of mirroring the practice of lighting fires on the hills.

Rosh Hodesh Candelighting   הַדְלָקַת נֵרוֹת רֹאשׁ חֹדֶשׁ
(pages 358–59)

Because Rosh Hodesh is not considered equivalent to the Sabbath or to the major festivals, no blessing is traditionally associated with Rosh Hodesh candlelighting customs. Nonetheless, I wanted to provide words to mark this ritual. Rather than mimic the form of **Sabbath Candlelighting**, which is a blessing of commandment, I have written a different kind of blessing, which might be thought of as a reflection. Personal in tone, it uses the first-person singular voice to address the moon in its renewal and in its antiquity (this personal address of the moon follows the example of the traditional *birkat hal'vanah* ritual; see the commentary to *Birkat Hal'vanah:* **Blessing of the Moon**, pp. 506–8). The moon in this new blessing is more than an image of the natural world; it is also a metaphor for Jewish tradition. The twin meanings (literal and metaphorical) are embedded in the opening images of the Hebrew, *Or ḥadash, ma'or kadmon*, "New light, ancient light [i.e., moon]." *Or ḥadash*, "new light," is a term borrowed from the blessing known as *yotzeyr or*, "creator of light," in the traditional synagogue liturgy, where it is a metaphor for Israel's redemption. The line in which it appears reads: *Or ḥadash al tziyon ta'ir, v'nizkeh khulánu m'heyrah l'oro*, "Cause a new light to shine on Zion, and may we all soon merit its light." The new candlelighting blessing juxtaposes *or ḥadash* with *ma'or kadmon*, "ancient light," an image calling to mind the biblical story of the creation of the great lights of the sun and the moon, *ham'orot hag'dolim* (Gen. 1:14–19). Together, *or ḥadash* and *ma'or kadmon* suggest the redemptive possibilities inherent in our thoughtful renewal of ancient tradition. In the English version, the play of old and new is slightly shifted: instead of "New light, ancient moon," we have "New moon, ancient light."

Blessing of the Children   בִּרְכַּת יַלְדָּה וָיֶלֶד
(pages 360–61)

In traditional ritual for the eve of holidays, the practice of blessing the children often takes place after candlelighting. I have therefore included the **Blessing of the Children** (also found in *Kabbalat P'ney Shabbat:* **Home Ritual Welcoming the Sabbath**) in the ceremony for Rosh Hodesh eve, immediately following **Rosh Hodesh Candlelighting**. For commentary to this blessing, see pp. 450–51.

Meditation for the Sanctification over Wine for Rosh Hodesh
כַּוָּנַת הַלֵּב לְקִדוּשׁ לְרֹאשׁ חֹדֶשׁ
(page 363)

The Hebrew term in the title, *kavanat haleyv*, literally, "direction of the heart" (rendered in the English title as "meditation"), is related to the concept of directing the heart in prayer, which is discussed in the commentary to **Putting on the Prayer Shawl**, pp. 458–59. The term *kavanat haleyv* itself is discussed in the commentary to the **Amidah: Sevenfold Prayer for the Sabbath** (p. 469).

This preparatory reading was inspired by Rosh Hodesh communities experimenting with new ritual. It meditates on the image of the "fruit of the vine" as a metaphor for community, which is implicit in every sanctification over wine in this book. The blessing of *eyn hahayim / matzmihat p'ri hagéfen*, "the source of life / that ripens fruit on the vine," is meant to be read not just as a blessing of appreciation for the gifts of the natural (botanical) world. Because the blessing over wine is recited at occasions when people gather to mark the sacred, this blessing may also be experienced as an appreciation of human interconnections. I have made this idea explicit in the **Meditation for the Sanctification over Wine for Rosh Hodesh** because Rosh Hodesh celebrations today are a tribute to the creative force of community building. The motif of weaving, which is also central in this meditation, is discussed immediately below.

Sanctification over Wine for Rosh Hodesh   קִדּוּשׁ לְרֹאשׁ חֹדֶשׁ
(pages 364–65; see also 396–97)

Sanctification over Wine for the Eve of Sabbath Rosh Hodesh
קִדּוּשׁ לְלֵיל שַׁבָּת רֹאשׁ חֹדֶשׁ
(pages 366–67)

Sanctification over Wine for the Day of Sabbath Rosh Hodesh
קִדּוּשׁ לְיוֹם שַׁבָּת רֹאשׁ חֹדֶשׁ
(pages 398–99)

The status of Rosh Hodesh in Jewish liturgical practice is ambiguous. Considered a half-holiday with special synagogue prayers, Rosh Hodesh goes unmarked in the home; a sanctification over wine (*kiddush*) is not recited. Nonetheless, like the intermediary days of the festivals of Passover and Sukkot (which also are not marked with a *kiddush*), Rosh Hodesh is assigned a *musaf* service, in which a seven-sectioned *amidah* prayer is recited; in the fourth section of this *amidah*, a blessing for *k'dushat hayom*, "sanctification of the day," is said.

Given the renewed significance of Rosh Hodesh in our time, which is illustrated, in part, by the practice of holding new ceremonies in the setting of the home, and given the importance of the *kiddush* in modern Jewish celebrations, Rosh Hodesh seems to call out for a *kiddush*. For this reason—and as a symbol for the broader renewal of Jewish ritual today—I have created a new sanctification over wine for this holiday. It follows the form of the other *kiddush* blessings in this book: **Sanctification over Wine for Sabbath Eve, Sanctification over Wine for Sabbath Day**, and **Sanctification over Wine for the Week.**

The **Sanctification over Wine for Rosh Hodesh** opens with a biblical quotation taken from Isaiah 66, the whole of which constitutes the *haftarah* (supplementary Bible reading) traditionally chanted in synagogue on Sabbath Rosh Hodesh (this is a remarkable *haftarah*, which includes, among other memorable images, a portrayal of God as a nursing mother). I have excerpted part of v. 23 from this chapter and followed it by part of v. 14, to create the introduction to the blessing: "It shall come to be from one month to the next / that your hearts will rejoice / and your bones will flower like young grass."

The biblical quotation is followed by the same blessing over wine that is found in my other sanctifications: *N'vareykh et eyn haḥayim / matzmiḥat p'ri hagéfen*, rendered in English as "Let us bless the source of life / that ripens fruit on the vine." This, in turn, is followed by a statement beginning with the word *unkadeysh*, "and let us sanctify": *unkadeysh et rosh haḥódesh / ba'arigat p'tiley ḥayéynu / l'tokh masékhet hadorot*, literally, "and let us sanctify Rosh Hodesh / by the weaving of the threads of our lives / into the mesh (or network, or web) of the generations."

Weaving is a craft historically associated with women, and in feminist writings today the image of weaving is often used to symbolize interconnectedness and nonhierarchical relation. I had these associations in mind when I first conceived this blessing, because Rosh Hodesh has been the product of much collaborative effort among women. But I chose the image equally for its resonances in Hebrew: in particular, the word *masékhet*, "mesh," or "network," or "web," has a particularly rich history of metaphorical use beginning in the Bible and continuing to today. As with the English "web," a *masékhet* may be the workings of a spider or of the human imagination; it may also be the product of a loom. In Isaiah 30:1, the phrase *linsokh maseykhah*, "to weave a web," means to create a plan, weave thoughts; thus the word *masékhet* (or, in Aramaic, *masekhta*) also refers to a tractate of Mishnah or Talmud. In this blessing I refer to *masékhet hadorot*, literally, "network of the generations," that is, the historical tradition, the fabric of history. This image is linked to another image of weaving, *arigat p'tiley ḥayéynu*, "the weaving of the threads of our lives"; like *masékhet*, *arigah*, "weaving," is biblical in origin. Rosh Hodesh is the holiday that, in modern times, has truly interwoven the old and the new, bringing new hands to the ancient looms.

The lines *ba'arigat p'tiley hayéynu / l'tokh masékhet hadorot* thematically echo the words of **Recalling Our Ancestors, Remembering Our Lives,** which is the first blessing of the **Amidah: Sevenfold Prayer for the Sabbath.** That blessing reads: *Nizkor et masóret hadorot / v'nishzor bah et sarigey hayéynu,* literally, "Let us recall the tradition of the generations / and let us weave into it the branches (or tendrils) of our lives." The word *nishzor,* "let us weave," is synonymous with a verbal form of *arigah (na'arog).* The phrase *sarigey hayéynu,* "branches of our lives," brings yet another association to the motif of weaving: *sarig,* spelled as here with the Hebrew letter *sin,* is "branch" or "tendril," but it is also a variant of *sarig* spelled with a *sámekh,* which is "grid," or "lattice," or "weaving." Finally, the phrases *masóret hadorot,* "tradition of the generations," and *masékhet hadorot,* "network of the generations," are similar in sound as well as meaning. These congruencies are meant to link the Rosh Hodesh ceremony to the place in the liturgy that is specifically devoted to recalling the past.

Before leaving the discussion of linguistic associations, I can't resist a final word for those who enjoy an embedded pun. A verbal form of *masékhet—nasakh,* "weave"—has a homonym meaning "pour [as a libation]." Needless to say, this association with the blessing over wine is purely coincidental.

Two variations of the **Sanctification over Wine for Rosh Hodesh—Sanctification over Wine for the Eve of Sabbath Rosh Hodesh** and **Sanctification over Wine for the Day of Sabbath Rosh Hodesh**—are provided for those days when Rosh Hodesh coincides with the Sabbath. These sanctifications are combinations of the blessings for the two coinciding occasions, with the blessing for the Sabbath preceding the blessing for Rosh Hodesh, since the Sabbath is considered the holiest of all days. The biblical quotation for Rosh Hodesh in these sanctifications contains an additional phrase *umidey shabbat b'shabbato,* "and from one Sabbath to the next," which is found in the original verse (Isa. 66:23).

Blessing for the New and for Renewal   שֶׁהֶחֱיָנוּ
(pages 368–69)

The traditional blessing for renewals, known as *birkat haz'man,* "blessing of time," and commonly referred to as *sheheheyánu* (from one of its key words, meaning "which [or who] has revived us"), is perhaps one of the best-known and most-loved blessings in modern Jewish life. It has historically been recited at the onset of holidays and new events, often uttered in conjunction with another blessing; for example, before tasting a fruit for the first time in its season, one utters a blessing for that fruit and then says the *sheheheyánu* blessing. On Rosh Hodesh it may be considered appropriate to say a blessing for renewals after the sanctification over wine, much as is done on other festivals. That Rosh Hodesh ceremonies today are largely new creations gives double resonance to the use of such a blessing to mark this holiday.

My **Blessing for the New and for Renewal** is closely related to its traditional counterpart, which reads: *Barukh atah, y-h-v-h elohéynu, mélekh ha'olam, sheheḥeyánu v'kiy'mánu v'higi'ánu laz'man hazeh*, literally, "Blessed are you, YHVH our God, king of the world, who has revived us and sustained us and brought us to this time." The significant change in the new blessing (besides the substitution of the active *n'vareykh*, "let us bless," for the passive *barukh atah*, "blessed are you") is that divinity is now celebrated as *ma'yan ḥayéynu*, literally, "the fountain of our lives," rendered in the English version as "the flow of life." The image of the flowing fountain is intended to call attention to the focus of the blessing, which is the passage of time. At the same time, because *ma'yan*, "fountain," is a grammatically masculine noun (though semantically neutral and etymologically related to the feminine noun *áyin*, which is part of the phrase *eyn haḥayim*, "source of life"), I was able to preserve intact the much-loved wording of the second half of the traditional blessing. To the traditional words *sheheḥeyánu v'kiy'mánu v'higi'ánu la'zman hazeh* I have added only a line break to emphasize their rhythm. As a new "blessing of time," the **Blessing for the New and for Renewal** celebrates process and time itself—past, present, and future as an unceasing flow.

Prayer for the New Month תְּפִלַּת הַחֹדֶשׁ
(pages 370–73)

See pp. 495–96; also see the commentary to *Birkat Haḥódesh:* **Heralding the New Month**, p. 494.

Personal Prayers תְּפִלּוֹת אִישִׁיוּת
(pages 374–75)

The creativity of today's new Rosh Hodesh ceremonies suggested to me the need for a special place in the liturgy where spontaneous, individual contributions would be invited. The rubric of **Personal Prayers** allows participants to add their own thoughts and wishes for the new month within a communal context. Although an innovation for Rosh Hodesh, this addition to the liturgy is in keeping with an old tradition for *havdalah*, the ceremony closing the Sabbath, in which individuals added their personal choice of biblical verses with which to bless the new week.

Handwashing Before the Meal   נְטִילַת יָדַיִם לִפְנֵי הָאֲרוּחָה
(pages 376–77)

See pp. 426–28.

Blessing Before the Meal   הַמּוֹצִיאָה
(pages 378–79)

See pp. 428–30.

Blessing After the Meal   בִּרְכַּת הַמָּזוֹן
(pages 380–81)

See pp. 430–31.

Closing Psalm   מִזְמוֹר סִיּוּם
(pages 382–83)

Because of the special significance that Rosh Hodesh has historically held for Jewish women, and because of the new flowering of Rosh Hodesh ceremonies among Jewish women's groups today, this new **Kabbalat P'ney Haḥódesh** ceremony concludes with a poem by the Hebrew poet Zelda that takes as its subject the gathering of women and the celebration of their time together. Although Zelda's poem was not written specifically for Rosh Hodesh, its evocation of the "treasure of leisure" can inspire and inform the creation of holiday time.

Blessings for the Morning of Rosh Hodesh
קִדּוּשׁ וּבְרָכוֹת לִתְפִלַּת שַׁחֲרִית
(pages 387–99)

This part of THE MONTHLY CYCLE is not self-contained; rather, it offers inclusions (individual blessings) with which to render the **Shaḥarit: Morning Service for the Sabbath** into a morning service for Rosh Hodesh. For this purpose, the fourth section of the **Amidah: Sevenfold Prayer for the Sabbath**, which is the section sanctifying the day, is changed (as explained in the instructions within the liturgy). Because a sanctification over wine is appended to the **Shaḥarit: Morning Service for the Sabbath** (for use immediately following the service), sanctifications over wine for Rosh Hodesh and for Sabbath Rosh Hodesh are included here as well.

Note that the traditional *shaḥarit* service for weekdays coinciding with Rosh Hodesh contains an *amidah* of nineteen sections (standard for weekdays) embellished by a supplementary prayer known as *ya'aleh v'yavo*, "may it ascend and come." Following the *shaḥarit*, a *musaf* service containing an *amidah* of seven sections (customary for Sabbaths and festivals) is traditionally recited. Because the communities using this book are likely to conduct only one service on Rosh Hodesh day, I have provided a means to create a holiday **Shaharit** in which the **Amidah** is modeled on that of the Rosh Hodesh *musaf* (hence it contains seven sections, the fourth of which, **Sanctifying Rosh Hodesh**, replaces or supplements the fourth section of the **Shaḥarit: Morning Service for the Sabbath**). I have also included in this **Amidah** a re-creation of the *ya'aleh v'yavo* prayer, which is strongly identified with traditional Rosh Hodesh celebration (this is the blessing entitled **May We Be Remembered**).

Sanctifying Rosh Hodesh   קְדֻשַּׁת רֹאשׁ חֹדֶשׁ
(pages 391–93)

The traditional blessing sanctifying Rosh Hodesh, which is found in the fourth section of the *amidah* recited at the *musaf* service on Rosh Hodesh day, contains citations and paraphrases of biblical passages concerning the establishment of this festival and its sacrificial offerings. It closes with a petition of blessings for the new month, some of which I have adapted and incorporated into the **Prayer for the New Month**. Its eulogy (concluding line) is *Barukh atah, y-h-v-h, m'kadeysh yisra'eyl v'rashey ḥodashim*, "Blessed are you, YHVH, who sanctifies Israel and the heads of the months [i.e., the New Moon festivals]"; the new blessing **Sanctifying Rosh Hodesh** is based on this line.

Just as the fourth blessing of the Sabbath **Amidah**, **Sanctifying the Sabbath Day**, echoes the **Sanctification over Wine for Sabbath Eve** and the **Sanctification over Wine for Sabbath Day**, this fourth blessing of the **Amidah** for Rosh Hodesh echoes the **Sanctification over Wine for Rosh Hodesh**. And just as a key phrase, *v'nishmor oto*, "and let us keep it," is introduced in **Sanctifying the Sabbath Day**, so here the phrase *unḥadeysh oto*, "and let us renew it," is introduced. The word *unḥadeysh*, "and let us renew," is related not only to the word *ḥadash*, "new"—and thus to the theme of newness characterizing the revival of this festival in our time—but also to the word *ḥódesh*, "month," and hence, the name Rosh Hodesh, which means "head of the month." Thus the blessing reads: *N'kadeysh et rosh* *haḥódesh / unḥadeysh oto / ba'arigat p'tiley ḥayéynu / l'tokh masékhet hadorot*, literally, "Let us sanctify Rosh Hodesh / and let us renew it / by the weaving of the threads of our lives / into the mesh (or network, or web) of the generations."

May We Be Remembered   יַעֲלֶה וְיָבֹא
(pages 394–95)

The prayer called *ya'aleh v'yavo*, literally, "may it ascend and come," which is inserted in the daily morning service on Rosh Hodesh and on the intermediary days of Passover and Sukkot festivals, is referred to in the ancient sources (Tosefta Berakhot 3:14) as a *k'dushat hayom*, "sanctification of the day." It contains many references to *zikaron* and *pikadon*, synonyms meaning "memory" or "remembrance," because of which it has been suggested that it was originally part of the *zikhronot*, "remembrance verses," recited during the *musaf* of Rosh Hashanah. *Ya'aleh v'yavo* is a prayer of sixty-eight Hebrew words divided into three statements, each filled with enumerations of synonymous or parallel phrases connected by commas or the word "and." While ostensibly a prayer of petition beseeching God to remember us with blessings, *ya'aleh v'yavo* is so much about memory itself that it is hard not to read it as an effort to connect the self with previous generations. As such, it fits in with a recurring motif in my new liturgy for Rosh Hodesh, which is the connecting of new practices with those of our past.

I have re-created this prayer in a shorter form, retaining the enumerative style and the use of repetitions (here, three appearances of forms of the noun *zikaron* and one of the related verb *l'hizakheyr*, "to be remembered"), which characterize the original *ya'aleh v'yavo*. In fact, fully two-thirds of the words in the Hebrew version of my prayer come directly from the traditional prayer. The last two lines of the new prayer, however, have a focus different from that of the traditional one, which is addressed solely to God; the new lines express the hope that we be remembered by future generations as part of a historical chain. Note too that the phrase *ya'aleh v'yavo*, "ascend and come," which in the original prayer applies to an ascension to God, may here be read as a rising to consciousness, as in the idiom *ya'aleh l'da'at*, which translates into English as "come to mind" or "cross the mind."

The closing phrase, *b'masóret hadorot*, "in the tradition of the generations," recalls the line *l'tokh masékhet hadorot*, "into the network of the generations," which closes the **Sanctification over Wine for Rosh Hodesh** and **Sanctifying Rosh Hodesh Day**. This echo is deliberate, linking this prayer with the other blessings of *k'dushat hayom*, "sanctification of the day." The phrase *masóret hadorot* is also found in the first blessing of the **Amidah: Sev-**

enfold Prayer (Recalling the Past, Remembering Our Lives) which, like **May We Be Remembered**, calls for a remembrance of the generations that preceded us, intertwining our own lives with those in our people's history.

Sanctification over Wine for Rosh Hodesh   קִדּוּשׁ לְרֹאשׁ חְֹדֶשׁ
(pages 396–97)

Sanctification over Wine for the Day of Sabbath Rosh Hodesh
קִדּוּשׁ לְיוֹם שַׁבָּת רֹאשׁ חֹדֶשׁ
(pages 398–99)

See pp. 499–501.

Birkat Hal'vanah: Blessing of the Moon   בִּרְכַּת הַלְּבָנָה
(pages 403–13)

There is, arguably, no more colorful and intriguing piece of liturgy in Jewish culture than *birkat hal'vanah*, "blessing of the moon," alternatively referred to as *kiddush hal'vanah*, "sanctification of the moon." Of ancient origin, it is first reported on in the Talmud (b. Sanhedrin 42a) and in Tractate Soferim. Based on the obligation to pronounce a blessing whenever one witnesses an important natural phenomenon, the ritual of blessing the moon differs from the ritual of blessing the month (*birkat haḥódesh*) in its focus on nature imagery and on the moon in particular. Thus it is to be performed in the open air, on a night when the waxing moon is clearly visible. Unique in form, *birkat hal'vanah* is an eclectic compilation of passages from both Bible and Talmud, along with popular greetings, sayings, code words, and a magical inversion of a biblical line. Some of it is expressed in the first-person singular voice, and some of it is addressed directly to the moon. It contains a formulaic blessing, of God who "renews months," which is discussed in the Talmud (b. Sanhedrin 42a), where the rabbis note that "even our women recite this blessing." (This seems to be evidence of an early women's liturgical tradition, but it is difficult to say much more about that tradition from this source.) The rabbis felt strongly about the importance of saying this blessing, as is clear from their statement in the talmudic discussion: "When one blesses the month at the appropriate time, it is as though one welcomes the Shekhinah."

Yet, sadly, the recitation of *birkat hal'vanah* is rather uncommon today; I never witnessed it when I was growing up. When I did see the ritual for the first time, in my thirties, the experience was unforgettable. Saturday night in the city of Jerusalem, I was leaving the home of the poet Zelda, where I had spent the better part of the Sabbath day. An Orthodox Jew of Hassidic descent, Zelda lived at the time in the religiously observant neighborhood Sha'arey Hesed. Wending my way through the narrow streets of that neighborhood back to my own home, I passed by a *shtibele*, a little synagogue, outside of which a dozen men, wearing the black coats and hats characteristic of ultra-Orthodox Jews, were praying. But this was prayer the likes of which I had not seen in a Jewish community! There they were, staring up at the moon, lifting themselves on tiptoe, reciting words clearly addressed *to* the moon itself: "Just as I dance before you and cannot touch you, so may my enemies be unable to touch me and cause me harm." Having recited this and other phrases three times, they turned to greet each other robustly with the words *Shalom aleykhem! Aleykhem shalom!* ("Peace to you!"). A medley of lines I recognized as being from Psalms and the Song of Songs followed, but I was too stunned to take it all in. Nothing I had seen in feminist Jewish rituals—or, indeed, in the rituals of many non-Jewish feminists—looked more open to the label of "paganism" (a label frequently used to censure Jewish feminist innovations) than what I was witnessing here, on the streets of Sha'arey Hesed, being enacted by members of a devout Jewish sect. Direct, personal address to a celestial body! Ecstatic movement (almost dance) toward and away from an inert source of light—and not just *any* light, but the moon itself, the object of ancient worship by peoples considered, in biblical terms, to be idolators!

Birkat hal'vanah is a remarkably transparent ritual, through which one may observe historical layers of the tradition. Vestiges of early belief in astrology and in the power of the moon remain embedded here (as they do in the common greeting *mazal tov*, which is found here and throughout Jewish life, and which means, literally, "good sign of the zodiac"). Although the Bible warned Israelites against participating in cults of the moon, which were prevalent in the ancient Near East, cultic practices and beliefs clearly had their influence. If Orthodox Jews today are comfortable with the ritual of *birkat hal'vanah*, which contains vestiges of these earlier times, it only attests to their sense of secure self-identification as Jews. They needn't be concerned that someone overhearing their prayers might think that they are literally worshiping the moon, for such a thought would be preposterous. Traditional Jews observing the practice of *birkat hal'vanah* seem unselfconsciously to enjoy the ritual with all its celebratory, nature-loving, "pagan" undertones—presumably aware that it is a link to their ancient history.

We might apply similar latitude to the interpretation of feminist Jewish practice. For example, some feminist Jews today seek to uncover and reclaim vestiges of early woman-centered and nature-centered traditions, finding meaning in unearthing and bringing to light rare pieces of our past. Often these resurrected fragments are not all that different from parts of the *birkat hal'vanah* ceremony. Other feminist Jews use metaphorical images drawn from nature to point toward experience of the divine. There is no more reason to assume literal "nature worship" on the part of these Jews than there is to assume it of Ortho-dox Jews celebrating *birkat hal'vanah*. In re-creating this ritual, I have tried to retain some of the mystery of the original while also giving expression to Jewish feminist yearnings.

Opening Psalms   מִזְמוֹרֵי פְּתִיחָה
(pages 409–11)

Two contemplative poems open the new **Birkat Hal'vanah** ritual, placed there to encourage personal attentiveness. They highlight an opportunity to find one's home in liminal places and times, including the unfamiliar (and therefore sometimes uncomfortable) terrains of new traditions.

Renewal of the Moon   הִתְחַדְּשׁוּת הַלְּבָנָה
(pages 412–13)

The new Hebrew prayer, which is based on the traditional *birkat hal'vanah* ritual, is woven of threads from several layers of tradition. The following is a literal translation:

> I lift my eyes to the hills,
> my help will come
> from the heavens and the earth.
> By day the sun will not harm me
> and by night the moon will guide me.
>
> The moon will renew itself
> for those borne from the belly
> and for every creature
> at the start of its way—
> that they may be renewed like it.
>
> May the light of the moon
> be as praised as the sun's
> and may we all merit
> its light soon—
> the light of the beginning of our creation.

The first stanza of this prayer is based on Psalm 121, which appears in its entirety in the traditional *birkat hal'vanah*. For **Renewal of the Moon**, I have excerpted and adapted vv. 1–2 and 6 of this psalm.

The second stanza takes its source from a passage in the Talmud (b. Sanhedrin 42a), also quoted in the traditional *birkat hal'vanah*, in which the moon is said to renew itself as a glorious crown for "those borne from the belly," *amusey váten*. The talmudic term *amusey váten* is in turn derived from Isaiah 46:3, which refers to the people of Israel as *amusim mini-véten* and *n'su'im mini-ráham*, "those borne [by God] from the belly" and "those carried [by God] from the womb"—that is, people sustained and supported by God from the time of their beginnings and thereafter. Thus the phrase implies an image of God as a pregnant mother, with Israel as the fetus. Here, in **Renewal of the Moon**, the term *amusim mini-véten*, "those borne from the belly," has as its primary meaning all creatures that grow in the womb and are later sustained in life on the planet. At the same time, the resonance from the biblical context, in which *amusim mini-véten* refers to the people of Israel, speaks to the particular significance of the new moon in Jewish liturgical culture.

The third stanza of **Renewal of the Moon** is based on the prophecy, in Isaiah 30:26, that "the light of the moon will be like the light of the sun," which is paraphrased in the traditional *birkat hal'vanah*. I interpret this prophecy to mean that the disempowered will regain power and entitlement, in keeping with the talmudic story (b. Hullin 60b) of the sun and the moon, in which God promises to atone for unfairly diminishing the moon's original status (this story is discussed in the introduction to THE MONTHLY CYCLE, p. 329). Thus **Renewal of the Moon** expresses the wish that the light of the moon be as praised, or blessed—*m'vorakh*—as the light of the sun.

Lines 13–14 of the prayer are based on the traditional liturgical line *v'nizkeh khulánu m'heyrah l'oro*, "and may we all soon merit its light." In its original liturgical context, "it" refers to *or hadash*, literally, "new light." The image of *or hadash* appears also in my **Rosh Hodesh Candlelighting**, where I use it as a metaphor for the new moon (see the commentary on p. 498). In ll. 13–14 of **Renewal of the Moon**, the referent of "it" is *hal'vanah*, "the moon," which is further portrayed, in l. 15, as *or reyshit b'ri'atéynu*, "the light of the beginning of our creation." (Note that because *hal'vanah* is grammatically feminine, whereas *or hadash* is grammatically masculine, the word *l'oro*, "its [masc.] light," becomes *l'orah*, "its [fem.] light," in the new blessing. Also note that the word *khulánu* is rendered as *kulánu* in the new blessing, in accordance with modern Hebrew usage.) This image of our primordial beginnings also recalls the embryonic origins alluded to in the second stanza of the prayer.

The length, variegated nature, and unique ambiance of the traditional *birkat hal'vanah* ritual led me to experiment with both style and form in creating **Renewal of the**

Moon, which might be characterized as a reverie combined with a wish. Scholars have argued that much of the traditional *birkat hal'vanah* ritual is related to the theme of redemption. I have treated this ritual as a focus of hope for redemption—although I believe that redemption depends not just on faith but on human effort, especially actions intended to bring about justice and peace. Of all the offerings in THE MONTHLY CYCLE, **Renewal of the Moon** is intended to address most pointedly the aspirations of feminist Jews trying to re-create Jewish tradition in redemptive ways.

Notes

AUTHOR'S PREFACE

1. *(p. xvii)* I presented an early version of my *Havdalah:* **Parting Ritual for the Sabbath** at the National Havurah Institute held at Rutgers University, New Brunswick, New Jersey, in August 1983. In November 1984, I delivered a speech, "A Blessing for This Day," at the conference "Illuminating the Unwritten Scrolls: Women's Spirituality and Jewish Tradition," sponsored by Hebrew Union College and the University of Southern California, Los Angeles; in this talk I offered a new blessing over wine and my **Blessing for the New and for Renewal.**

2. *(p. xvii)* "What About God? New Blessings for Old Wine" (*Moment* 10:3 [March 1985]: 32–36). This essay introduced my new blessings into print; it was reprinted in revised form as "Notes on Composing New Blessings: Toward a Feminist-Jewish Reconstruction of Prayer" in *Journal of Feminist Studies in Religion* (3:1 [Spring 1987]: 39–53); also in *Reconstructionist* (53:3 [December 1987]: 10–15, 22), where it occasioned a symposium among rabbis and scholars of the Reform, Reconstructionist, and Conservative movements. See essays by Edward L. Greenstein, David Ellenson, Ruth H. Sohn, and David Teutsch in "New Blessings: A Symposium," *Reconstructionist* (53:7 [June 1988]: 13–22, 30). Also see the responses to these by Judith Plaskow and Edward L. Greenstein in *Reconstructionist* (54:2 [October–November 1988]: 2, 34). A further revised excerpt of the essay that appeared in *JFSR* was later anthologized in Judith Plaskow and Carol Christ, eds., *Weaving the Visions* (San Francisco: Harper & Row, 1989), pp. 128–38.

3. *(p. xvii)* While the major movements of non-Orthodox Judaism in the United States have all produced new prayer books in recent decades, most have not made substantial changes to the basic prayers of the Hebrew liturgy or added significant variations to the traditional Hebrew terms for the divine. Rather, changes to the Hebrew mostly take the form of excisions, both large and small, and slight revisions of phrases and lines. Whole new prayers are rarely offered; when they are, they are closely based on the traditional prayers and share the same theological perspective. The first prayer book of the Reconstructionist movement, *Sabbath Prayer Book* (New York: Jewish Reconstructionist Foundation, 1945), did contain a number of original Hebrew texts; however, the traditional depiction of God as Lord and king remained intact throughout. The new Reconstructionist prayer book, *Kol Haneshamah: Shabbat Veḥagim*, ed. David Teutsch (Wyncote, PA: Reconstructionist Press, 1994), and its provisional (somewhat more experimental) edition, *Kol Haneshamah: Shabbat Eve*, ed. David Teutsch (Wyncote, PA: Reconstructionist Press, 1989), are notably innovative in that they offer an extensive variety of attributes characterizing divinity ("Beloved One," "Ancient One," etc.); significantly, however, these variations in "God-language" are primarily in English. As might be expected, more radical changes to the liturgy have been made outside the standard prayer books of the major movements, in the publications of individual synagogues, women's groups, Jewish renewal communities, and the like. Even here, however, the creative innovations have largely taken the form of new English renditions of the traditional Hebrew prayers and of new English prayers and supplementary readings.

   In Israel, of course, whatever changes are made to the prayer book are in Hebrew; until recently, however, such changes have not been either extensive or theologically challenging. While the Rabbinate has produced a few new compositions—including a prayer for the State of Israel, a service for Israeli Independence Day, and a new version of the traditional prayer for taking a journey—these conform closely to traditional liturgical expression and do not alter or supplement traditional depictions of the divine. With the development of a liberal alternative to Orthodox Judaism in Israel, however, liturgical innovation may become more creative; there are signs that this development is under way. The Movement for Progressive Judaism includes modern Hebrew poetry and prose in its new prayer book and provides its own prayers for new holidays such as Israeli Independence Day. Once again, however, the basic prayers of the Hebrew liturgy remain, by and large, unchanged. See *Ha'avodah Shebaleyv: Siddur T'filot Limot Haḥol, L'shabbatot Ulmo'adey Hashanah* (Jerusalem: Movement for Progressive Judaism in Israel, 1982). Innovation is also taking place on a grass-roots level in Israel, and here one may expect more radical experimentation. For example, in Kibbutz Lotan in the Negev, a committee has been formed to produce new prayer services that will be responsive to the theological perspectives of its members, at least some of whom have serious feminist concerns.

4. *(p. xvii)* Responding to letters to the editor of *Moment* (10:8 [September 1985]: 7–9), I wrote: "I have not 'resolved the issue of naming God' for myself or for anyone else; I don't believe in a resolution of that issue. Rather, I am calling for a revival of the process of naming, a process that should not be resolved, completed, or stopped. I agree wholeheartedly that 'the problem belongs to us all,' and the solutions, therefore, should be in the hands of the entire community. My own blessings are intended as examples of what might flow from the community if we were to take the responsibility for naming upon ourselves."

5. *(p. xvii)* This use of the line *N'vareykh et eyn haḥayim* became quite common in some circles, and at one point it found its way into a new prayer book, which proposed its use as an "alternative formula." See *Kol Haneshamah* (1994), p. 5 and passim.

6. *(p. xviii)* In his essay on the creative process, "The Figure a Poem Makes," Robert Frost writes, "No surprise for the writer, no surprise for the reader." Writing a blessing is, for me, like writing a poem; ideally, I would have the process be as Frost described it: "begin[ning] in delight and end[ing] in wisdom." Hyde Cox and Edward Connery Lathem, eds., *Selected Prose of Robert Frost* (New York: Holt, Rinehart and Winston, 1966), pp. 18–19.

7. *(p. xx)* Readers may wonder what I mean when I refer to or quote from "the traditional liturgy," as I do throughout this book. Modern Jewish prayer books exist in various renditions, most of them prepared with emendations deemed suitable for given denominations—Reform, Reconstructionist, Conservative, and so forth. All of these are dependent upon a relatively standard text generally labeled Orthodox, which itself is available in two different versions—Ashkenazic and Sephardic. These Orthodox versions have been subject to enormous change over the centuries. Today's standardized texts are largely the result of nineteenth-century scholars who collected extant variants in early printed editions and compared them to manuscripts in their possession, and whose editorial work necessarily required them to make subjective decisions as to what should be included and what not. Thus even today there is no single, reliable, altogether authentic Orthodox version of our prayers; rather, there exist many standard prayer books, each the result of the particular editorial policy adopted by its twentieth-century publisher.

I have selected one such work as representative of the whole: Philip Birnbaum's now classic American edition of the traditional liturgical corpus, which has been in use for almost fifty years in congregations worldwide (*Daily Prayer Book: Ha-Siddur Ha-Shalem* [New York: Hebrew Publishing Company, 1949]). (Birnbaum's is the prayer book of choice among many scholars, as, for example, Lawrence A. Hoffman, who regularly cites it as his standard reference.) I chose Birnbaum's Ashkenazic version over his Sephardic version because the former will be more familiar to most of my readers. I have, of course, also consulted many other prayer books, especially for the purpose of informing my own re-creations. But when quoting the traditional liturgy in my Commentary, I based my citations on Birnbaum's text, making changes in punctuation as I deemed necessary for clarity and consistency. To avoid identification with any particular movement and to indicate my sense that our received text is the spiritual property of all Jews, I generally refer to citations based on Birnbaum's text simply as "traditional."

INTRODUCTION TO THE DAILY CYCLE

8. *(p. 4)* In a forthcoming volume of *The Book of Blessings* that treats ordinary and extraordinary events of the life cycle, I will provide blessings for unanticipated moments, such as seeing something beautiful in nature.

9. *(p. 5)* Some of the blessings in this sequence are troubling in their implication that physical disabilities are defects—imperfections that God may miraculously remove. This is liturgical evidence of a problematic aspect of rabbinic theology that is gaining attention today. While I cannot treat this subject in depth here, I would note that it is an integral part of the rabbinic view of the body in relation to the spirit and in relation to God, a view that I outline further on in this introduction.

10. *(p. 6)* Bill Moyers, *Healing and the Mind* (New York: Doubleday, 1993), p. 189.

INTRODUCTION TO THE WEEKLY CYCLE

11. *(p. 44)* Abraham Joshua Heschel, *The Sabbath: Its Meaning for Modern Man*, expanded ed. (New York: Farrar, Straus, 1952). See especially pp. 14–15.

12. *(p. 44)* Ibid., p. 3.

13. *(p. 44)* Ibid., p. 10.

14. *(p. 45)* Ibid., p. 3.

15. *(p. 46)* This blessing also implies a value-laden distinction between "light" and "darkness"; I overturn the hierarchy of this dualism elsewhere in my liturgy (see **Blessing of Creation**, pp. 166–67, and the commentary to it on pp. 464–65).

16. *(p. 49)* For discussion of the themes of creation, revelation, and redemption as they relate to the three parts of the Sabbath day, see Franz Rosenzweig, *The Star of Redemption*, trans. William W. Hallo from the 2d ed. of 1930; foreword by N. N. Glatzer (Boston: Beacon Press, 1972), pp. 310–15. For further discussion of these themes, with particular emphasis on the meaning of revelation for the modern Jew, see Martin Buber, "The Man of Today and the Jewish Bible," in Martin Buber, *Israel and the World: Essays in a Time of Crisis*, trans. Olga Marx (New York: Schocken Books, 1948), pp. 89–102.

17. *(p. 50)* Pinchas Peli, *The Jewish Sabbath: A Renewed Encounter* (New York: Schocken Books, 1991), p. ix.

INTRODUCTION TO THE MONTHLY CYCLE

18. *(p. 327)* The first documentation of the modern feminist revival of Rosh Hodesh is Arlene Agus's "This Month Is for You: Observing Rosh Hodesh as a Woman's Holiday," in Elizabeth Koltun, ed., *The Jewish Woman* (New York: Schocken Books, 1976). Agus cites 1972 as the year in which "a small group of women . . . began observing the day with a special ceremony and feast, combining traditional practices associated with the holiday with additions from contemporary sources" (p. 84).

19. *(p. 329)* Although the symbolic association of lunar and menstrual cycles still has currency today, I do not see it as a promising basis for feminist revisioning of the tradition; it rests too heavily on a reductionist identification of women with menstruation. It seems to me that if, as Jews, we wish to acknowledge life-cycle events, such as menstruation and childbirth, and passages like menarche and menopause, it is more appropriate to mark them ritually in their own contexts than to merge them with Rosh Hodesh celebrations. Blessings for the life cycle will be provided in a forthcoming volume of *The Book of Blessings*.

INTRODUCTION TO THE COMMENTARY

20. *(p. 419)* Moses Cordovero was a leading figure in Kabbalah (Jewish mystical tradition); this quotation is from his Shi'ur Komah, Modena Manuscript, 206b, as cited in translation in Daniel C. Matt, *The Essential Kabbalah* (San Francisco: HarperSanFrancisco, 1995), p. 24. In his book *God and the Big Bang* (Woodstock, VT: Jewish Lights, 1996), Matt explicates his own view of God as "the oneness of it all" from which the self is not fundamentally separate. He finds historical precedents for his theology in kabbalistic teachings, specifically in the ideas of *eyn sof*, "the boundless," and *áyin*, "nothingness." (This *áyin* [אַיִן] is a different word from *áyin* [עַיִן] meaning "wellspring" or "source," which I discuss in the commentary to **Blessing Before the Meal**; so too, the *eyn* of *eyn sof* [אֵין סוֹף] is different from the *eyn* in my liturgical appellation *eyn haḥayim* [עֵין הַחַיִּים], "source [or wellspring] of life.")

21. *(p. 419)* Mordecai Kaplan (1881–1983) was an influential rabbi, philosopher, and teacher of Conservative rabbis in the United States. Reconstructionism is based on his writings, the most comprehensive and central of which is *Judaism as a Civilization: Toward a Reconstruction of American-Jewish Life* (New York: Macmillan, 1935). Kaplan believed that God was "the Power that makes for Salvation," that is, a force that runs through us and allows us to achieve redemptive goals. For Kaplan, God was neither a Person who acted on the world nor an outside force, but rather the organic interrelationship of all the laws of the universe, which act not upon us but through us. A useful compendium of Kaplan's writings may be found in Emanuel S. Goldsmith and Mel Scult, eds., *Dynamic Judaism: The Essential Writings of Mordecai M. Kaplan* (New York: Schocken Books/Reconstructionist Press, 1985).

22. *(p. 420)* Ira Eisenstein, "Prayer as 'Passionate Reflection,'" *Reconstructionism Today* 2:2 (Winter 1994–95): 9–10.

23. *(p. 420)* Rachel Adler, "And Not Be Silent: Towards Inclusive Worship," chapter in her forthcoming book, *Engendering Judaism* (Philadelphia: Jewish Publication Society, 1997).

24. *(p. 420)* Lawrence A. Hoffman, "A Response to Marcia Falk," *Tikkun* 4:4 (July–August 1989): 57.

25. *(p. 420)* For me, theology begins with personal experience; this approach is one I share with other feminist theologians. In an insightful essay providing an overview of Jewish feminist the-

ology, Ellen M. Umansky writes: "What differentiates feminist theology from many theologies of the past, and some of the present, is both a willingness to acknowledge openly the autobiographical nature of experience and a consequent reluctance if not refusal either to assert universal truths or to make universal claims" (Umansky, "Jewish Feminist Theology," chap. 13 in Eugene B. Borowitz, *Choices in Modern Jewish Thought: A Partisan Guide*, 2d ed. [West Orange, NJ: Behrman House, 1995], p. 314).

26.   *(p. 420)* I have discussed this subject in an essay, "Toward a Feminist Jewish Reconstruction of Monotheism" (*Tikkun* 4:4 [July–August 1989]: 53–56).

27.   *(p. 420)* Arthur Green, *Seek My Face, Speak My Name: A Contemporary Jewish Theology* (Northvale, NJ: Jason Aronson, 1992), pp. 8–9.

28.   *(p. 421)* Ibid., pp. 16–17.

29.   *(p. 422)* Hoffman, "Response," p. 57.

30.   *(p. 422)* Judith Plaskow, "Spirituality and Politics: Lessons from B'not Esh," *Tikkun* 10:3 (May–June 1995): 32. Plaskow discusses the issue of anthropomorphic "God-language" in chap. 4 of her groundbreaking work *Standing Again at Sinai: Judaism from a Feminist Perspective* (San Francisco: Harper & Row, 1990); see especially pp. 154–69. In the same chapter, pp. 128–34, she critiques the image of God as dominating Other.

31.   *(p. 423)* Eisenstein, "Prayer," p. 9.

COMMENTARY TO THE DAILY CYCLE

32.   *(p. 426)* In her essay "In Your Blood, Live: Re-Visions of a Theology of Purity" (*Tikkun* 8:1 [January–February 1993]: 38–41), Rachel Adler writes, "For the feminist Jew, impurity seems to mean the violation of physical or sexual integrity, death by invasion." Adler discusses the use of *mikveh* (immersion in the ritual bath) for purification of the body after sexual violation.

33.   *(p. 428)* Franz Rosenzweig, *The Star of Redemption*, trans. William W. Hallo from the 2d ed. of 1930, foreword by N. N. Glatzer (Boston: Beacon Press, 1972), p. 316.

34.   *(p. 435)* A blessing for the posting of *m'zuzot* will be included in a forthcoming volume of *The Book of Blessings* intended for ordinary and extraordinary events of our lives.

35.   *(p. 438)* The relationship between personal intention (*kavanah*) and fixed prayer (*kéva*) is the subject of much discussion not only in talmudic texts but in later writings. A useful summary of the history of this discussion may be found in Jakob J. Petuchowski, "Spontaneity and Tradition," chap. 1 in Petuchowski, *Understanding Jewish Prayer* (New York: Ktav, 1972), pp. 3–16.

COMMENTARY TO THE WEEKLY CYCLE

36.   *(p. 440)* Kabbalah first emerged in Provence in the twelfth century and in Spain in the thirteenth century. Kabbalistic liturgical tradition developed in the Spanish Diaspora and in Palestine in the sixteenth century and thereafter also came to influence eastern European (Ashkenazic) tradition. Hassidism (the eighteenth-century eastern European revivalist movement) represents a popularization of Kabbalah that remains influential in some forms of Jewish worship today.

37.   *(p. 442)* The rabbis do not explicitly lay out the reasons why many commanded acts do not require a blessing; the subject is certainly worth pondering in the context of understanding the function and purpose of prayer. Beyond the explanation I have proposed here, it seems reasonable to speculate that tradition does not wish to treat human beings instrumentally; therefore

one does not say a blessing of commandment over an act of which another person is the beneficiary.

38. *(p. 445)* See Lawrence A. Hoffman, "Welcoming Shabbat: The Power of Metaphor," *Liturgy* 8:1 (1989): 17–23.

39. *(p. 452)* For more information about the Song of Songs and a translation of the full Hebrew text, see Marcia Falk, *The Song of Songs: A New Translation and Interpretation* (San Francisco: HarperSanFrancisco, 1990).

40. *(p. 452)* Lawrence A. Hoffman explains this body as follows: "Whenever the rabbis encountered a liturgical tradition that they assumed to be sound, but whose origins were shrouded in the dim past, they classified it as an innovation of the Men of the Great Assembly. This was tantamount to saying that the prayer or practice or doctrine under discussion was authentic, but so old that it was impossible to know for sure the name of the sage who had created it." *Beyond the Text: A Holistic Approach to Liturgy* (Bloomington and Indianapolis: Indiana University Press, 1987), p. 29.

41. *(p. 454)* Note that in this citation the word *adonay*, "Lord," appears in the text followed by the Tetragrammaton, *y-h-v-h* (in this instance *adonay* does not represent the rabbinic substitution for the Tetragrammaton). Whenever the written word *adonay* appears in conjunction with *y-h-v-h*, as it does here, tradition pronounces the latter as *elohim*, which means, literally, "God."

42. *(p. 459)* For explanation of the concept of *kavanah* in kabbalistic and Hassidic thought and of the related kabbalistic doctrine of *kavanot*, "intentions," see Louis Jacobs, *Hasidic Prayer* (New York: Schocken Books, 1973).

43. *(p. 464)* The scholar of Jewish liturgy Ismar Elbogen, for example, calls the change "a slight alteration at the end of the verse to suit it for the service." See *Jewish Liturgy: A Comprehensive History*, trans. Raymond P. Scheindlin (Philadelphia: Jewish Publication Society, 1993), p. 17. Joseph H. Hertz, the former British Chief Rabbi and the editor of a standard prayer book, implies that the emendation is a rabbinic clarification of the theology of the biblical verse, rather than an actual departure from its meaning. In *The Authorized Daily Prayer Book* (New York: Bloch, 1948), he writes: "Some see in this declaration of absolute monotheism [Isa. 45:7] a protest against the ancient Persian belief in two gods—one a god of light and goodness, and the other, of darkness and evil. Jewish teaching emphasizes that nothing coming from God is in itself evil, that even the lower passions may be made agencies for good. Hence the change of 'create evil' into 'createst all things.' God is the sole Source of everything" (p. 427). If God is the source of everything, yet nothing coming from God is evil, it would seem that Hertz defines "everything" as "everything except evil."

44. *(p. 470)* The foremothers are included in the new prayer book of the Reconstructionist movement, *Kol Haneshamah: Shabbat Veḥagim*, ed. David Teutsch (Wyncote, PA: Reconstructionist Press, 1994), and in the latest version of the Reform movement's prayer book, *Gates of Prayer for Shabbat and Weekdays: A Gender Sensitive Prayerbook*, ed. Chaim Stern (New York: Central Conference of American Rabbis, 1994). While the foremothers are not mentioned in the Conservative movement's new prayer book, *Siddur Sim Shalom: A Prayerbook for Shabbat, Festivals, and Weekdays*, ed. Jules Harlow (New York: Rabbinical Assembly/ United Synagogue of America, 1985), the insertion of their names was made permissible in 1993 by the Committee on Jewish Law and Standards of the Rabbinical Assembly (see the res-

ponsum by Joel Rembaum, "Regarding the Inclusion of the Names of the Matriarchs in the First Blessing of the Amidah," 1990; also the summary paragraph in *Summary Index of the Committee on Jewish Law and Standards*, Rabbinical Assembly, December 1993, sec. 9, p. 19).

45. *(p. 471)* See *Gates of Prayer: The New Union Prayerbook*, ed. Chaim Stern (New York: Central Conference of American Rabbis, 1975), p. 38 and passim; and *Kol Haneshamah* (1994), p. 95 and passim.

46. *(p. 474)* In Kabbalah, the image of the Shekhinah was both "female" and "feminine"; it conformed to kinship roles and gender constructs associated with women at the time. In what is considered the earliest text of Kabbalah, Sefer Habahir (late twelfth century, Provence), the Shekhinah is portrayed as the daughter of *hakadosh barukh hu*, "The-Holy-One-Blessed-Be-He." In the Zohar, considered Kabbalah's classical text (thirteenth century, Spain), the Shekhinah is God's wife. See Gershom Scholem, "Shekhinah: The Feminine Element in Divinity," in *On the Mystical Shape of the Godhead* (New York: Schocken, 1991), pp. 140–96.

47. *(p. 477)* Martin Buber, "The Man of Today and the Jewish Bible," in *Israel and the World: Essays in a Time of Crisis*, trans. Olga Marx (New York: Schocken Books, 1948), p. 94.

48. *(p. 478)* See *Kol Haneshamah* (1994), p. 385.

49. *(p. 480)* The writing of Mordecai Kaplan, the founding theologian of the Reconstructionist movement, is a good place to begin consideration of this topic. Kaplan rejected chosenness as a viable concept for modern Judaism, and the Reconstructionist movement as a whole adopted this position. See Mordecai M. Kaplan, *The Future of the American Jew* (New York: Macmillan, 1948), chap. 13; also Rebecca T. Alpert and Jacob J. Staub, *Exploring Judaism: A Reconstructionist Approach* (New York: Reconstructionist Press, 1985), pp. 25–28.

50. *(p. 480)* Of course, there is no reason why the new **Torah Blessings** offered here as part of the Sabbath morning service cannot be adopted for Torah study at other times as well.

51. *(p. 481)* See *Kol Haneshamah* (1994), pp. 685–93.

52. *(p. 481)* See Rivkeh Haut, "From Women: Piety, Not Rebellion," *Sh'ma* 15 (May 7, 1985): 110.

53. *(p. 482)* See *Kol Haneshamah* (1994), pp. 685–93; *Siddur Sim Shalom*, pp. 142–45, 402–9.

54. *(p. 483)* Further blessings under this rubric will be included in a forthcoming volume of *The Book of Blessings* intended for events of the life cycle.

55. *(p. 490)* Today's science confirms what Proust described novelistically—that smell is an important trigger of early childhood memories, enabling us to recall entire contexts of personal experience. It is well known that smell is used to identify both kin and foe in many animal species and that sexual attraction between animals, including humans, is strongly identified with the individual's smell. In humans, smell is the most "primal" sense, in that it developed earliest in the species and also develops earliest in the individual human brain; therefore our earliest memories are of smell. Scientific studies show that human newborns recognize their mothers by smell even before they can recognize them by sight, and I have heard of a recent finding that smell is a more reliable identifier than sight for newly delivered mothers as well!

56. *(p. 491)* See Louis Jacobs, "The Uplifting of the Sparks in Later Jewish Mysticism," in Arthur Green, ed., *Jewish Spirituality: From the Sixteenth-Century Revival to the Present* (New York: Crossroads, 1988), pp. 99–126.

Bold type indicates titles of new liturgical offerings presented in this book.

Marcia Falk received her B.A. in philosophy from Brandeis University and her Ph.D. in English and comparative literature from Stanford. As a Fulbright Scholar and a Postdoctoral Fellow at the Hebrew University of Jerusalem, she studied Bible, Hebrew language, and Hebrew literature. She has taught at SUNY Binghamton, the Claremont Colleges, and Stanford, and now lectures widely.

Marcia Falk's other books include two poetry collections, *This Year in Jerusalem* and *It Is July in Virginia*, and two volumes of translation, *The Song of Songs: A New Translation and Interpretation* and *With Teeth in the Earth: Selected Poems of Malka Heifetz Tussman* (translated from the Yiddish). Her writing has also appeared in numerous journals and anthologies. She is currently working on further volumes of *The Book of Blessings*—for the major and minor festivals, the High Holidays, the Passover Haggadah, and the ordinary and extraordinary events of the life cycle.